Time for Socialism

Time for Socialism

Dispatches from a World on Fire, 2016–2021

THOMAS PIKETTY

Yale UNIVERSITY PRESS

New Haven and London

Yale University Press books may be purchased in quantity for educational, business, or promotional use. For information, please email sales.press@yale.edu (U.S. office) or sales@yaleup.co.uk (U.K. office).

Set in Minion Pro by Westchester Publishing Services.

Printed in the United States of America.

Library of Congress Control Number: 2021935893
ISBN 978-0-300-25966-7 (hardcover: alk. paper)
A catalogue record for this book is available from the British Library.

This paper meets the requirements of ANSI/NISO Z39.48-1992 (Permanence of Paper).

10 9 8 7 6 5 4 3 2 1

Contents

Long Live Socialism! 1

Toward a Different Globalization, 2016–2017

Hillary, Apple, and Us 29

The IMF, the Inequality Debate, and
Economic Research 33

The French Right and the European
Budgetary Rules 43

Gender Pay Inequality: 19% or 64%? 47

Agenda for Another Globalization 50

Basic Income or Fair Wage? 54

The Passing of Anthony B. Atkinson 58

On Productivity in France and in Germany 62

Long Live Populism! 84

On Inequality in China 88

For a Democratic Eurozone Government 92

Public Capital, Private Capital 95

What Would a Democratic Eurozone Assembly
Look Like? 99

What Reforms for France? 2017–2018

Inequality in France 113

What Reforms for France? 117

Reagan to the Power of Ten 121

Will Macron's Marchers Take Power? 125

The CICE Comedy 134

Rethinking the Capital Code 138

Suppression of the Wealth Tax: A Historical Error 142

Budget 2018: French Youth Sacrificed 147

The Catalan Syndrome 154

Trump, Macron: Same Fight 159

2018: The Year of Europe 163

Parcoursup: Could Do Better 168

Toward a Union in the Union 173

Capital in Russia 178

May 1968 and Inequality 182

The Transferunion Fantasy 186

Europe, Migrants, and Trade 190

Social-Nativism: The Italian Nightmare 195

Brazil: The First Republic under Threat 200

Le Monde and the Billionaires 204

To Love Europe Is to Change It, 2018–2020

Manifesto for the Democratization of Europe 211

Yellow Vests and Tax Justice 217

1789: The Return of the Debt 222

Wealth Tax in America 226

To Love Europe Is to Change It 231

Basic Income in India 235

Europe and the Class Cleavage 240

The Illusion of Centrist Ecology 244

Will Money Creation Save Us? 249

What Is a Fair Pension System? 253

Toward a Circular Economy 257

Surpassing Identity Conflict via Economic Justice 262

Several Universal Retirement Schemes
Are Possible 267

After the Climate Denial, the Inequality Denial 272

Social-Federalism vs. National-Liberalism 276

The Franco-German Assembly, a Unique Opportunity
for Tax Justice in Europe 281

Sanders to the Aid of Democracy in the
United States 286

Avoiding the Worst 291

The Age of Green Money 296

Confronting Racism, Repairing History 301

Reconstructing Internationalism 305

The Fall of the U.S. Idol, 2020–2021

Can the Left Unite on Europe? 313

What to Do with Covid Debt 317

Global Inequalities: Where Do We Stand? 321

The Fall of the U.S. Idol 329

Index 335

Long Live Socialism!

I f someone had told me in 1990 that I would publish a collection of articles in 2020 entitled *Vivement le socialisme!* in French, I would have thought it was a bad joke. As an 18-year-old, I had just spent the autumn of 1989 listening to the collapse of the communist dictatorships and "real socialism" in Eastern Europe on the radio. In February 1990, I took part in a French student trip to support the young people in Romania who had just gotten rid of the regime of Ceauşescu. We arrived in the middle of the night at the Bucharest airport, then went by bus to the rather sad and snowy city of Braşov, nestled in the arc of the Carpathian Mountains. The young Romanians proudly showed us the impact of bullets on the walls, witnesses of their "Revolution." In March 1992, I made my first trip to Moscow, where I saw the same empty shops and the same gray avenues. I had succeeded in becoming one of the participants in a Franco-Russian conference entitled "Psychoanalysis and Social Sciences," and it was with a group of French academics, who were a bit lost, that I visited the Lenin Mausoleum and Red Square (the "Shrine of the Russian Revolution"), where the Russian flag had just replaced the Soviet flag.

Born in 1971, I belong to a generation that did not have time to be tempted by communism, and which became adult when the absolute failure of sovietism was already obvious. Like many, I was more liberal than socialist in the 1990s, as proud as a peacock of my judicious observations, and suspicious of my elders and all those who were nostalgic. I could not stand those who obstinately refused to see that the market economy and private property were part of the solution.

But now, thirty years later, in 2020, hypercapitalism has gone much too far, and I am now convinced that we need to think about a new way of going beyond capitalism, a new form of socialism, participative and decentralized, federal and democratic, ecological, multiracial, and feminist.

History will decide whether the word "socialism" is definitively dead and must be replaced. For my part, I think that it can be saved, and even that it remains the most appropriate term to describe the idea of an alternative economic system to capitalism. In any case, one cannot just be "against" capitalism or neoliberalism: one must also and above all be "for" something else, which requires precisely designating the ideal economic system that one wishes to set up, the just society that one has in mind, whatever name one finally decides to give it. It has become commonplace to say that the current capitalist system has no future, as it deepens inequalities and exhausts the planet. This is not false, except that in the absence of a clearly explained alternative, the current system still has many days ahead of it.

As a social science teacher-researcher, I have specialized in the study of the history of inequalities and the relationship between economic development, wealth distribution, and political conflict, which led me to publish several voluminous books.[1]

---

1. See in particular *Top Incomes in France in the Twentieth Century: Inequality and Redistribution, 1901–1998* (Cambridge, MA: Harvard University

I have also contributed to the creation of the World Inequality Database, a vast collective and participatory project aimed at bringing more transparency to the evolution of income and wealth inequalities in the different societies of the planet.[2]

Drawing on the lessons of this historical research, and of course on my experience as a citizen-observer of the period 1990–2020, I have tried in my last book to outline some "elements for a participatory socialism"; I will summarize the main conclusions here.[3] However, I must make it clear that these "elements" are only a small starting point among others, a tiny contribution to a huge process of collective elaboration, open discussion, and social and political experimentation, a process which will have to be a long-term one, approached with humility and tenacity, especially in view of the scale of past failures and the challenges to come.

The interested reader will also find some of my considerations in the present study, in which are reproduced all my monthly articles published in the newspaper *Le Monde* from September 2016 to February 2021, without any modification or rewriting. I have simply added a few additional graphs, tables, references, and texts published on my blog hosted by

---

Press, 2018); *Capital in the Twenty-First Century* (Cambridge, MA: Harvard University Press, 2014); and *Capital and Ideology* (Cambridge, MA: Harvard University Press, 2020). For a more complete bibliography and a large number of texts, extracts, and data available online, see piketty.pse.ens.fr.

2. All these data, as well as thousands of pages of studies and documentation on more than 100 countries, are available online at WID.world. See also Facundo Alvaredo, Lucas Chancel, Thomas Piketty, Emmanuel Saez, and Gabriel Zucman, eds., *World Inequality Report 2018* (Cambridge, MA: Belknap Press, 2018), also available online at WID.world.

3. For a more detailed presentation of these elements for participatory socialism, see Thomas Piketty, *Capital and Ideology*, chapter 17.

Le Monde.[4] I would like to point out at the outset that some of the columns have aged less well than others, and I apologize in advance for any repetition. These texts represent nothing more than an imperfect attempt by a social scientist to descend from his ivory tower and his thousand-page books and get involved in the life of the city and in current events, with all the risks that this entails. I hope that the indulgent reader will find some useful leads for his or her own reflections and commitments.

The Long March toward Equality and Participatory Socialism

Let's start with a statement that some may find surprising. If we take a long-term perspective, then the long march toward equality and participatory socialism is already well under way. No technical impossibility prevents us from continuing along this already open path, as long as we all get on with it. History shows that inequality is essentially ideological and political, not economic or technological.

This optimistic point of view may certainly seem paradoxical in these times of gloom. Yet it corresponds to reality. Inequalities have been sharply reduced over the long term. This is thanks in particular to the new social and fiscal policies introduced during the twentieth century. Much remains to be done, but the fact is that it is possible to go much further by drawing on the lessons of history.

4. See lemonde.fr/blog/piketty. The interested reader will also find on the site links to the data files used in the graphs and tables; some additional data are available on WID.world or on piketty.ps.ens.fr.

Consider, for example, the evolution of property concentration over the past two centuries. First of all, we can see that the share of the richest 1% of the total property (i.e., the total real estate, financial, and professional assets, net of debt) was at an astronomical level throughout the nineteenth century and until the beginning of the twentieth century—which shows, by the way, that the promise of equality of the French Revolution was more theoretical than real, at least as far as the redistribution of property is concerned. It can then be observed that the share of the richest 1% of the population fell sharply during the twentieth century: it was around 55% of total wealth on the eve of World War I and is now close to 25%. However, it should be noted that this share is still about five times higher than that held by the poorest 50%, who currently own just over 5% of the total wealth (despite the fact that they are by definition fifty times more numerous than the richest 1%). The cherry on the cake is that this low share has also been declining since the 1980s and 1990s, a trend that can also be observed in the United States, Germany, and the rest of Europe, as well as in India, Russia, and China.

To sum up: the concentration of ownership (and therefore economic power) has clearly decreased over the past century, but it is still extremely high. The reduction of property inequalities has mainly benefited the "property-owning middle class" (i.e., the 40% of the population between the top 10% and the bottom 50%), but has benefited very little the poorest half of the population. In the end, the share of wealth of the richest 10% has fallen significantly, from 80–90% to around 50–60% (which is still considerable), but the share of the poorest 50% has never stopped being tiny (see figure 1). The situation of the poorest 50% has improved more in terms of income than in terms of wealth (their share of total income has grown

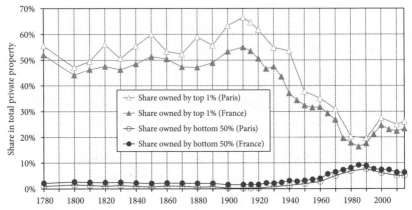

Figure 1. The failure of the French Revolution: The proprietarian inequality drift in nineteenth-century France. In Paris, the richest 1% owned about 67% of total private property in 1910 (all assets combined: real, financial, business, etc.), versus 49% in 1810 and 55% in 1780. After a small drop during the French Revolution, the concentration of property rose in France (and particularly in Paris) during the nineteenth century until World War I. In the long run, the fall in inequality occurred following the two world wars (1914–1945), rather than following the Revolution of 1789. *Sources and series:* see piketty.pse.ens.fr/ideology.

from barely 10% to around 20% in Europe), although here again the improvement is limited and potentially reversible (the share of the poorest 50% has fallen to just over 10% in the United States since the 1980s).[5] The poorest 50% of the world's population is still the poorest 50% of the world's population.

5. For a detailed discussion of the historical evolution of income and wealth inequality, see Thomas Piketty, *Capital and Ideology,* especially charts 4.1–4.3, 5.4–5.7, 10.1–10.7, 11.1–11.8, and 13.8–13.9. All these charts and series are available online at piketty.pse.ens. en/ideology.

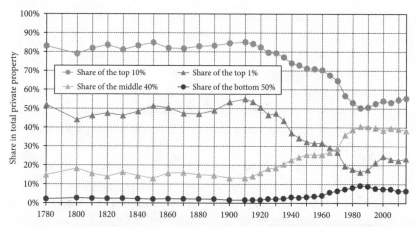

Figure 2. The concentration of property in France, 1780–2015. The share of the richest 10% in total private property (total real estate, business, and financial assets, net of debt) was between 80% and 90% in France between the 1780s and the 1910s. The fall in the concentration of property started following World War 1 and was interrupted in the 1980s. It occurred mostly to the benefit of the "patrimonial middle classes" (the middle 40%), here defined as the intermediate group between the "lower classes" (bottom 50%) and the "upper classes" (top 10%). *Sources and series:* see piketty.pse .ens.fr/ideology.

The Social State as a Vehicle for Equal Rights

How can we account for these complex and contradictory developments, and in particular, how can we explain the reduction in inequalities observed over the past century, particularly in Europe? In addition to the destruction of private assets as a result of the two world wars, the positive role played by the considerable changes in the legal, social, and tax systems introduced in many European countries during the twentieth century must be emphasized.

One of the most decisive factors was the rise of the welfare state between 1910–1920 and 1980–1990, with the development of investment in education, health, retirement and disability pensions, and social insurance (unemployment, family, housing, etc.). At the beginning of the 1910s, total public expenditure in Western Europe amounted to barely 10% of national income, and a large part of it was regalian/public expenditure related to policing, the army, and colonial expansion. Total public expenditure reached 40–50% of national income in the 1980s and 1990s (before stabilizing at this level) and was mainly expenditure on education, health, pensions, and social transfers.[6]

This development has led to a certain equality of access to the basic goods of education, health, and economic and social security in Europe during the twentieth century, or at least a greater equality of access to these basic goods than had been available to all previous societies. However, the stagnation of the welfare state since the 1980s and 1990s, even though needs have continued to increase, particularly as a result of longer life expectancy and higher levels of schooling, shows that nothing can ever be taken for granted. In the health sector, we have just bitterly noted with the Covid-19 health crisis the inadequacy of the hospital and human resources available. One of the major issues at stake in the epidemic crisis of 2020 is precisely whether the march toward the social state will resume in rich countries and will finally be accelerated in poor countries.[7]

6. See Piketty, *Capital and Ideology,* figures 10.14, 10.15.
7. See "Avoiding the Worst," April 14, 2020. (References indicated with a title and date are articles by Thomas Piketty that were published on lemonde.fr/blog/piketty and appear in this volume.)

Take the case of investment in education. At the beginning of the twentieth century, public spending on education
at all levels was less than 0.5% of national income in Western
Europe (and slightly higher in the United States, which at the
time was ahead of Europe). In practice, this meant extremely
elitist and restrictive education systems: the mass of the population had to make do with overcrowded and poorly funded
primary schools, and only a small minority had access to secondary and higher education. Investment in education increased more than tenfold over the twentieth century, reaching
5–6% of national income in the 1980s and 1990s, allowing for a
very high level of educational expansion. All available evidence suggests that this development has been a powerful
factor driving both greater equality and greater prosperity
over the past century.

Conversely, all the evidence suggests that the stagnation
in total educational investment observed in recent decades, despite the sharp increase in the proportion of an age group
moving to higher education, has contributed both to the rise
in inequality and to the slowdown in the rate of growth of average income.[8] It should also be pointed out that extremely
high social inequalities in terms of access to education persist.
This is obviously the case in the United States, where the prob-
ability of access to higher education (largely private and fee-
paying) is powerfully determined by parental income. But it
is also the case in a country such as France, where total public investment in education (all levels) is very unevenly distributed within an age group, particularly in view of the huge
inequalities between the resources allocated to selective and

8. I will return later to the way in which in the future the concept of
"growth" should be used.

non-selective courses of study.[9] In general, the number of students in France has risen sharply since the middle of the 2000s (from just over 2 million to almost 3 million today), but public investment has not followed suit, especially in general university courses and short technical courses, so that investment per student has fallen sharply, representing a considerable social and human waste.[10]

Toward Participatory Socialism: Enabling Greater Circulation of Power and Ownership

Educational equality and the welfare state are not enough: to achieve real equality, the whole range of relationships of power and domination must be rethought. This requires, in particular, a better sharing of power in companies.

Here again, we have to start from what worked well during the twentieth century. In many European countries, particularly in Germany and Sweden, the trade union movement and social democratic parties succeeded in imposing a new division of power on shareholders in the middle of the twentieth century, in the form of so-called co-management systems: elected employee representatives have up to half of the seats on the boards of directors of large companies, even without any share ownership. The point is not to idealize this system (in the event of a tie, it is always the shareholders who have the decisive vote), but simply to note that this is a considerable transformation of the classic shareholder logic. In particular,

9. See Piketty, *Capital and Ideology*, graphs 0.8 and 17.1. See also "Parcoursup: Could Do Better," February 13, 2018.

10. See "Budget 2018: French Youth Sacrificed," October 21, 2017.

this implies that if employees also hold a minority stake of 10% or 20% in the capital, or if a local authority holds such a stake, then the majority can be tipped, even in the face of an ultra-majority shareholder in the capital. But the fact is that such a system, which gave rise to loud cries from shareholders in the countries concerned when it was set up, and which required intense social, political, and legal struggles,[11] has in no way harmed economic development—quite the contrary. There is every indication that this greater equality of rights has led to greater employee involvement in the long-term strategy of companies.

Unfortunately, shareholder resistance has so far prevented a wider dissemination of these rules. In France, the United Kingdom, and the United States, shareholders continue to hold almost all the power of the company.[12] It is interesting to note that French Socialists, like British Labour, favored a nationalization-centered approach until the 1980s, often finding the Swedish and German Social Democrats' strategies of power-sharing and voting rights for employees too timid. The nationalization agenda then disappeared after the collapse of

---

11. In particular, the German constitutional laws of 1919 and 1949 defined property as a social relationship involving several types of stakeholders, thus allowing for this kind of reform, which would, for example, be much more difficult to implement with the current French Constitution, which is based on a much more conservative view of strictly private property. Rather than focusing on the transition to the Sixth Republic or the establishment of a Constituent Assembly (although the nature of the envisaged constitutional amendment is not always clear), French discussions on constitutional reform on these issues would benefit from more substantial socioeconomic objectives, particularly on the issue of property and progressive taxation. See Piketty, *Capital and Ideology,* chapter 17.

12. One seat (out of twelve) has been introduced in France on the boards of directors of large companies since 2013.

Soviet communism, and both French Socialists and British Labour almost abandoned in the 1990s and 2000s any prospect of a transformation of the ownership regime. Discussions on Nordic-German co-management have been going on for about ten years now, and it is high time to generalize these rules to all countries.

Next, and more importantly, it is possible to extend and amplify this movement toward a better sharing of power. For example, in addition to the fact that employee representatives should have 50% of the votes in all companies (including the smallest), it is conceivable that within the 50% of voting rights going to shareholders, the share of voting rights held by an individual shareholder may not exceed a certain threshold in sufficiently large companies.[13] In this way, a single shareholder who is also an employee of his company would continue to have the majority of votes in a very small company, but would have to rely more and more on collective deliberation once the company becomes more significant in size.[14]

13. For example, an individual shareholder could hold a maximum of 90% of shareholder voting rights in small companies (less than ten employees), and this threshold would gradually be lowered to 10% of shareholder voting rights for larger companies (above 100 employees). Where there is a single shareholder, unallocated shareholder voting rights would be added to employee voting rights. See Piketty, *Capital and Ideology*, chapter 17. This system generalizes to all sectors of activity the voting rights cap rules already proposed for media companies. See Julia Cagé, *Saving the Media: Capitalism, Crowdfunding, and Democracy* (Cambridge, MA: Harvard University Press, 2016).

14. With the rules described above, a single shareholder of a company employing five employees (including herself) would hold 56% of the votes: 45% of the votes as shareholder (90% of 50%) and 11% of the votes as employee (55%/5). In the case of a company employing 20 employees (including himself), he would hold 43% of the votes: 40% of the votes as shareholder (80% of 50%) and 3% of the votes as employee (60%/20). With

Important as it is, this transformation of the legal system will not be enough. In order to ensure a genuine circulation of power, the tax and inheritance system must also be mobilized to encourage a greater circulation of property itself. As we have seen above, the poorest 50% own almost nothing, and their share in total wealth has barely improved since the nineteenth century. The idea that it would be enough to wait for the general increase in wealth to spread ownership is not very meaningful: if this were the case, we would have seen such a development long ago. This is why I support the idea of a more proactive solution, in the form of a minimum inheritance for all, which to give an idea could be on the order of 120,000 euros (i.e., about 60% of average wealth per adult in France today) or $180,000 (i.e., about 60% of the average wealth per adult in the United States today) paid out at the age of twenty-five.[15] Such an inheritance for all would represent an annual expenditure of around 5% of national income, which could be financed by a mixture of an annual progressive property tax (i.e., on real estate, financial, and professional assets, net of debts) and a progressive inheritance tax.

What I have in mind is that this minimum inheritance for all (which can also be referred to as a "universal capital endowment") should be financed by a combination of annual

---

100 employees, he would hold less than 11% of the votes: 10% of the votes as a shareholder and 0.9% as an employee (90%/100). It goes without saying that these parameters are given here for illustrative purposes only and should be the subject of extensive historical experimentation.

15. Currently, the average wealth of the poorest 50% is equivalent to about 10% of the average wealth (hence a share of barely 5% of the total wealth). The measure discussed here would therefore result in a six-fold increase in the average wealth of the poorest 50%. The amount envisaged (60% of average wealth) is slightly above the current median wealth.

wealth taxes and inheritance taxes and would constitute a relatively small part of total public expenditure. To clarify my ideas further, one can indeed envisage, in the context of consideration of the ideal tax system, revenues of a total of around 50% of national income (close to the current level in Western Europe, but this would be more fairly distributed, which would allow for possible future increases). These would be composed of, on the one hand, a system of progressive property and inheritance taxes (which would bring in around 5% of national income and finance the universal capital endowment), and, on the other, an integrated system of progressive income tax, social contributions, and carbon tax (with an individual carbon card to protect low incomes and responsible behavior, and to concentrate efforts on the highest individual emissions, which would be heavily taxed), which would bring in a total of about 45% of national income and finance all other public expenditure, and in particular articulate all social expenditure (education, health, pensions, social transfers, basic income, etc.) and environment-related measures (transport infrastructure, energy transition, thermal renovation, etc.).

Several points deserve to be clarified here. First of all, no valid environmental policy can be carried out if it is not part of a global socialist project based on the reduction of inequalities, the permanent circulation of power and property, and the redefinition of economic indicators.[16] I insist on this last point: there is no point in circulating power if we keep the same economic objectives. We therefore need to change the framework, both at the individual and local level (in particular with the introduction of an individual carbon card) and at the national

16. See "The Illusion of Centrist Ecology," June 11, 2019; "Towards a Circular Economy," October 15, 2019.

Table 1. The circulation of property and progressive taxation

Progressive tax on property (funding of the capital endowment allocated to each adult)			Progressive tax on income (funding of basic income and social and ecological state)	
Multiple of average wealth	Annual tax on property (effective tax rate) (%)	Tax on inheritance (effective tax rate) (%)	Multiple of average income	Effective tax rate (including social contributions and carbon tax) (%)
0.5	0.1	5	0.5	10
2	1	20	2	40
5	2	50	5	50
10	5	60	10	60
100	10	70	100	70
1,000	60	80	1,000	80

Source: See piketty.pse.ens.fr/ideology.

Interpretation: The proposed tax system includes a progressive tax on property (annual tax and inheritance tax) funding a capital endowment for all young adults and a progressive tax on income (including social contributions and progressive tax on carbon emissions) funding the basic income and the social and ecological state (health, education, pensions, unemployment, energy, etc.). This system favoring the circulation of property is one of the constituting elements of participatory socialism, together with a 50–50 split of voting rights among workers' representatives and shareholders in corporations.

Note: In the example given here, the progressive property tax raises about 5% of national income (allowing the funding of a capital endowment of about 60% of average net wealth, to be allocated to each young adult at twenty-five years of age) and the progressive income tax of about 45% of national income (allowing the funding of an annual basic income of about 60% of after tax income, costing about 5% of national income, and the social and ecological state for about 40% of national income).

level. Gross domestic product must be replaced by the notion of national income (which implies deducting all capital consumption, including natural capital), attention must focus on distributions and not on averages, and these indicators in terms of income (essential for building a collective standard of justice) must be complemented by environmental indicators (in particular regarding carbon emissions).[17]

I would also stress that the "universal capital endowment" represents only a small share of total public spending, because the just society as I see it here is based above all on universal access to a set of fundamental goods (education, health, retirement, housing, environment, etc.), enabling people to participate fully in social and economic life and cannot be reduced to monetary capital endowment. However, as long as access to these other fundamental goods is guaranteed, including of course access to a basic income system,[18] then the minimum inheritance for all represents an important additional component of a just society. The fact of owning 100,000 or 200,000 euros or dollars in wealth indeed changes a lot compared to owning nothing at all (or only debts). When you own nothing, you have to accept everything: any salary, any working conditions, or almost anything, because you have to be able to pay your rent and provide for your family. Once you

17. On the global inequality of carbon emissions and the concentration of the highest individual emissions in the United States and Europe, see Piketty, *Capital and Ideology,* figure 13.7, and Thomas Piketty and Lucas Chancel, "Carbon and Inequality: From Kyoto to Paris," WID.world, Working Paper Series No. 2015/7.

18. The basic income is an integral part of the ingredients of a just society, provided that it is included in a larger whole and that it does not become a miracle solution. See "Basic Income or Fair Wage?" December 13, 2016.

have a small property, you have access to more choices: you can afford to refuse certain proposals before accepting the right one, you can consider setting up a business, or you can buy a home and no longer need to pay rent every month. By thus redistributing property, we can help to redefine the whole set of relations of power and social domination.

I would also like to point out that the rates and amounts given here are for illustrative purposes only. Some people will consider excessive the tax rates in the 80–90% range that I plan to apply to the highest incomes, estates, and assets. This is a complex debate, which obviously deserves extensive deliberation. I would simply like to recall that such rates have been applied in many countries during the twentieth century (notably in the United States from 1930 to 1980), and that all the historical elements at my disposal lead me to conclude that the record of this experience is excellent. In particular, this policy has not hindered innovation in any way, quite the contrary: growth in national income per capita in the United States was twice as low between 1990 and 2020 (after fiscal progressivity was halved under Reagan in the 1980s) as it had been in the preceding decades.[19] American prosperity in the twentieth century (and more generally, economic prosperity in history) has been based on a clear educational lead[20] and certainly not on an inequality lead. On the basis of the historical elements at my disposal, the ideal society seems to me to be one where everyone would own a few hundred thousand euros, where a few people would perhaps own a few million, but where the higher

19. See Piketty, *Capital and Ideology,* graph 11.13. See also "Toward a Circular Economy," October 15, 2019.

20. In the United States, 90% of an age group were enrolled in secondary education in the 1950s, compared to just 20–30% in Western Europe and Japan at the same time.

holdings (several tens or hundreds of millions, and a fortiori several billions) would only be temporary and would quickly be brought down by the tax system to more rational and socially more useful levels.

Others will find the rates and amounts too timid. In fact, under the tax and inheritance system outlined here, young adults from modest backgrounds who currently inherit nothing at all would receive 120,000 euros, while wealthy young adults who currently inherit 1 million would receive 600,000 euros.[21] We are therefore a long way from the complete equalization of chances and opportunities, a theoretical principle that is often proclaimed but rarely applied consistently. In my opinion, it is possible and desirable to go much further.

In any case, the rates and amounts indicated here are for illustrative purposes only, and are part of an exercise of reflection and deliberation on the ideal system that one wishes to build in the long term, and do not prejudge the gradualist strategies that may be chosen here and there, depending on the particular historical and political contexts. For example, in the current French context, it can be considered that the first priority is to reintroduce a modernized wealth tax (ISF), based on preprepared wealth declarations and much stricter control than in the past, which would at the same time reduce the property tax, which is a particularly burdensome and unfair wealth tax, especially for all indebted households in the process of becoming homeowners.[22]

---

21. After operation of the inheritance tax and the universal endowment.

22. See "Suppression of the Wealth Tax: A Historical Error," October 10, 2017; "Yellow Vests and Tax Justice," December 11, 2018.

Social Federalism: Toward a Different Organization of Globalization

Let's say it again clearly: it is quite possible to move gradually toward participatory socialism by changing the legal, fiscal, and social system in this or that country, without waiting for the unanimity of the planet. This is how the construction of the social state and the reduction of inequalities took place during the twentieth century. Educational equality and the social state can now be relaunched country by country. Germany or Sweden did not wait for authorization from the European Union or the United Nations to set up co-management, and other countries could do the same now. France's wealth tax revenues were growing at a brisk pace before it was abolished in 2017, which shows the extent to which the argument of widespread tax exile was a myth and confirms that it is possible to reintroduce a modernized wealth tax without delay.

In the United States, given the size of the country, governments can be even more ambitious. The new Democratic administration which took office in January 2021 will need to reconcile the country, especially after the events at Capitol Hill, and this will require taking decisive steps in the direction of social justice and redistribution.[23] I continue to believe that the Biden team would be well inspired to take up some of the key proposals made by Bernie Sanders and Elizabeth Warren during the U.S. presidential primary campaign, for instance, regarding the wealth tax on top billionaires. The U.S. federal government has the capability to effectively enforce such a tax,

23. See "The Fall of the U.S. Idol," January 12, 2021.

whose proceeds could contribute to upgrade the modest U.S. welfare state.

Having said that, it is quite clear that it is possible to go even further and faster by adopting an internationalist perspective and trying to rebuild the international system on a better basis. In general, to give internationalism a chance again, we need to turn our backs on the ideology of absolute free trade that has guided globalization in recent decades and put in place an alternative economic system, a model of development based on explicit and verifiable principles of economic, fiscal, and environmental justice. The important point is that this new model must be internationalist in its ultimate objectives but sovereignist in its practical modalities, in the sense that each country, each political community, must be able to set conditions for the pursuit of trade with the rest of the world, without waiting for the unanimous agreement of its partners. The difficulty is that this universalist sovereignty will not always be easy to distinguish from the nationalist type of sovereignty that is currently gaining momentum.

I would like to emphasize once again here how the different approaches can be distinguished, which seems to me to be a central issue for the future.[24] In particular, before considering possible unilateral sanctions against countries practicing social, fiscal, and climate dumping (sanctions in any case must remain incentive-based and reversible), it is essential to propose to other countries a cooperative model based on universal values of social justice, reduction of inequalities, and

---

24. See "Reconstructing Internationalism," July 14, 2020. I return to these questions in several other columns: "Agenda for Another Globalization," November 15, 2016; "Europe and the Class Cleavage," May 14, 2019; "Social-Federalism vs. National-Liberalism," February 11, 2020.

preservation of the planet. This requires in particular indicating precisely which transnational assemblies should be in charge of global public goods (climate, medical research, etc.) and common fiscal and climate justice measures (common taxes on the profits of large companies, the highest incomes, wealth, and carbon emissions). This applies in particular at the European level, where there is an urgent need to move away from the unanimity rule and meetings behind closed doors. The proposals contained in the Manifesto for the Democratization of Europe (tdem.eu) make it possible to move in this direction, and the creation in 2019 of a Franco-German Parliamentary Assembly (unfortunately without real powers) shows that it is perfectly possible for a subgroup of countries to build new institutions without waiting for the unanimity of the other countries.[25]

Beyond the European case, these discussions on social federalism also have a much broader scope. For example, the countries of West Africa are currently trying to redefine their common currency and definitively break away from colonial rule. This is an opportunity to put the West African currency at the service of a development project that is based on investment in youth and infrastructure (and not only for the mobility of capital and the richest). Moreover, it is too often forgotten in Europe that the WAEMU (West African Economic and Monetary Union) is in some ways more advanced than the eurozone. For example, in 2008 it introduced a directive establishing a common corporate tax base and obliging each country to apply a tax rate of between 25% and 30%, which the

25. See "Manifesto for the Democratization of Europe," December 10, 2018; "The Franco-German Assembly, a Unique Opportunity for Tax Justice in Europe," February 21, 2020.

European Union has so far been unable to agree on. More generally, the new monetary policies set up at the global level over the past ten years require a rethinking of the balance between monetary and fiscal approaches, and a comparative, historical and transnational perspective is again essential.[26]

At the global level, I believe that social-federalism and transnational parliamentary assemblies will also be necessary to regulate international economic relations and design adequate financial, fiscal, and environmental regulations (e.g., between the United States, Canada, and Mexico; between the United States and Europe; between Europe and Africa; and so on).

For a Feminist, Multiracial, and Universalist Socialism

The participatory socialism I am calling for is based on several pillars: educational equality and the social state, the permanent circulation of power and property, social federalism, and sustainable and fair globalization. On each of these points, it is essential to take stock without concession of the inadequacies of the various forms of socialism and social democracy experienced in the twentieth century.

Among the many limitations of the multiple socialist and social-democratic experiences of the past century, it must also be emphasized that the issues of patriarchy and postcolonialism have not been sufficiently taken into account. The important point is that these different issues cannot be thought of in isolation from one another. They have to be dealt with within

26. See "Will Money Creation Save Us?" July 9, 2019; "Time for Green Money," May 12, 2020.

the framework of a comprehensive socialist project based on the real equality of social, economic, and political rights.

All human societies up to the present day have been patriarchal societies in one way or another. Male domination has played a central and explicit role in all the inegalitarian ideologies that succeeded one another until the beginning of the twentieth century, whether ternary, proprietarist, or colonialist. Over the course of the twentieth century, the mechanisms of domination became more subtle (but no less real): formal equality of rights has gradually been established, but the ideology of a woman's place as being the home reached its apogee in the prosperous 1945–1975 period, known as the "thirty glorious years" in France. In the early 1970s, almost 80% of wage earners were men.[27] Here again, the question of indicators and their politicization is crucial. All too often, we are simply informed that the gender difference in pay for "the same job" is 15% or 20%. The problem is precisely that women do not have access to the same jobs as men do. At the end of their careers, the average pay gap (which will then continue throughout retirement, not including career breaks) is actually 64%. If we look at access to the best-paid jobs, we can see that things change only very slowly: at the current rate, it would take until the year 2102 to reach parity.[28]

In order to accelerate the movement and truly move away from patriarchy, it is essential to put in place binding, verifiable, and sanctioned measures, both for positions of responsibility in companies, administrations, and universities and in political assemblies. Recent work has shown that this improved representation of women could go hand in hand with an

27. See Piketty, *Capital and Ideology*, chapter 13.
28. See "Gender and Pay Inequality: 19% or 64%?," November 7, 2016.

improvement in the representation of disadvantaged social categories, which are currently virtually absent from assemblies. In other words, gender parity must advance in tandem with social parity.[29]

The issue of gender discrimination must also be considered in relation to the fight against ethno-racial discrimination, particularly in terms of access to employment. This also involves the necessary collective and civic reappropriation of colonial and postcolonial history. Some people are surprised today to see demonstrators of all origins attacking the statues of slave traders that still adorn many European and American cities. Yet it is essential to consider the extent of this shared history.

In France, it is all too often ignored that Haiti had to pay back a considerable debt to the French state between 1825 and 1950, all in order to have the right to be free and to finance financial compensation to slave owners (unjustly deprived of their property, according to the ideology of the time). Today Haiti is claiming reparations from France for this iniquitous tribute; it is difficult not to agree with Haiti, and this issue should no longer be postponed, particularly when today restitution is still being organized for spoliations that took place during the two world wars. More generally, it is easy to forget that the abolition of slavery in France and the United Kingdom was always accompanied by the payment of compensation to the owners, and never to the slaves themselves. Compensation to former slaves had been mentioned at the end of the U.S. Civil War (the famous forty acres and a mule), but nothing was ever paid out, in 1865 or a century later, in 1965, when legal segregation ended. In 1988, however, $20,000 in

29. See Julia Cagé, *Libres et égaux en voix* (Paris: Fayard, 2020).

compensation was awarded to Japanese-Americans unjustly interned during World War II. Compensation of the same type paid today to African-Americans who were victims of segregation would have a strong symbolic value.[30]

However, this legitimate and complex debate on reparations, which is essential to build confidence in a common standard of deliberation and justice, must be framed within a universalist perspective. In order to repair society from the damage of racism and colonialism, one cannot be satisfied with a logic based on eternal intergenerational compensation. Above all, we must also look to the future and change the economic system, based on the reduction of inequalities and equal access for all to education, employment, and property, including a minimum inheritance for all, regardless of their origins, in addition to compensation such as that enjoyed by Japanese-Americans and which could be enjoyed by African-Americans. The two perspectives, that of reparations and that of universal rights, should complement, not oppose, each other.

The same is true at the international level. The legitimate debate on reparations, such as those concerning Haiti, must take place in conjunction with a necessary reflection on a new universal system of international transfers. In particular, the current epidemic crisis can be an opportunity to reflect on a minimum health and education allocation for all the world's inhabitants, financed by a universal right for all countries to a share of the tax revenues paid by the most prosperous economic actors around the world: large companies and households with high incomes and assets. This prosperity is, after all, based on a global economic system—and incidentally on the unbridled exploitation of the world's natural and human

30. See "Confronting Racism, Repairing History," June 16, 2020.

resources for centuries. It therefore now requires global regulation to ensure its social and ecological sustainability.[31]

Let's conclude by insisting on the fact that the participatory socialism I'm calling for will not come from the top: it is useless to wait for a new proletarian vanguard to come and impose its solutions. The devices mentioned here aim to open the debate, never to close it. Real change can only come from the reappropriation by citizens of socioeconomic questions and indicators that allow us to organize collective deliberation. I hope that these words and the texts that follow can contribute to this.

February 2021

---

31. See "Avoiding the Worst," April 14, 2020. See also Simon Reid-Henry, "Global Public Investment: Redesigning International Public Finance for Social Cohesion," London, Queen Mary, 2020.

Toward a Different Globalization, 2016–2017

Hillary, Apple, and Us

September 13, 2016

In less than two months, the United States will have a new president. If Donald Trump wins, it would be a catastrophe for his country but also for the rest of the world. Racist, vulgar, full of himself and of his fortune, he epitomizes the worst of America. And the fact that Hillary Clinton has had so much difficulty in outdistancing him in the opinion polls should give us all food for thought.

Trump's strategy is classical: he explains to the poorer whites, who have been the losers in globalization, that their enemy is the poor Black, the immigrant, the Mexican, or the Muslim and that things will get better if the big white millionaire gets rid of all of them. He exacerbates the racial and identity conflict in order to avoid the class conflict which might well not be to his advantage. This predominance of ethnic cleavages has played a central role throughout the history of the United States and explains to a large extent the lack of solidarity and the weakness of the social state in America. Trump is happy to push this strategy to extremes with, however, several major innovations. In the first instance, he relies on an ideology of the well-deserved fortune and of the sacrosanct mantra of the market and private property which has reached unprecedented heights over the past few decades in the United States. This structuring of the political conflict is now tending to spread throughout the world today, in particular in Europe. In many places, we witness the rise in working-class constituencies of a mixture of attraction for xenophobia and resigned acceptance of the laws of globalized capitalism. Since it is unrealistic to expect anything much from the regulation of finance and multinationals, let's focus on immigrants and foreigners; it won't do us any harm even if we don't get much out of it. Many of those who vote for Trump or Le Pen have a fundamental conviction which is very simple: it is easier to attack immigrants than financial capitalism or to imagine another economic system.

Confronted with this fatal threat, the response of the left and the center is somewhat hesitant. At times it consists of siding with the dominant rhetoric in identity mode (as witness the miserable French polemic this summer over the burkini, supported by a prime minister who considers himself progressive). Or else, in most instances, of abandoning the working classes to their fate, guilty of voting against their party, or of low electoral turnout, and also of contributing less to the cost of their political campaigns (there is nothing like a few rich donors to get things going!). Thus left-wing and center parties find themselves also promoting the cult of the all-powerful market, differentiating themselves from the populist right mainly by their defense—at least formally, which is better than nothing—of racial and cultural equality. This enables them to keep the vote of the minorities and immigrants, while losing a considerable proportion of the local working classes, whence an increasingly marked retreat into the defense of the most privileged and best-equipped groups in the global market place.

The challenge is immense, and nobody has the miracle solution. It's a question of keeping solidarity alive within very large-scale political communities, riddled with multiple divides, which is not simple. In the United States, in 2008 Hillary Clinton was the instigator of a social project which in many ways was more ambitious than that of Barack Obama, for example, the project of universal health insurance coverage. Today, people are weary of the Clinton dynasty, the fees received from Goldman Sachs, the time spent with her husband's donors: Hillary increasingly appears as the candidate of the establishment. Now she has to learn from the Sanders vote and show the working-class electorate that she is the best placed to improve their situation. This will involve proposals for the minimum wage, public education, and fiscal justice. Several Democratic leaders are urging her to finally announce strong measures on taxation of multinationals and of the largest fortunes. In particular; she could build on the recent European decision to make Apple pay tax on its Irish profits, which would also enable her to oppose the conservative position of the U.S. Treasury and financial circles (whose dream is a fiscal amnesty for the profits repatriated from multinationals). The best solution would be to offer Europe the introduction of a significant minimum tax rate—at least 25% or 30%—on the profits of all European and American multinationals. This would force the European authorities to at long last apply a joint minimal tax rate on large firms (whereas the recent decision merely requested the application of the Irish rate of 12.5%, which is much too low, and once again puts Europe in the hands of the Competition Law judges). A speech of this sort would be proof of a genuine desire for a change in approach to globalization. For if firms like Apple and its consorts have obviously given the world huge innovations, the truth is that these giants could not have come into existence without decades of public research and community infrastructures, while benefiting from lower rates of taxation than small and medium businesses in America, as in Europe (and if the manager of Apple and his colleagues claim the contrary, they should finally publish detailed accounts). This complexity must be explained, which demands transparency and political courage. The time has come for Hillary Clinton to demonstrate this.

The IMF, the Inequality Debate, and Economic Research

September 21, 2016

A few weeks ago, the IMF published a study challenging some of the inequality-generating mechanisms described in my book *Capital in the Twenty-First Century*.[1]

To make it clear, I am very pleased that my book has made a contribution to stimulating public discussion about inequality, and all the contributions to this debate are worth taking on board!

In this instance however, the IMF study does seem to me to be rather weak and not very convincing, and I would like to briefly explain why here. To be precise, I had already replied to similar arguments in my book (which unfortunately is very long!), as well as in several shorter and more recent articles.[2]

---

1. Carlos Góes, "Testing Piketty's Hypothesis on the Drivers of Income Inequality: Evidence from Panel VARs with Heterogeneous Dynamics," IMF Working Paper, 2016. https://www.imf.org/external/pubs/ft/wp/2016/wp16160.pdf.

2. See, for example: Thomas Piketty, "About *Capital in the Twenty-First Century*," *American Economic Review* 105, no. 5 (2015): 48–53; Piketty,

But it is only normal that the discussion should continue, particularly when it concerns questions which are as complex and also as controversial.

Briefly, the IMF study aims to demonstrate that there is no systematic relationship between inequality on one hand and the r-g gap separating the return on capital, r, and the economy's rate of growth, g, on the other. To this end, the study uses a measure of inequality for a number of developed countries between 1980 and 2012, a measure of the r-g gap for these same countries and these same years and attempts to estimate whether there is a statistical relationship between these two variables. Technically, they run a statistical regression between a measure of the inequality and a measure of $r - g$. The idea of undertaking a regression of this type is not unreasonable as such—on condition, however, that adequate data are available. Now the problem is that for both terms of the regression, the IMF uses totally inappropriate data, both for inequality and for the r-g gap, with the result that it is almost impossible to learn anything useful from this exercise.

Let's begin with the measurement of inequality. The first problem is that the IMF uses a measurement of inequality of income and not of inequality of wealth. This poses a major difficulty insofar as inequality of income is determined mainly by income from labor (that is to say, the wages of salaried employees and incomes of self-employed persons, which represent the vast majority of incomes, far above dividends, interest,

---

"Putting Distribution Back at the Center of Economics: Reflections on Capital in the Twenty-First Century," *Journal of Economic Perspectives* 29, no. 1 (2015): 67–88; Piketty, "Vers une économie politique et historique. Réflexions sur le capital au xxiᵉ siècle," *Annales. Histoire, sciences sociales* 70, no. 1 (2015): 125–138. Other texts are available at http://piketty.pse.ens.fr /fr/articles-de-presse/97.

rents, and other incomes from capital; the exact labor vs. capital share varies over time and country, but typically amounts to 70% vs 30% for the countries and periods considered by the IMF). Now the range of employment incomes depends on all sorts of mechanisms influencing the working of the labor market (inequality in access to education and skills, technical change, and international competition, evolution of the role of trade unions and of the minimum wage, corporate governance and rules for determining the salaries of managers, etc.), and is in no way dependent on the r-g gap (which only applies to the dynamics of the income from capital and its distribution).

As I analyze in my book[3] as well as in the articles referred to above, the explanation for the rise in inequality of income in a great many countries since the 1980s, in particular the United States, is due in the first instance to mechanisms affecting the labor market and the inequality of labor incomes. There are legitimate disagreements about the respective weights of these various mechanisms in enabling us to account for the rise in inequality of labor incomes. For example, I insist on the role of institutional and political differences between countries, in particular, in matters of inequality of access to education, the minimum wage, the salaries of managers and how they are influenced by progressivity of the tax system. Others insist more on the role of technical change and international competition (which I do not deny but which does not enable us to explain why inequality has increased much more sharply in the United States and in the United Kingdom than in Germany, Sweden, France, or Japan). In any event, these various mechanisms have absolutely nothing to do with the

3. Thomas Piketty, *Capital in the Twenty-First Century* (Cambridge, MA: Harvard University Press, 2014), in particular, chapters 7–9.

gap between the return on capital, r, and the rate of growth, g. In these circumstances, doing a regression analysis between a general measurement of income inequality (which therefore depends primarily on inequality of income from employment) and the r-g gap makes little sense.

It would have been more justified to use a measure of inequality of wealth. This would have made it possible to estimate the dynamic multiplier effect on the dispersion of wealth of a bigger r-g gap, all things being equal (in particular the saving rates of the various income groups), and for a given level of labor income inequality. In fact, as I demonstrate in my book,[4] the historical data available on wealth show that it is necessary to use a multiplier mechanism of this sort to explain the very high level of concentration of wealth observed historically in all countries, particularly in the nineteenth century and until World War I. Unfortunately at the moment, these data only exist for a small number of countries over the long-term (France, the United Kingdom, the United States, and Sweden). This is too few to carry out a regression of the type favored by the IMF. But this is the best we have at this stage, and it shows the importance of this amplifier mechanism. Intuitively, a higher return on capital (and not chiseled off by taxation, inflation, or destruction, as was the case in the nineteenth century and until 1914) and a lower growth rate lead to multiplying and prolonging the inequalities in wealth constituted in the past.[5] The French

4. Thomas Piketty, *Capital in the Twenty-First Century* (Cambridge, MA: Harvard University Press, 2014), in particular, chapters 10–12.

5. For a given level of inequality in employment and models and simulations, see Thomas Piketty and Gabriel Zucman, "Wealth and Inheritance in the Long Run," in *Handbook of Income Distribution*, vol. 2B, ed. Anthony B. Atkinson and François Bourguignon (Amsterdam: Elsevier, 2015), 1303–1368.

individual inheritance data which we have retrieved with Gilles Postel-Vinay and Jean-Laurent Rosenthal in the property registers archives from the time of the French Revolution to the present-day also confirms the importance of this mechanism in accounting for the historical evolution of the wealth distribution and the age-wealth profile by age.[6] All this in no way means that the r-g mechanism is the only factor responsible: The history of inequality is complex and multidimensional, and research is ongoing. But at the very least, this indicates that the multiplier mechanism of inequality in wealth is part of the issue to be considered, provided that we take the time to examine appropriate data.

In fact, to further our research, we have to continue our work on the collection of data on income and wealth, carefully distinguishing between mechanisms which apply on the one hand to inequality in employment, in qualifications, and in wage formation, and on the other, inequality in capital, in accession to property, and to the returns on wealth. These two series of mechanisms are linked but bring into play specific approaches. It is precisely this long-term endeavor which we have undertaken in the context of the World Wealth and Income Database,[7] a database which my colleagues Facundo Alvaredo, Tony Atkinson, Emmanuel Saez, Gabriel Zucman, and I have been assembling for the past fifteen years. Today this project brings together more than ninety researchers from

6. See in particular, Thomas Piketty, Gilles Postel-Vinay, and Jean-Laurent Rosenthal, "Wealth Concentration in a Developing Economy: Paris and France, 1807–1994," *American Economic Review* 96, no. 1 (2006): 236–256; Piketty, Postel-Vinay, and Laurent Rosenthal, "Inherited vs Self-Made Wealth: Theory & Evidence from a Rentier Society (Paris, 1872–1927)," *Explorations in Economic History* 51, no. C (2014): 21–40.

7. World Inequality Database (WID), http://www.wid.world.

almost seventy countries all over the world. From this point of view, one of the most beneficial effects of the discussions following the publication of *Capital in the Twenty-First Century* (which is, to a large extent, based on this database) is that we now have access to the fiscal and financial archives of a large number of countries, in particular in Asia, Africa, and Latin America, which we could not previously use. We are gradually putting on-line the totality of the new data produced, with all the technical details concerning their construction, and a new website providing more accessible visualization tools will be available in the coming months.

Instead of heading into poorly constructed statistical regressions and the defense of outdated ideological positions, the IMF economists would do better to spend more time participating in the collective endeavor toward financial transparency and the collection of improved data on inequality.

The second problem posed by the IMF study, at least as serious as the first, is the way in which the gap between r and g is measured. To estimate the return on capital, r, the IMF uses measurements of interest rate on the sovereign debt. The difficulty here is that the large portfolios and great amounts of wealth are not invested in Treasury bills (contrary to what the IMF seems to imagine). As I demonstrate in my book,[8] it is impossible to account for the expansion in the biggest fortunes at world level over recent decades if one does not take into account the fact that different levels of wealth have access to very different returns. In other words, the holder of a little *Livret A* (savings bank passbook) and the owner of a considerable portfolio invested in shares and financial derivatives do

8. Thomas Piketty, *Capital in the Twenty-First Century* (Cambridge, MA: Harvard University Press, 2014), see in particular chapter 12.

Table 2. The growth rate of top global wealth, 1987–2013

Measure	Average real growth rate per year (after deduction of inflation), 1987–2013 (%)
The top 1/(100 million) highest wealth holders (about thirty adults out of 3 billion in 1980s, and forty-five adults out of 4.5 billion in 2010s)	6.8
The top 1/(20 million) highest wealth holders (about 150 adults out of 3 billion in 1980s, and 225 adults out of 4.5 billion in 2010s)	6.4
Average world wealth per adult	2.1
Average world income per adult	1.4
World adult population	1.9
World GDP	3.3

Sources: See piketty.pse.ens.fr/capital21c; Thomas Piketty, *Capital in the Twenty-First Century* (Cambridge, MA: Harvard University Press, 2014), p. 693.
Interpretation: Between 1987 and 2013, the highest global wealth fractiles have grown at 6–7% per year, vs. 2.1% for average world wealth and 1.4% for average world income. All growth rates are net of inflation (2.3% per year between 1987 and 2013).

not have access to the same capital return, or r. If one chooses to totally ignore this fact, then this makes it difficult to identify the impact on the returns on capital of the dynamics of inequality in wealth.

In fact, if we examine the data available on global rankings of fortunes (data which are very far from perfect, but which do give a more realistic image of the top levels of the distribution than the data from official surveys based on self-declaration), we observe that the highest levels of wealth have risen at a rate of around 6–7% per year in the world since the

1980s, compared with 2.1% for the average wealth and 1.4% for average income.

This evolution is itself the product of multiple and complex phenomena. The new technological fortunes and the innovators have certainly played their role, as have the waves of privatization of natural resources (the Russian millionaires did not invent the oil or natural gas reserves: they simply became their owners and then diversified their portfolios) and of former public monopolies (for example, in telecommunications, often sold at low prices to happy beneficiaries, like Carlos Slim in Mexico, as in many other countries). We also observe that above a certain level of fortune, wealth tends to grow mechanically at a higher rate than the average.

This is confirmed by an examination of the data available on the returns obtained by the financial endowments of the major American universities (data which at least have the merit of being made public, which is not the case for individual portfolios). We observe extremely high returns (an average of 8.2% per year between 1980 and 2010, after deduction of inflation and all the administrative costs) with a high graduation depending on the size of the endowment (6% for the smallest endowments to over 10% for the bigger ones).

In other words, the capital endowments of American universities have not been placed in Treasury bills for quite some time: The detailed data available to us show that, on the contrary, these very high returns are obtained by investments in extremely risky and sophisticated assets (commodity and equity derivatives, unquoted companies, etc.) which are not accessible to small portfolios. Unfortunately, we do not have such detailed data for individual portfolios, but everything leads us to believe that this same type of effect is in play (not perhaps to the same extent). In any event, it does not seem to me to be very serious to claim to be studying the unequal

Table 3. The return on the capital endowments of U.S.
universities, 1980–2010

Endowment	Average real annual rate of return, 1980–2010 (%)
All universities (850)	8.2
Harvard-Yale-Princeton	10.2
Endowments greater than $1 billion (60)	8.8
Endowments between $500 million and $1 billion (66)	7.8
Endowments between $100 and $500 million (226)	7.1
Endowments less than $100 million (498)	6.2

Sources: See piketty.pse.ens.fr/capital21c; Thomas Piketty, *Capital in the Twenty-First Century* (Cambridge, MA: Harvard University Press, 2014), p. 716.
Interpretation: Between 1980 and 2010, U.S. universities earned an average real return of 8.2% on their capital endowments, and more for larger endowments. All returns reported here are net of inflation (2.4% per year between 1980 and 2010) and of all administrative costs and financial fees.

impact of the r-g gap on the dynamics of wealth by simply ignoring this inequality of returns obtained by the various investors and by attributing to each the interest rate of the sovereign debt.

One last point: I would like to make it clear that this type of controversy seems to me to be perfectly natural and healthy for democratic debate. Some would prefer that the "experts" in economic questions come to an agreement to enable the rest of the world to draw the necessary conclusions. I quite understand this standpoint, and at the same time, it seems to me unrealistic. Research in the social sciences, of which economics is an integral part, whatever some may think, is and always will be hesitant and imperfect. It is not designed to produce ready-made certainties. There is no universal law of economics: There is only a multiplicity of historical experiences and imperfect data, which we have to examine patiently to endeavor to draw some provisional and uncertain lessons. Everyone must gain an understanding of these questions and of these materials to draw their own conclusions without allowing themselves to be intimidated by the well-argued opinions of others.

The French Right and the European Budgetary Rules

October 18, 2016

One does sometimes wonder why the French are so morose. The answer is fairly simple. As a result of the errors of their governments, the countries in the eurozone have just experienced the longest period of stagnation since World War II. In 2017, the level of economic activity in the area will with difficulty rise to its 2007 level, with huge regional and social disparities. In particular, young people and the less privileged were faced with a sharp rise in underemployment. In the meantime, the rest of the world will have continued to grow. China, of course, but also the United States, which was at the origin of the crisis in 2008, but which has shown more budgetary flexibility in relaunching its economy. In France the unemployment rate at the end of 2007 was just under 7% and at the end of 2016 will be in the region of 10%—in other words, a rise of 50%. Contrary to what one still hears too frequently in government circles in Paris, Brussels, or Berlin, this massive rise has nothing to do with a labor market which has suddenly become less flexible or with bus routes insufficiently deregulated. This is not to say that these discussions on the much-discussed structural reforms

aimed at the introduction of more flexibility and more competition are not worth our attention (even if they are often very
poorly formulated). All we mean is that it would be easier to
achieve them if we began by recognizing that the explosion in
unemployment since 2008 is in the first instance due to austerity programs, or more precisely, to an attempt to reduce
budgetary deficits too quickly. This led to a fall in economic
activity in the eurozone in 2011–2013, from which we have
barely recovered. The facts are not disputed if they are exam-
ined calmly.[1] It is now time for the various policy makers in
France and in Germany, who participated in these decisions,
to agree on a common diagnosis of what happened during this
period and above all to accept to learn from their mistakes for
the future.

From this point of view, the fact that the candidates in
the right-wing primary—the winner of which stands a good
chance of winning the presidential and parliamentary elections in spring 2017—seem to be in no hurry to reduce the
deficits is good news—but on two conditions. In the first instance, the lean budgetary margins thus obtained must enable
the defense of the most vulnerable, and investment in the
future and should not finance gifts for the most wealthy (e.g.,
elimination of the wealth tax, reductions in high rates of taxation for large estates and high incomes). In choosing to ignore
the lowest incomes and giving preference to the richest, the
right-wing candidates are in the wrong time period. They are
also on the point of ensuring a clear route to the National
Front, who will present themselves as the defenders of those

1. See Thomas Piketty, "2007–2015: Such a Long Recession," *Le Monde,*
February 27, 2016, https://www.lemonde.fr/blog/piketty/2016/02/27/2007
-2015-such-a-long-recession/.

who pay less tax while at the same time claiming primacy in matters of identity and xenophobia. As far as tax cuts are concerned, priority should go to relief in the property tax for those who wish to become property owners and the structural reduction of the tax burden on labor instead of the CICE (*Crédit d'impôt pour la compétitivité et l'emploi,* or tax credit scheme for employment and competitiveness), an incomprehensible and inefficient scheme invented by the Left in power. Let's also hope that the Right will not be stupid enough to abolish the withholding of income tax at source, at long last voted by the Left. They would do better to continue the somewhat overdue upgrading of our fiscal and social system by unifying the retirement schemes for the younger generations.

Finally, and above all, it is time for policy makers in France, both on the Left and on the Right, to bring to the table proposals for the reform of the European budgetary criteria. We cannot simply continue to violate these without proposing anything in their place. The main lesson in the past few years has been that the circumvention of democracy by automatic regulations does not enable budgetary policy to adapt to unforeseen economic situations. This is what led to the reversal in recovery in 2011–2013. There are not an infinite number of solutions. The rigid rules must be replaced by a majority vote in a true eurozone parliamentary chamber, in which each country would be represented in proportion to its population (that is, 24% of the seats to Germany and 51% for France, Italy, and Spain combined) following a public and adversarial debate. An instance of this sort would also confer the democratic legitimacy required for a genuine eurozone budget. If France were to make a specific proposal, then Germany would have to accept a compromise, perhaps with a combination of indicative rules and qualified majorities. Reform is particularly urgent as the budgetary criteria have been considerably toughened by the 2012 Treaty. The aim now is to work toward a maximum deficit of 0.5% of gross domestic product (GDP). As soon as the interest rates rise again, this will imply huge primary surpluses for decades (as a reminder: the interest on the debt already represents 200 billion euros per year in Europe, vs 2 billion per year for the Erasmus program). In passing, it has been forgotten that in the 1950s, Europe was built on the cancellation of past debts, in particular, to the benefit of France and Germany, to enable investment in the future. The French Right is perhaps preparing to come to power in a very difficult context. Let's hope that it will be equal to the challenge.

Gender Pay Inequality:
19% or 64%?
November 7, 2016

F rance is mobilizing today to denounce gender pay inequalities. The figure today is 19%, which is an estimate of the average wage gap between men and
women for the same job. In other words, it is as if
women were working for men beginning on November 7 at
16:34 (i.e., 4:34 p.m.). As emblematic as it is, this figure should
not make us forget that things are actually much worse than
that, because women still do not have access to the same jobs
as men do—far from it.

Let's start by looking at the evolution of the ratio of the
average working income of men to women (all jobs combined,
and including unemployed people) according to age in France
in 2014.[1] We see that inequality increases very sharply with
age, from just over 1.2 at the beginning of a career to more than
1.6 at the end of a career.

1. These results are based on research conducted with Bertrand
Garbinti and Jonathan Goupille-Lebret on the dynamics of inequality in
France. For a more complete presentation, see http://piketty.pse.ens.fr
/files/GGP2016DINASlides.pdf.

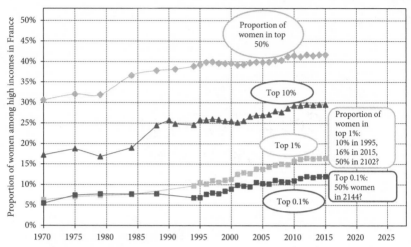

Figure 3. The persistence of patriarchy in France in the twenty-first century. The proportion of women in the top percentile (top 1%) of the distribution of labor income (wages and self-employment income) increased from 10% in 1995 to 16% in 2015 and should reach 50% by 2102 if the trend continues at the same speed as during the 1995–2015 period. For the top 0.1%, parity could wait until 2144. *Sources and series:* see piketty.pse.ens.fr/ideology.

In other words, around the age of twenty-five, women work almost as often as men, and on average work in relatively comparable jobs, so that the income gap observed (25%) roughly corresponds to the wage gap measured in equivalent jobs (usually between 10% and 20%, according to estimates; hence there is some confusion about the figure for today, especially since the gap can be expressed in two ways: if women earn on average 16% less than men do, then men earn 19% more than women do; I choose this second way). But as careers progress, women are less often promoted than men in the highest-paid jobs, so the gap soars with age: it exceeds 60% around the age of fifty, and reaches 64% on the eve of retirement. This

graph quite clearly illustrates the limits of the "all things being equal" reasoning applied to gender inequality: true, for the
same job, the same qualifications, the gap is "only" 10% or 20%
(which is already considerable); but the fact is that women do
not work in "equal" jobs.

One could be reassured by noting that this graph also illustrates the fact that women of older generations (those currently in their fifties or sixties) had less continuous professional
careers than do the younger generations, and that they suffered
more from occupational discrimination and sexist biases than
younger generations. In other words, everything gradually
settles down, and you just have to wait a little while for the
curve shown above to flatten naturally. Unfortunately, there is
a risk of a long wait, as the following graph illustrates; it shows
the evolution of women's share among the various high-income
groups in the labor market since 1970.

Women continue to be massively underrepresented in
the highest-paying jobs. A particularly extreme case is that of
the 1% of the highest paid; the share of women has increased
in recent decades, but at an extremely slow rate: between 5%
and 10% of women in the 1970s, 10% in 1994, 16% in 2012. If we
continue the observed evolution, then we have to wait until
2102 to reach parity. It's a long wait.

Agenda for Another Globalization

November 15, 2016

L et it be said at once: Trump's victory is primarily due to the explosion in economic and territorial inequality in the United States over several decades and the incapacity of successive governments to deal with these. Both the Clinton and the Obama administrations frequently only went along with the move to liberalization and sacralization of the market launched under Reagan, then Bush, father and son; at times they even exacerbated their predecessors. The financial and commercial deregulation carried out under Clinton is an example. The suspicion of proximity with finance and the inability of the Democrats' politico-media elite to learn the lessons from the Sanders vote sealed the deal. Hillary won the popular vote by a whisker, but the participation of the youngest and the lowest income groups was too low to enable key states to be won.

The tragedy is that Trump's program will only strengthen the tendency to inequality. He intends to abolish the health insurance laboriously granted to low-paid workers under Obama and to set the country on a headlong course into fiscal dumping, with a reduction from 35% to 15% in the rate of federal tax on corporation profits, whereas to date, the United States had resisted this perpetual race against time which came from Europe. In addition, the increasing ethnicization in politics in America does not bode well for the future if new compromises are not found. Here is a country where structurally 60% of the white majority votes for one party, while over 70% of the minorities vote for the other and where the majority is on the verge of losing its numerical superiority (70% of the votes cast in 2016, as compared with 80% in 2000, and 50% forecast in 2040).

The main lesson for Europe and the world is clear: As a matter of urgency, globalization must be fundamentally reoriented. The main challenges of our times are the rise in inequalities and global warming. We must therefore implement international treaties enabling us to respond to these challenges and to promote a model for fair and sustainable development. Agreements of a new type can, if necessary, include measures aimed at facilitating exchanges in goods and services. But the question of liberalizing trade should no longer be the main focus. Trade must once again become what it should never have ceased to be: a means in the service of higher ends. In concrete terms, there must be an end to the signature of international agreements reducing customs duties and other commercial barriers without inclusion in the same treaty, and from the outset, of quantified and binding measures to combat fiscal and climate dumping. For example, there could be common minimum rates of corporation tax and targets for carbon emissions which can be verified and sanctioned. It is no longer possible to negotiate trade treaties for free trade with nothing in exchange.

From this point of view, the EU-Canada Comprehensive Economic and Trade Agreement (CETA) is a treaty which belongs to another age and should be rejected. It is a strictly commercial treaty and contains absolutely no binding measures concerning fiscal or climate issues. However, it does contain a considerable reference to the "protection of investors," enabling multinationals to sue states in private arbitration courts, bypassing the public tribunals available to one and all. The legal supervision proposed is clearly inadequate, in particular, concerning the key question of the remuneration of the arbitrators, and will lead to all sorts of abuses. At the very time when American legal imperialism is gaining in strength and imposing its rules and its dues on our companies, this decline in public justice is an aberration. The priority, on the contrary, should be the construction of strong public authorities, with the creation of a European prosecutor and justice system capable of enforcing their decisions.

What sense is there in signing under the Paris Accords a purely theoretical aim of limiting global warming to 1.5 degrees (which would, for example, require the oil found in the tar sands in Alberta to be left in the ground, whereas Canada has just started mining there again) then, a few months later, to sign a binding commercial treaty without a single mention of this question? A balanced treaty between Canada and Europe, aimed at promoting a partnership for fair and sustainable development, should begin by specifying the emission targets of each signatory and the practical commitments to achieve these.

In matters of fiscal dumping and minimum rates of taxation on corporation profits, this would obviously mean a complete change in paradigm for Europe, which was constructed as a free trade area with no common fiscal policy. This change is, however, essential. What sense is there in agreeing on a common fiscal policy (which is the one area in which Europe has achieved a little bit of progress for the moment) if each country can then fix a near-zero rate and attract all the major company headquarters? It is time to change the political discourse on globalization: trade is a good thing, but fair and sustainable development also demands public services, infrastructures, and health and education systems. In turn, these themselves demand fair taxation systems, failing which, Trumpism will prevail.

Basic Income or Fair Wage?

December 13, 2016

The debate on basic income has at least one virtue, namely, that of reminding us that there is a degree of consensus in France on the fact that everyone should have a minimum income. Disagreements exist over the amount. At the moment, the Revenu de Solidarité Active or RSA (the French minimum income scheme) granted to single individuals with no dependent children is 530 euros per month, a sum which some people find sufficient, and others would like to increase to 800 euros. But on both the Right and the Left, everyone seems to agree on the existence of a minimum income around this level in France as, moreover, in numerous other European countries. In the United States, the childless poor have to make do with food stamps, and the social state often assumes the guise of guardian or even prison. In contrast, the French and European consensus is to be commended, but at the same time, we cannot consider it satisfactory.

The problem with the discussion about basic income is that in most instances, it leaves the real issues unexplored and in reality expresses a concept of social justice on the cheap. The question of justice is not simply a matter of 530 euros or

800 euros a month. If we wish to live in a fair and just society, we have to formulate more ambitious objectives which cover the distribution of income and wealth in its entirety and consequently, the distribution of access to power and opportunities. Our ambition must be that of a society based on a fair return to labor, in other words, a fair wage and not simply a basic income. To move in the direction of a fair wage, we have to rethink a whole set of institutions and policies which interact with one another: these include public services, and in particular, education, labor law, and organizations and the tax system.

In the first instance, we have to challenge the hypocrisies in our educational system, which too frequently reproduces or even exacerbates inequalities. This is the case in higher education. Those university tracks that are the most attended by disadvantaged students are massively underfunded compared with the elitist grande ecoles tracks that are more often attended by better-off students. The situation has only gotten worse, with the result that today, whole generations cram into overcrowded lecture halls.

The same is true for schools and technical colleges. In practice, the underprivileged establishments have many more inexperienced teachers on short-term contracts than the others, with the result that effective public expenditure per pupil is in reality less than elsewhere. In the absence of a transparent and verifiable policy of allocation of means, the focus has been on stigmatizing establishments by categorizing them as being in an educational priority area or ZEP (Zone d'éducation prioritaire), without increasing their resources, whereas the authorities should have done the exact opposite.

If in addition we bear in mind the fact that nothing has been done to promote a mix of social classes and that private schools are allowed to recruit whomever might be thought fit, while benefiting from public financing, we are very far from the equality of opportunity vaunted in the advertising slogans in electoral campaigns.

To move toward fair pay, we must stop denigrating the role of trade unions, the minimum wage, and salary scales. We should reconsider the role assigned to the employees' representatives. In countries where they play an active role on the executive boards—between one-third and half of the votes in Sweden and Germany—we find a narrower range of salary scales, greater investment of the employees in the firms' strategy, and as a result, higher productivity. In addition, there is nothing to prevent us from imagining original forms of power sharing, with the board members being elected by a combination of employees and shareholders (to go beyond the interaction between paid administrators and shareholders with the latter automatically holding the majority).

To restrict the power of capital and its perpetuation, the tax system must also play its role fully, in particular, by means of a progressive tax on property, which enables the transformation of the right of ownership into a temporary right, at least for the largest property owners. This is in effect what inheritance taxes do for intergenerational transmissions (family property is no longer permanent), and annual progressive taxes on property do the same within a lifetime. Instead, the right-wing wishes to suppress our meager wealth tax (ISF—Impôt Sur la Fortune); this should instead be brought closer to the property tax (taxe foncière), to reduce this for smaller property owners.

Finally, a progressive income tax rate should contribute to the fair wage by reducing the income gap to the strict minimum. Historical experience shows that high marginal tax rates on very high incomes—82% on average between 1930 and 1980 in the United States—enabled an end to giant salaries, to the considerable benefit of lower salaries and economic efficiency.

The last point is that with deduction of income tax at source, a progressive income tax enables the basic income due to low-wage earners to be paid directly in the paycheck or remuneration statement. At the moment, a full-time employee paid at the minimum wage rate (the SMIC) earns 1,150 euros net, after deduction from his gross wage of 1,460 euros of 310 euros for the CSG (Generalized Social Contribution) and other contributions. On application, several months later, the employee is eligible for an activity allowance, equivalent to 130 euros per month. It would be infinitely preferable to reduce the deduction at source and raise the net salary by an equivalent amount.

For the same reason, I have difficulty understanding those who insist on wishing to pay a basic income of 500 euros per month to those earning a salary of 2,000 euros, and then get back the same sum by raising their taxes deducted at the source.

It is now time for the debate on justice to ask the right questions.

The Passing of
Anthony B. Atkinson

January 3, 2017

A nthony B. Atkinson passed away on the morning of January 1, 2017, at the age of 72, after a long illness. This leaves us with an inestimable loss.

Anthony "Tony" Atkinson occupies a unique place among economists. During the past half-century, in defiance of prevailing trends, he placed the question of inequality at the center of his work, while demonstrating that economics is first and foremost a social and moral science.

Tony was born in 1944 and published his first book in 1969. Between 1969 and 2016, he wrote over forty books and more than 350 scholarly articles. They have brought about a profound transformation in the broader field of international studies of inequality, poverty, and the distribution of income and wealth. Since the 1970s, he has also written major theoretical papers devoted in particular to the theory of optimal taxation. Atkinson was always interested in practical issues of public policy and social justice, and understood that marrying theoretical analysis with a careful look at the actual data was the most powerful way to make progress.

Atkinson's most important and profound work has to do with the historical and empirical analysis of inequality, carried out within a theoretical frame that he deploys with impeccable mastery and utilizes with caution and moderation. With his distinctive approach, at once historical, empirical, and theoretical; with his extreme rigor and his unquestioned probity; with his ethical reconciliation of his roles as researcher in the social sciences and citizen of, respectively, the United Kingdom, Europe, and the world, Atkinson has himself for decades been a model for generations of students and young researchers.

Together with Simon Kuznets, Atkinson single-handedly originated a new discipline in the social sciences and political economy: the study of historical trends in the distribution of income and wealth. Of course, the question of distribution and long-term trends already lay at the heart of nineteenth-century political economy, particularly in the work of Thomas Malthus, David Ricardo, and Karl Marx. But these writers could draw only on limited data and were frequently obliged to limit themselves to purely theoretical speculation.

It was not until the second half of the twentieth century and the research of Kuznets and Atkinson that analyses of distribution of income and wealth could actually be based on historical sources. In his 1953 masterwork, *Shares of Upper Income Groups in Income and Savings,* Kuznets combined the first systematic records of American national income and property (records that he himself had helped to create) and the data produced by the federal income tax (established in 1913, in the aftermath of a prolonged political battle), to establish the very first historical account of year-by-year income distribution.

In 1978, in *The Distribution of Personal Wealth in Britain,* a fundamental book (co-written with Allan Harrison),

Atkinson outstripped and overtook Kuznets: He made systematic use of British probate records from the 1910s to the 1970s to analyze in magisterial fashion the extent to which different economic, social, and political forces can help us understand the developments observed in the distribution of wealth, a distribution that was particularly under scrutiny during this period of exceptional turbulence. Compared to Kuznets's book, which was mostly concerned with the construction of the statistical database, Atkinson's book goes a step further, in the sense that it better articulates the data collection with the historical and theoretical analysis.

All subsequent work on historic trends in income and wealth inequality to a certain extent follow in the wake of Kuznets's and Atkinson's groundbreaking studies. In particular, the World Wealth and Income Database (WID.world) can be viewed as a mere continuation of the Atkinson-Kuznets agenda.

At a more personal level, I was very fortunate to meet Tony when I was a young student at the London School of Economics in the fall of 1991. His many advices, always delivered with infinite care and kindness, had a decisive impact on my trajectory. Soon after I published *Top Incomes in France in the Twentieth Century,* in 2001, I had the chance to benefit from his enthusiastic support. Tony was the first reader of my historical work on inequality in France, and he immediately took up the British case (where historical income data had not been exploited yet) as well as a number of other countries. Together, we edited two thick volumes that came out in 2007 and 2010, covering twenty countries in all. These works are at the origin of the database WID.world, and also of my 2014 book *Capital in the Twenty-First Century,* which could not have existed without the support of Tony.

Leaving aside his historic and pioneering writings, Atkinson has been for decades one of the leading international specialists doing comparative investigations on the measurement of inequality and poverty in contemporary society. He has also been the tireless architect of projects for international cooperation on these subjects.

In his most recent book, published in 2015, *Inequality: What Can Be Done?*—wholly focused on a plan of action—he provided us with the broad outlines of a new radical reformism based on his many decades of research analyzing inequality and public policy. Witty, elegant, and profound, this book brings us the finest blend of what political economy and British progressivism have to offer.

Atkinson was a generous and rigorous scholar, a unique source of inspiration for all of us. He was also the kindest of mentors. Although he had been fighting a long illness in the last years of his life, he remained extremely active until the very end, continuing work on several big projects, and interacting with his colleagues and friends even in recent weeks. Atkinson dies at a time when inequality has become probably the most pressing issue that our societies are facing. His life has been about creating the tools to measure, understand, and tackle inequality. His work will live on as we continue confronting the problem of inequality. We will miss him deeply.

On Productivity in France and in Germany

January 5, 2017

At the start of 2017, with the elections in France in the spring and then in Germany in autumn, it may prove useful to return to one of the fundamental issues which plagues discussion at the European level, that is, the alleged economic asymmetry between Germany with its reputation as prosperous and France, which is described as on the decline. I use the term "alleged" because, as we shall see, the level of productivity of the German and French economies—as measured in terms of GDP per hour worked, which is by far the most relevant indicator of economic performance—is almost identical. Furthermore, it is at the highest world level, demonstrating incidentally that the European social model has a bright future, despite what the Brexiters and Trumpers of every hue might think. This will also enable me to return to several of the issues addressed in this blog in 2016 (in particular concerning the long European recession and the reconstruction of Europe[1])

1. See Thomas Piketty, "2007–2015: Such a Long Recession," *Le Monde,* February 27, 2016, https://www.lemonde.fr/blog/piketty/2016/02/27/2007

as well as in my December 2016 article "Basic Income or Fair Wage?"[2]

Let's start with the most striking fact. If we calculate the average labor productivity by dividing the GDP (the gross domestic product, that is, the total value of goods and services produced in a country in one year) by the total number of hours worked (by both salaried and nonsalaried employees), we then find that France is at practically the same level as the United States and Germany, with an average productivity of approximately 55 euros per hour worked in 2015, or more than 25% higher than the United Kingdom or Italy (roughly 42 euros) and almost three times higher than in 1970 (less than the equivalent of 20 euros in 2015; all figures are expressed in purchasing power parity and in 2015 euros, that is, after taking into account inflation and price levels in the different countries).

Let us state at the outset that the data at our disposal to measure the number of hours worked is not perfect and that the accuracy of these figures should not be exaggerated. Furthermore, the very concept of "GDP per hour worked" is in itself somewhat abstract and simplistic. In reality, in these comparisons it is the totality of the economic system and the organization of labor and production in each country which comes into play, with a wide range of variations between sectors and firms; and it is somewhat unrealistic to claim to subsume the totality in a single indicator. But if productivity between countries has to be compared (an exercise which has

-2015-such-a-long-recession/; Piketty, "Reconstructing Europe after Brexit," *Le Monde,* June 30, 2016, https://www.lemonde.fr/blog/piketty/2016/06/30/reconstructing-europe-after-brexit/.

2. Thomas Piketty, "Basic Income or Fair Wage?" *Le Monde,* December 13, 2016, https://www.lemonde.fr/blog/piketty/2016/12/13/basic-income-or-fair-wage/.

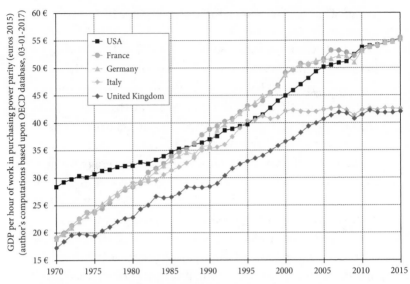

Figure 4. Labor productivity (GDP per hour of work), 1970–2015
(2015 euros). Labor productivity, as measured by GDP per hour
worked (in constant 2015 euros and purchasing power parity), rose
from 18 euros in Germany and France in 1970 to 55 euros in 2015.
Germany and France caught up with (or slightly exceeded) the
level of the United States around 1985–1990, while the United
Kingdom remained 20% lower. Author's computation based on
Organisation for Economic Co-operation and Development
(OECD) database 3/1/17. *Sources and series:* see piketty.pse.ens
.fr/ideology.

its utility, as long as we recognize its limits; it may enable us to
go beyond nationalist prejudices and to set a few orders of magnitude), then the GDP per hour worked is the most meaningful concept that can be used.

We should also state that the figures for hours worked
which we use here are taken from the series in the OECD database. International series for hours worked are also established by the BLS (the U.S. Government's Bureau of Labor

Statistics). Apart from slight differences between series, all the sources available—in particular, those of the OECD and the BLS—confirm that the number of hours worked is roughly at the same level in France, in Germany, and in the United States (with differences between these three countries which are so minimal that it is doubtless impossible to make a distinct separation, given the inaccuracy of this measurement), and that countries like the United Kingdom, Italy, and Japan are approximately 20–25% lower. For the present state of the data available, these orders of magnitude can be considered valid.

It should also be noted that no country in the world significantly exceeds the level of labor productivity observed in France, Germany, and the United States, or at least no country of comparable size and economic structure. We do find significantly higher levels of GDP per hours worked in small countries based on very specific economic structures, for example, oil-producing countries (the Emirates or Norway) or tax havens (Luxembourg), but these are the outcome of very different rationales.

At the sight of the figure of an average production of 55 euros per hour worked in France today, some readers will perhaps be tempted to go straight to their manager to ask for a raise in pay. Yet others, rather more in number, will question the meaning of this figure. We would like to state clearly that this is an average: the average production of goods and services per hour worked may be between 10 and 20 euros in some sectors and jobs and between 100 and 200 euros per hour in others (not necessarily the most arduous). It may also obviously happen that in the interaction and balance of forces in wage negotiations, some workers may appropriate a larger share of the production than others. This average production figure of 55 euros per hour worked tells us nothing about these subtleties.

We should also specify that the concept of gross domestic product (GDP) poses a number of problems. In particular, it would be preferable for statistical institutes to concentrate on the "net domestic product," that is, after deduction of the consumption of fixed capital, which corresponds to the depreciation of capital and equipment (repair of buildings and machinery, replacement of computers, etc.). This capital depreciation does not constitute income for anyone, be they wage earners or shareholders, and furthermore, it tends to rise over time. The consumption of fixed capital represented about 10% of GDP in advanced economies in the 1970s; today it exceeds 15% of GDP (a sign of the acceleration of the obsolescence of equipment). This means that a (small) proportion of the growth in labor productivity measured above is an illusion. Similarly, if the consumption of natural capital were to be taken into account correctly, then a proportion of the growth in world GDP would disappear (the annual extraction of natural resources is close to the world growth in GDP, or roughly 3% per year at the moment and tends to rise over time, depending on how this is valued). But again, this would not affect the comparisons across countries on which we focus here.

Another way of expressing the findings outlined above consists of measuring the productivity of each country by comparison with the productivity observed in the United States, which has long been far in advance of others. We then obtain the findings shown in the figure.

In summary, in 1970, productivity in France and Germany was in the range of 65–70% of the American level; both countries caught up with the United States in 1970–1980 and since 1990 were at the same level as the United States (slightly above until the crisis in 2008 and since then, a little below but with relatively small differences. Moreover, it is permissible to

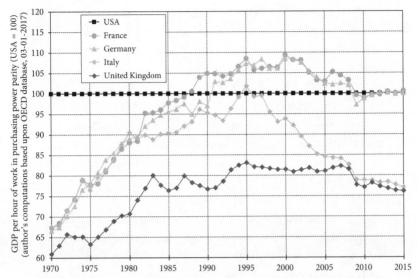

Figure 5. Labor productivity (GDP per hour of work) relative to the United States. Labor productivity, as measured by GDP per hour worked (in constant 2015 euros and purchasing power parity), was twice as low in Western Europe as in the United States in 1970. Germany and France caught up (or slightly exceeded) the U.S. level in 1985–1990, while the United Kingdom was still around 20% lower. Author's computation based on OECD database 3/1/17. *Sources and series:* see piketty.pse.ens.fr/ideology.

hope that the eurozone will succeed in recovering from the crisis better than it has done to date).

If we were to go back to the immediate post–World War II period, when Franco-German productivity was barely 50% of the American level, the catch-up effect would be even more striking. It must also be borne in mind that the European disparity in terms of productivity was of much longer standing (it was already very considerable in the nineteenth century and at the beginning of the twentieth, on the eve of World War I, and was amplified by the wars). The classic explanation is the relative disparity in educational level. The small American population was fully literate from the beginning of the nineteenth century, whereas a similar level was not achieved in France until the end of the century, by which time the United States had already progressed to the following stage (mass secondary education, then higher education). It was the investment in education in the *Trente Glorieuses* (the thirty years' postwar boom) which enabled France and Germany to catch up with the United States between 1950 and 1990. The real issue today is to maintain and extend this evolution.

In contrast, the persistent backwardness in British productivity, which never reached the American level, is usually attributed to the historical weaknesses in the educational system. Similarly, according to a recent study,[3] the slower rate in Italy since the mid-1990s can in part be explained by the lack of investment in education made by the Italian public authorities (engulfed in the repayment of an interminable public debt which France and Germany had gotten rid of through inflation and postwar debt cancellations).

We should also stress that the high level of American activity at the moment is accompanied by considerable inequality. The United States was more egalitarian than old Europe in the nineteenth century and until the mid-twentieth century, but in recent decades, the country has become much less egalitarian. In particular in the educational sector, there is a glaring contrast between the excellent, top-ranking universities (unfortunately reserved for those with higher incomes)

3. See Thomas Piketty, "2007–2015: Such a Long Recession," *Le Monde*, February 27, 2016, https://www.lemonde.fr/blog/piketty/2016/02/27/2007-2015-such-a-long-recession/.

on one hand, and on the other a somewhat mediocre second-ary and higher educational system accessible to the greatest number. This largely explains why the incomes of the 50% of the less well-off Americans have not risen since 1980, whereas the incomes of the highest 10% have risen considerably.[4]

While there is no need to boast (particularly as the challenges to be met are numerous, with the demographic evolution in Germany and the modernization of the fiscal-social system in France), we do have to admit that the social, educational, and economic model constructed in France and Germany is more satisfactory. These two countries have achieved the highest level of productivity in the world, as high as that in America, but with a much more egalitarian form of distribution.

Let's now examine the GDP per capita. We see that it is approximately 35,000 euros per annum (just below 3,000 euros per month) in Europe—a little higher in Germany, a little lower in France and the United Kingdom—or approximately 25% lower than in the United States (roughly the equivalent of 45,000 euros per year).

But the important point is that this higher GDP per capita in the United States comes solely from a greater of number of hours worked and not from a higher level of productivity than in France and in Germany. Similarly, the United Kingdom succeeds in compensating for its lower productivity and raising itself to the same level of GDP per capita as France solely as a result of working longer hours.

4. Thomas Piketty, Emmanuel Saez, and Gabriel Zucman, "Distributional National Accounts: Methods and Estimates for the United States," National Bureau of Economic Research, Working Paper 22945, 2016; https://www.nber.org/papers/w22945.

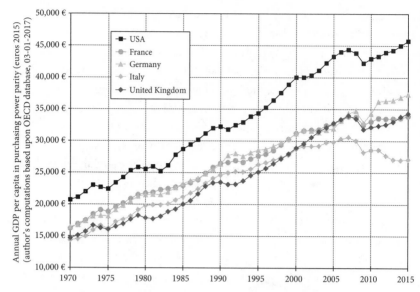

Figure 6. Annual GDP per capita, 1970–2015 (2015 euros). Author's computation based on OECD database 3/1/17. *Sources and series:* see piketty.pse.ens.fr.

For a better understanding of these discrepancies in hours worked, a distinction has to be made between what comes under number of hours worked per job and what comes under number of jobs per capita. Let's begin with the number of hours worked per job.

We observe that the annual average hours worked per job is lower in Germany than in France (the consequence of a higher rate of part-time work, which is not always a choice, but which may be more satisfactory than no employment). Beyond this gap, there again we observe a degree of proximity between the trajectories of France and of Germany: these two countries have chosen to use the very high growth rate of the *Trente Glorieuses* to appreciably reduce the length of the working day

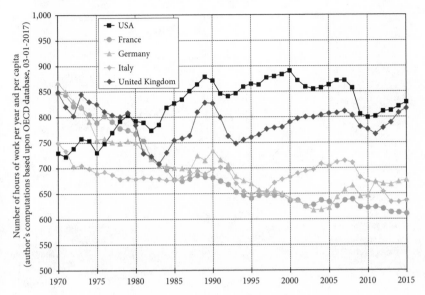

Figure 7. Number of hours of work per year and per capita,
1970–2015. Author's computation based on OECD database 3/1/17.
Sources and series: see piketty.pse.ens.fr.

since the 1960s, going from an average length of almost 2,000
hours per year in 1970 (which roughly corresponds to 42 hours
per week for 48 weeks per year) to less than 1,500 hours per year
today (or almost 35 hours per week for 44 weeks per year). In
contrast, the United States and the United Kingdom have
barely reduced the amount of time worked; as a result, the
weeks have remained very long and the paid leave very short
(often restricted to two weeks, in addition to public holidays).

Obviously, I am not attempting to claim that it is always
preferable to reduce the working day and to lengthen the va-
cations, and the question of the rate at which the time worked
should be reduced is an extremely complex and sensitive problem. But it does appear to be clear that one of the aims of the
growth in productivity in the long term is to enable the benefit

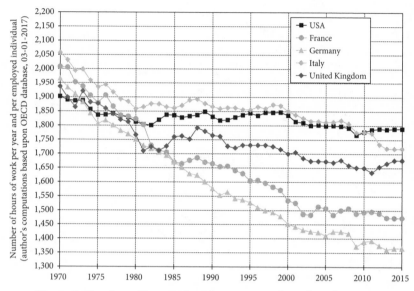

Number of hours of work per year and per employed individual (author's computations based upon OECD database, 03-01-2017)

Legend:
- USA
- France
- Germany
- Italy
- United Kingdom

Figure 8. Number of hours of work per year and employed individual, 1970–2015. Author's computation based on OECD database 3/1/17. *Sources and series:* see piketty.pse.ens.fr.

of more time for private and family life, and cultural and recreational activities, and that the trajectories of France and Germany seem to give more consideration to this aim than those of the United States and the United Kingdom.

Now let us turn to what is much less successful, beginning with the low rate of employment in France, where the difference with the rate of employment in Germany was relatively low in 2005 (only 2 points difference: 42 jobs per 100 inhabitants in France, 44 in Germany) and has considerably increased since the crisis (more than seven points difference, with an employment rate of 42% in France as compared with over 49% in Germany).

If we break down these developments into age groups, we see that the employment rate for the 25–54-year-old group has

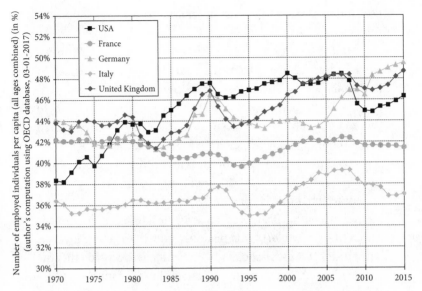

Figure 9. Number of employed individuals per capita (%), 1970–2015. Author's computation based on OECD database 3/1/17.

always been around 80% in France, as in other countries, and that it is among the 15–24-year-old and the 55–64-year-old groups that the discrepancy has been more marked in recent years, simultaneously with the rise in unemployment.

I will not return here to the multiple reasons for this weakness in employment in France. The very poor budgetary policies adopted in the eurozone are partly responsible for provoking a ridiculous fall in economic activity in 2011 to 2013,[5] from which we are only just recovering (the fault is primarily due to the successive French and German governments, which

5. Thomas Piketty, "2007–2015: Such a Long Recession," *Le Monde*, February 27, 2016, https://www.lemonde.fr/blog/piketty/2016/02/27/2007-2015-such-a-long-recession/.

concluded an ill-conceived budgetary treaty that should be reformed).[6]

But there are other specifically French factors: less promising industrial specializations than in Germany, where in particular use has been made of a greater investment of employees in the governance and strategies of firms,[7] and where there is a much better system of vocational training which France could well try to match. In France, the system of financing social protection falls too heavily on the wage bill of the private sector; an overall reform of the taxation system[8] would be required but this is constantly postponed (instead, stopgap measures have been adopted, such as the CICE (*Crédit d'impôt compétitivité emploi*). This has only added a further layer of complexity to a fiscal-social system which was already incomprehensible. It is also time to consolidate and unify the retirement system,[9] which is complex and split between too many regimes. In particular, this reform would reassure the younger generations (at the moment our retirement system is well financed—it is the second-most expensive in Europe, the Italians being in the lead—while at the same time, it is so opaque that nobody understands anything about their future rights).

6. Thomas Piketty, "Reconstructing Europe after Brexit," *Le Monde*, June 30, 2016, https://www.lemonde.fr/blog/piketty/2016/06/30/reconstructing -europe-after-brexit/.

7. "Basic Income or Fair Wage?" December 13, 2016.

8. Camille Landais, Thomas Piketty, and Emmanuel Saez, *Pour une révolution fiscale. Un impôt sur le revenu pour le xxi e siècle* (Paris: Seuil, 2011).

9. Antoine Bozio and Thomas Piketty, *Pour un nouveau système de retraite. Des comptes individuels de cotisations financés par répartition* (Paris: Rue d'Ulm, 2008).

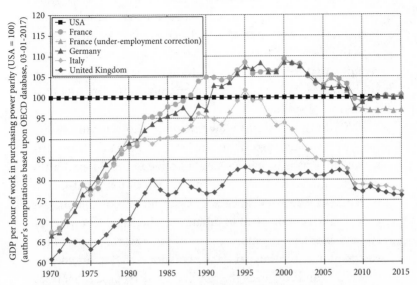

Figure 10. Labor productivity (GDP/hour of work): under-employment correction. Author's computation based on OECD database 3/1/17.

Here, I wish simply to stress two elements. On the one hand, the present weakness of employment in France implies that the estimates of productivity indicated above are doubtless overly optimistic, because the people excluded from the labor market are often the least well qualified. In fact, if we correct the series for productivity by assuming that the number of hours worked have followed the same trend as in Germany since 2005 and by assuming that these new jobs would have had a rate of productivity 30% lower on average than that of the present jobs, then we obtain the findings shown in figure 10.

In other words, we observe a tendency for French productivity to fall between 2000 and 2015. Of course, we are still far from the decline in productivity seen in Italy, and whatever the hypotheses adopted to account for the underemployment, French productivity remains distinctly above the British figures and very close to Germany and the United States. The fact remains that this trend is potentially worrying and must be countered if France wishes to maintain the momentum achieved in 1950–1990.

From this point of view, the main shortcoming of the five-year term now ending is the weakness in educational investment. This is in particular applicable to the budgets allocated to universities and other higher education institutions, which have stagnated since 2012 (with microscopic, nominal growth barely equivalent to inflation), whereas the number of students has risen by almost 10%. In other words, the real investment in education per student distinctly fell in France between 2012 and 2017, even though all the talk is of the economics of innovation, of the knowledge society, etc. Instead of losing time in poorly conducted and poorly prepared discussions about labor flexibility,[10] the government would have done better to bear in mind that long-term economic performance is primarily determined by investment in training.

The second point on which I would like to insist is the following. Too frequently, the economic debate about France and Germany is focused on the difference in "competitiveness" between the two countries, that is to say, on the gap between the French trade deficit and the German trade surplus. Now the correct concept for the evaluation of the economic performance of a country is its productivity and not its "competitiveness," which is a fairly nebulous concept. Different countries

10. Thomas Piketty, "Labor Law Reform in France: An Appalling Mess," *Le Monde*, June 2, 2016, https://www.lemonde.fr/blog/piketty/2016/07/02/labour-law-reform-in-france-an-appaling-mess/.

with similar levels of productivity may temporarily find themselves in totally different situations in terms of balance of trade for a host of voluntary or involuntary reasons. For example, some countries may choose to export more than they import, in order to have reserves for the future in the form of assets held abroad. This may be justified for an aging country which anticipates a fall in its working population, and this classical explanation is often used to explain a part of the trade surplus observed in aging countries, such as Germany or Japan, in comparison with younger countries like the United States, the United Kingdom, or France. These may require consuming and investing more in their territories, which may give rise to trade deficits. But the important point is that these situations of trade surplus or trade deficit can only last for a limited time and must be compensated for in the long run. In particular, there is no point in having a permanent trade surplus (this would amount to eternally producing for the benefit of the rest of the world, which is of no interest).

Let us see what happens in practice.

At the outset, we see that the overall level of exports and imports (expressed as a percentage of GDP) has risen significantly since the 1970s (this is the well-known phenomenon of intensification of international trade and corporate globalization) and that it is much higher in France and Germany than in the United States or Japan. This expresses the fact that European economies are smaller in size and are much less strongly integrated with one another, in particular, in matters of trade.

We also observe that the phases of trade surplus and trade deficit tend to even out over time. For example, Japan had a trade surplus in the 1990s and the 2000s (usually between 1% and 2% of GDP per year), and it has experienced considerable deficits since 2011 (−3% of GDP at the moment). France had a trade surplus every year from 1992 to 2004 (usually 1–2% of

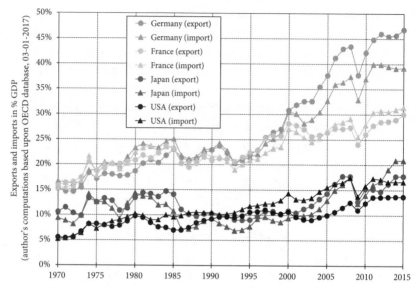

Figure 11. Exports and imports (% of GDP), 1970–2015. Author's computation based on OECD database 3/1/17.

GDP) and has had a deficit since 2005 (−1.4% of GDP in 2015). If we take the average over the period 1980–2015, France has an almost perfect balance in trade: −0.2% of GDP (+0.1% for 1990–2015). For Japan, we observe that the dominant trend is a trade surplus (+1.0% in the period 1980–2015, +0.6% in the period 1990–2015), which explains why Japan has accumulated comfortable financial reserves abroad, on which it is drawing at the moment.

However there are situations which are less balanced. For example, the United States is in an almost permanent trade deficit with an average of −2.6% of GDP over the period 1980–2015 (−2.9% during 1990–2015). The country's external financial indebtedness is, however, less distinctly negative than that which the accumulation of trade deficits should have produced, because the United States pays a low return on its debts (due to the confidence in its currency and political regime), and it obtains a high yield on its investments (thanks in particular to its investment system and merchant banks).

An even more extreme case of imbalance, and in the opposite direction, is that of Germany, which was in an almost break-even trade balance situation similar to France until 2000 and then had an average trade surplus of +5.0% of GDP over the period 2000–2015 (+3.2% in the period 1990–2015, +1.7% in the period 1980–2015, while we note an average trade deficit of −0.9% from 1980–2000, as compared with +0.2% in France). The German trade surplus has risen to over 6% of GDP since 2012 and rose to almost 8% of GDP in 2015.

In plain terms, this means that a very significant share of goods and services produced in Germany are neither consumed nor invested in Germany: They are consumed and invested in the rest of the world. Another—perfectly equivalent—way of representing the extent of the imbalance consists of calculating what the domestic consumption and investment would represent (that is pursued on the territory of the country considered) as a percentage of GDP (that is, of the total production of goods and services manufactured on this same territory).

A ratio above 100% means that a country consumes and invests more than it produces, in other words, it has a trade deficit. In contrast, a ratio below 100% is simply the counterpart of a trade surplus. For most countries, this ratio is on average very close to 100%. In Germany, on the contrary, this ratio fell to 92% in 2015, which is totally unprecedented in economic history.

In summary, France and Germany have similar productivities, but they use their high rates of productivity in very different ways. In recent years, when France produced 100 units

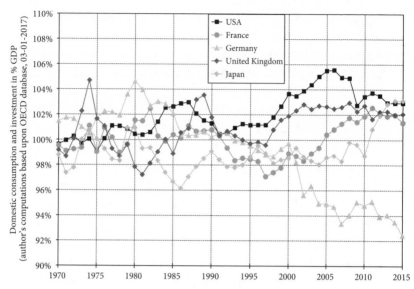

Figure 12. Domestic consumption and investment (% of GDP), 1970–2015. Author's computation based on OECD database 3/1/17.

of goods and services, it consumed and invested 101 and 102 units, respectively, on its territory. On the contrary, when Germany produces 100 units, it only consumes and invests 92 units. The gap may seem narrow, but when it occurs every year, it leads to financial and social imbalances of considerable size, which today threaten to undermine Europe.

How has this happened, and what can be done? In the first instance, we should point out that while the aging of the population and the demographic decline in Germany may explain a certain amount of trade surplus by the need to constitute reserves for the future, this is not sufficient to rationally account for such huge surpluses. The truth is that this trade surplus is not really a choice: It is the outcome of decentralized decisions made by millions of economic actors and in the absence of an adequate mechanism for correction. To put it simply: There is no pilot in the plane, or at least the pilots available are not very accurate.

After unification, the German governments were very afraid of a drop-off in the competitiveness of the "German production site." They adopted wage-freeze policies to increase productivity, and they probably went too far in this direction. At the same time, the entry of Central and Eastern European countries into the European Union enabled German firms to achieve an increased and highly advantageous integration with these new countries. This can be seen in particular with the explosion of the general level of imports and exports, which were very similar to the level in France in 2000 (close to 25–30% of GDP) and which in 2015 rose to 40–45% of GDP in Germany (as compared with 30% in France; see figure 12).

This all led to a trade surplus which was doubtless not entirely foreseeable and is in large part due to contingent factors. In its own way, it is an illustration of the strength of the economic forces at play in globalization which public authorities have not yet learned to regulate correctly.

We must also stress the fact that there is quite simply no example in economic history (at least not since the beginning of trade statistics, that is, since the beginning of the nineteenth century) of a country of this size which has experienced a comparable level of trade surplus on a long-term basis (not even China or Japan, which in most instances have not risen above 2–3% in trade surplus). The only examples of countries experiencing trade surpluses in the region of 10% of GDP are oil-producing countries with a relatively small population and with a GDP much lower than that of Germany.

Another indication of the fact that the German surpluses are objectively excessive is due to the poor foreign investments made by firms and the financial system; in contrast to the United States, the financial assets accumulated by Germany in the rest of the world are much lower than the amount which the addition of the trade surpluses should have produced.

The solution today would of course be to boost wages, consumption, and investment in Germany, both in the educational system as well as the infrastructure. Unfortunately, this is being implemented too slowly. The German leaders have an enormous responsibility here; they have other fine qualities (in particular, in their reception policies for migrants), but on this basic point, they have not explained the issues to their public and have even tended to present the trade surplus as a subject for national pride, even a proof of German virtue, which is quite simply beside the point. The German tendency to lecture the rest of Europe and to explain that everything would be fine if everyone copied Germany is logically absurd. If every country in the eurozone had a trade surplus of 8% GDP, there would be nobody in the world to absorb a surplus of this size (simply because there is on the planet no country of the size of the eurozone that is ready to have a trade deficit of 8%). This irrational tendency is unfortunately one of the risks of globalization and the heightened competition among countries; we all try first to find a refuge and then to survive.

Fortunately, there are other forces in play, in particular, the attachment to the European idea. If the other countries, beginning with France, Italy, and Spain (or a total of 50% of the population and the GDP of the eurozone, compared with 27% for Germany), were to decide democratically in a joint parliamentary chamber on the formulation of a detailed proposal for a democratic refoundation of the eurozone, including a spur to economic growth and a moratorium on public debts, I am convinced that a compromise can still be found. But it is unlikely that any solution will come from Germany, and the transition may be far from smooth. Considerable wrangling will doubtless be required. All that we can hope for is that the clashes will not be too violent; after Brexit, nobody can claim to be unaware of how far this might go.

I would like to end on a positive note. If we compare France and Germany with the United States, the United Kingdom, and other, still farther, parts of the globe, then they have much in common. In the decades following the self-destructive behavior of the years 1914–1945, these two countries have succeeded in constructing institutions and policies which have enabled the development of the most social and the most productive economies in the world. France and Germany still have major tasks to accomplish together to promote a model of fair and sustainable development. But they must not get lost in mistaken comparisons which prevent them from advancing toward the future and accepting the idea that they each have a lot to learn from the other and from history.

Long Live Populism!

January 17, 2017

In less than four months, France will have a new president, but will the president be a man or a woman? After Trump and Brexit, there is a risk that the opinion polls will be wrong once again and that Marine Le Pen's nationalist right wing will come close to winning. Even if the cataclysm is avoided this time, there is a real risk of her succeeding in appearing to be the only credible opponent to the liberal right for the next elections. On the radical left, hopes are of course pinned on Jean-Luc Mélenchon but unfortunately, he is not the most likely winner.

These two candidates do have one point in common: They both challenge the European treaties and the present system of cutthroat competition between countries and territories, which does attract many of those who have been left behind by globalization. They do also have fundamental differences: Mélenchon, despite divisive rhetorical outbursts and at times an alarming geopolitical imagination, does nevertheless tend toward a progressive and internationalist approach.

The risk of this presidential election is that all the other political forces—and the mainstream media—will simply castigate these two candidates and put them in the same box,

labeling them as "populists." This new ultimate political in-
sult, which has already been used with notable success in the
United States in relation to Sanders, may blind us to the fundamental issues. Populism is merely a somewhat confused but
legitimate response to the feeling of abandonment experienced by the working classes in the advanced countries in the
face of globalization and the rise of inequalities. To construct
specific answers to these challenges, we have to build on the
most internationalist populist elements—therefore on the
radical left—represented here and there by Podemos, Syriza,
Sanders, or Mélenchon, whatever their limits; otherwise the
retreat into nationalism and xenophobia will prevail.

Unfortunately, it is the strategy of denial which the candidates on the liberal right (Fillon) and center (Macron) intend to
adopt, as both are going to defend the integral status quo of the
2012 European Budgetary Treaty. There is nothing surprising
about this: Fillon negotiated it, and Macron applied it. All the
opinion polls confirm that these two candidates appeal primarily to those who have gained from globalization, with interesting differences (Catholics rather than the trendy middle classes
or *bobos*) but which are, in the last resort, secondary in relation
to the social question. They claim to represent a rational approach: Once France has regained the confidence of Germany,
Brussels, and the markets, by opening up the labor market, reducing expenditure and deficits, eliminating the wealth tax and
raising VAT, the time will have come to invite our partners to
show some goodwill in matters of austerity and the debt.

The problem with this apparently rational rhetoric is
that it is not in the slightest rational. The 2012 Treaty was a
monumental mistake which has ensnared the eurozone in a
fatal trap, by preventing it from investing in the future. Historical experience demonstrates that it is impossible to reduce

a public debt of this size without resorting to exceptional measures. The only way out is to forcibly produce primary surpluses
for decades, which puts severe pressure on any investment
capacity.

Thus from 1815 to 1914, the United Kingdom spent a whole
century in achieving huge primary surpluses to repay its own
annuitants and reduce the massive debt which was the outcome of the revolutionary wars (over 200% of GDP). This ill-
judged choice contributed to the underinvestment in education
and the later slow-down in productivity of the country. On the
contrary, between 1945 and 1955, a combination of debt cancellations, inflation, and one-off levies on private capital enabled Germany and France to quickly get rid of a similar debt.
This meant they could invest in growth. The same thing should
be done today, by imposing on Germany a eurozone parliamentary chamber to reduce the debts with full democratic
legitimacy. If not, the lag in investment and the slowdown in
productivity already observed in Italy will end up by spread-
ing to France and the whole eurozone (there are already signs
of this).[1]

It is by going back into the depths of history that we will
overcome the current stumbling blocks, as we have just been
reminded by the authors of the magnificent *World History of
France,*[2] a real antidote to the identity-related tensions in
France.

From a more mundane and less rosy point of view, we do
also have to accept participation in the primary organized by

1. Thomas Piketty, "Of Productivity in France and in Germany," *Le
Monde,* January 9, 2017, https://www.lemonde.fr/blog/piketty/2017/01/09
/of-productivity-in-france-and-in-germany/.

2. Patrick Boucheron, ed., *France in the World: A New Global History*
(New York: Other Press, 2019).

the left wing of the government (we refer to it in these terms, since the attempt to organize a joint primary with the radical left was unsuccessful, with the risk that it may be permanently excluded from government). It is essential that this primary designate a candidate who is committed to an in-depth review of the European regulations. Hamon and Montebourg seem closer to this line than Valls or Peillon, provided that they go beyond their positions on the universal income and the "made in France" issue, and that they finally formulate specific proposals in place of the 2012 Budgetary Treaty (hardly mentioned in the first televised debate, perhaps because they all voted for it five years ago: But this is precisely why it is all the more urgent to clarify things by presenting a detailed alternative). All is not lost, but it is urgent to act now, if we wish to avoid putting the National Front in a position of power.

On Inequality in China

February 14, 2017

With Trump and Brexit, the Western-type democratic model is under fire. The Chinese media are having a field day. In column after column, the *Global Times* (China's official daily newspaper) condemns the explosive cocktail of nationalism, xenophobia, separatism, TV-reality, vulgarity, and "money reigns supreme," the outcome of the so-called free elections and the wonderful political institutions which the West would like to impose on the world. No more lessons!

Recently the Chinese authorities organized an international colloquium on "The Role of Political Parties in Global Economic Governance." The message sent to the colloquium by the Chinese Communist Party (CCP) was perfectly clear. Reliance on solid intermediary institutions such as the CCP (which includes 90 million members, or roughly 10% of the adult population, almost as much as the turnout in the American or French presidential primaries) enables the organization of discussions and decision-making and the design of a stable and harmonious development model, in which identity conflicts and the centrifugal forces wrought by the electoral supermarket can be overcome.

By so doing, the Chinese regime may well be overconfident. The limits of the model are well known, beginning with the total lack of transparency and the ferocious repression suffered by all those who condemn the opacity of the regime.

According to the official statistics, China is still a passably egalitarian country in which the benefits of economic growth are fairly distributed. In fact this is far from certain, as we see from the findings of a recent study carried out with Li Yang and Gabriel Zucman.[1] By combining unpublished sources (in particular, by checking fiscal and wealth data against national accounts and surveys), we show that the official data considerably underestimates the level of inequality in China and its evolution.

Between 1978 and 2015, it is undeniable that growth in China enabled the country to emerge from poverty. The country's share of global GDP rose from just under 4% in 1978 to 18% in 2015 (whereas its share in world population declined slightly, falling from 22% to 19%). Expressed in terms of parity of purchasing power and in 2015 euros, per capita national income rose from barely 150 euros per month in 1978 to almost 1,000 euros per month in 2015. While the average income in the country remains between three and four times lower than in Europe or in North America, the richest 10% of the Chinese population—or some 130 million persons all the same—do have an average disposable income equivalent to that of the rich countries.

The problem is that the growth in income of the poorest 50% of the Chinese population has only been half the average.

1. Thomas Piketty, Li Yang, and Gabriel Zucman, "Capital Accumulation, Private Property and Rising Inequality in China, 1978–2015," *American Economic Review* 109, no. 7 (2019): 2469–2496.

According to our estimates, which must be considered as lower bound levels of inequality in China, the share of the poorest 50% in the national income in China fell from 28% to 15% between 1978 and 2015, while the income of the 10% richest rose from 26% to 41%. The extent of the phenomenon is impressive: The levels of inequality in China are clearly higher than in Europe and are rapidly approaching those observed in the United States.

We find the same evolution, but even more dramatically, for the concentration of private property. Between 1995 and 2015, the share of private wealth held by the richest 10% rose from 41% to 67%. In twenty years, China has gone from a level lower than that observed in Sweden to a level approaching that of the United States. This conveys strong inequality in the access to property wealth (almost entirely privatized during this period) and a process of partial privatization of companies, reserved for small groups of people under extremely opaque conditions. At this pace, China runs the risk of developing a form of *pluto-communism,* with a stronger concentration of private property than in capitalist countries, all guaranteed by a single Communist Party.

We should, however, stress a fundamental difference. The share of the Chinese state in the national capital of China (property, companies, land, infrastructure, and utilities) has dropped considerably but remains very substantial. According to our estimates, this share of public capital constituted 70% of national capital in 1978, and has stabilized around 30% since 2006, with even a slight rise since the crisis, the sign of an uptick in public companies.

In capitalist countries, the share of public capital was in the range of 20–30% during the main period of the mixed economy (1950–1980), but this share has collapsed since 1980, as public assets were privatized, and the debt was allowed to rise. In 2007, only Italy had negative public capital (with debts greater than assets). In 2015, this situation was found in the United States, the United Kingdom, and Japan (France and Germany have barely positive net public capital). In other words, private property owners own not only the totality of national capital, but they also have drawing rights on future tax revenues. This is a serious burden on the regulatory capacity of public authorities.

The position of the Chinese state is more promising, but only as long as the authorities show that this potential can be put at the service of the greatest number. The Chinese do not wish to be taught lessons by the West. Nor is it certain that they will listen to those of their supreme leaders for very much longer.

For a Democratic Eurozone Government

February 15, 2017

The eurozone needs a proper government: a joint budget, common rules of taxation, an investment and borrowing capacity, a growth strategy, and a model for sustainable and equitable development. But to achieve all these some day, the eurozone must first focus on creating democratic institutions that enable common decision making. There is no point in discussing a government for the eurozone if the democratic authority to which this government will be responsible is not clearly stated.

At the moment, the main decision-making body in the eurozone is the Council of Finance Ministers. The problem is that this council is usually incapable of making decisions. For years now, the eurozone has been responsible for adjudicating the restructuring of the Greek debt, which everyone knows is unsustainable, but these decisions are constantly deferred.

Reasons for Inaction

Take another example: For years now, there have been a growing number of corporate income tax scandals. Everyone knows now that there is widescale avoidance of this tax by multinationals, which often pay rates that are derisory. However, the eurozone has still not been capable of making the slightest tangible decision. We are still at the stage of discussing the setting up of a common tax base, and we have still not seriously considered the question of a common minimal tax rate. What meaning is there in agreeing on a common tax base if each country can then fix a rate close to zero and attract all the company head offices?

The reason for this lack of action is that in operation, the Council of Finance Ministers usually observes the principle of unanimity: On taxation, a veto from Luxembourg is enough to block everything. Some rare decisions can in principle be taken with a majority vote, but in practice, the major countries have a right of veto. Thus Germany and its minister for finance stick obstinately to the absurd idea that Greece must produce a huge primary budgetary surplus of 3.5% of GDP for decades to come, and this idea blocks any decision.

The problem lies in the very structure of the Council of Finance Ministers, which is a machine for opposing national interests against one another (or erroneously perceived as such) and leads to inertia. As soon as one single person represents a country of 80 million inhabitants (Germany) or 65 million inhabitants (France), it is almost impossible for this person to quietly accept being outvoted. This prevents any level-headed majority decision—and even any public deliberation.

A New Parliamentary Assembly for the Eurozone

Therefore the Council of Finance Ministers should be replaced by a true parliamentary assembly for the eurozone, in which each country would be represented by a certain number of elected members from their respective national parliaments, in a number proportionate to the country's population and the various political groups. For example, there would be thirty members from the German Bundestag and twenty-five from the French National Assembly, on an all-party basis. We would quickly realize that opinions on the Greek debt or corporate taxation rates vary considerably within each country, including in Germany, and it would become possible to take majority decisions which enable them to move beyond national oppositions. We should also bear in mind here that Germany makes up 24% of the population in the eurozone, while France, Italy, and Spain together constitute 51%, with Belgium, Greece, Portugal, and the other countries constituting 25%.

An alternative solution would be to fall back on a sub-formation from the eurozone within the European Parliament. It seems to me distinctly preferable to base the Eurozone Parliamentary Assembly on the national parliaments. This is because on the one hand, they have the requisite democratic legitimacy to engage national taxpayers, and on the other, it is essential, by means of this major democratic innovation, to formally recognize the existence of a core that is more closely integrated than the European Union as a whole and has its own institutions.

Whatever the case may be, it is essential for the candidates in the forthcoming elections to finally make specific proposals concerning the setting up of a democratic government for the eurozone, without which all the discussions on re-launching Europe and the economic government will remain wishful thinking.

Public Capital, Private Capital
March 14, 2017

The present economic debate is overdetermined by two realities which, moreover, are connected, as we sometimes tend to forget. On the one hand, we have the steady rise in public debt, and on the other, the prosperity of privately owned wealth. The figures for the level of public debt are well known; almost everywhere the level approaches or exceeds 100% of national income (the equivalent of almost one year of gross domestic product) as compared with barely 30% in the 1970s. Far be it from me to minimize the extent of the problem: It is the highest level of public debt since World War II, and historical experience demonstrates that it is difficult to reduce this level of debt by ordinary means. This is precisely why, to get a clear idea of the issues at stake and the alternatives, it is essential to put this reality into perspective by relating it to developments in the structure of property as a whole.

Briefly, the totality of what is owned in a country can be broken down into public capital, which is the difference between public assets (these include buildings, land, infrastructure, financial portfolios, shares in companies, etc., held by public authorities in different forms: state, municipalities, etc.)

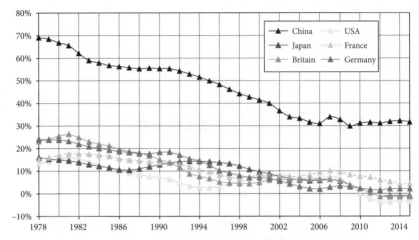

Figure 13. The decline of public property (% of public wealth in national wealth). Share of net public wealth (public assets minus public debt) in net national wealth (private + public). China: Piketty, Yang, and Zucman (2019). Other countries: Piketty and Zucman (2014) and WID.world updates.

and public debt on one hand; and private capital (that is, the difference between household assets and debts) on the other.

During the postwar boom (the *Trente Glorieuses*), public assets were very considerable (approximately 100–150% of national income, as a result of a very large public sector, a consequence of postwar nationalizations) and were significantly higher than public debt (which was historically low at less than 30% of national income—after inflation, the cancellation of debts, and the one-off levies on private capital in the years 1945–1955).

In total, public capital—net of debt—was largely positive, in the range of 100% of national income, despite the rising prices in real estate and on the stock market. At the same time, the public debt was approaching 100% of national income, with the result that net public capital became almost zero. On the eve of the crisis in 2008, it was already negative in Italy. The most recent data available for 2015–2016 shows that net public capital has become negative in the United States, Japan, and the United Kingdom. In all these countries, the sale of total public assets would not be sufficient to repay the debt. In France and Germany, net public capital is only just positive.

But this does not mean that rich countries have become poor: It is their governments which have become poor, which is very different. In fact, at the same time, private wealth—net of debt—has risen spectacularly. In the 1970s, private wealth represented 300% of national income, whereas in 2015 it had risen to, or exceeded, 600% in all the rich countries. This prosperity in private wealth is due to multiple causes: the rise in property prices (conglomeration effects in larger metropolitan areas), the aging of the population and decline in its growth (which automatically increases savings accumulated in the past in relation to current income and contributes to inflating the prices of assets), and also, of course, the privatization of public assets and the rise in debt (which is held in one form or another by private owners, via the banks). One might add the very high returns obtained by the highest financial assets (which structurally grow faster than the size of the world economy) and an evolution in the legal system globally very favorable to private property owners (both in real estate and in intellectual property). The fact remains that private capital grew much faster than the decline in public capital, and that rich countries themselves hold even a little more (in total, rich countries hold more financial assets in the rest of the world than the contrary).

Why be so pessimistic in the face of such prosperity? Simply because the ideological and political balance of power is such that public authorities are not able to make the main beneficiaries of globalization contribute their fair share. The perception of this impossibility of a fair tax sustains the flight toward debt. This feeling of disempowerment is reinforced by the unprecedented extent of economic and financial interdependence; each country is owned by its neighbors, particularly in Europe, where there is a profound impression of loss of control.

Historically, major changes in the structure of property ownership often come together with profound political changes. We see this with the French Revolution, the American Civil War, the European/World Wars in the twentieth century, and the *Libération* in France. The nationalist forces at work today could lead to a return to national currencies and inflation, which would promote a chaotic redistribution of resources, at the expense of severe social stress and an ethnicization of political conflicts. In the face of this fatal risk to which the present status quo could lead, there is only one solution. We must chart a democratic pathway out of the impasse and organize the necessary redistribution of resources within the framework of the rule of law.

What Would a Democratic Eurozone Assembly Look Like?

March 22, 2017

What would a Democratic Assembly of the eurozone look like? What would the political composition be, and would it be in a position to outvote austerity measures or not? Would it allow the establishment of a genuinely democratic eurozone government?

It should be pointed out straightaway that there is no miracle parliament or perfect treaty and that any change in the institutions cannot on its own reconcile Europe with its citizens. The project of a treaty for the democratization of the governance of the eurozone (T-Dem),[1] is simply an initial basis for discussion which would need to be debated at length and improved through proposals from all.

This draft treaty has been prepared by recognized specialists in European law—Stéphanie Hennette, professor of public law at Paris-Nanterre University, and Guillaume Sacriste and

---

1. "Treaty on the Democratization of the Economic and Social Government of the European Union," http://tdem.eu/en/treaty/.

Antoine Vauchez, professors and research fellows in political science at the Paris-I-Panthéon-Sorbonne University and at the Centre National pour la Recherche Scientique (CNRS). It does have the virtue of existing and demonstrating that there are solutions available to make Europe more democratic and more social, which do not involve the revision of all the existing treaties and are based solely on the countries that wish to move ahead. These include at the outset France, Germany, Italy, and Spain; these four countries together represent 76% of the population and the GDP of the eurozone. This project for democratization is in stark contrast to the somewhat vague proposals usually put forward by the political leaders and enables the discussion to be opened on a clearly structured basis.

In real terms, what would the composition and the political orientation of the Eurozone Parliamentary Assembly instituted by the Treaty for Democratization be? There are several possible scenarios, depending on whether we envisage a restricted Assembly (approximately 100 members) or a larger one (with a maximum of 400 members provided for in the T-Dem, article 4).

In the case of a restricted Assembly, if we take as a basis a total of 100 members from national parliaments, then Germany would send twenty-four members (because it represents 24% of the eurozone), France twenty members, Italy eighteen members, Spain fourteen, and so on. To guarantee that each member state has at least one seat (T-Dem, article 4), five extra seats will be required, hence a total of 105 members from national parliaments. If we add twenty-five members from the European Parliament, the final total would be 130 members. Thus, 105 would come from national parliaments (80%) and twenty-five from the European Parliament (20%) (as provided for in T-Dem, article 4). The small size of this assembly could mean improved efficiency in decision-making (see table 4).

Table 4. Assembly of the eurozone: Allocation of seats
among countries

	Population (millions)[a]	Population (% eurozone)	Number of seats in the Assembly of the eurozone[b]
Germany	82	24	24
France	67	20	20
Italy	61	18	18
Spain	46	14	14
Netherlands	17	5	5
Belgium	11	3	3
Greece	11	3	3
Portugal	10	3	3
Austria	9	3	3
Finland	5	2	2
Slovakia	5	2	2
Ireland	5	1	1
Lithuania	3	1	1
Slovenia	2	1	1
Lettonia	2	1	1
Estonia	1	0	1
Cyprus	1	0	1
Luxembourg	1	0	1
Malta	0	0	1
Total	340	100	105
Representatives of the European Parliament			25
Total number of seats in the Assembly			130

[a] *Eurostat estimates as of January 1, 2016.*
[b] *In proportion to population on the basis of 100 seats, with the addition of at least one seat for the smallest countries, hence a total of 105 seats.*

In contrast, an enlarged assembly would make it possible to take political plurality more fully into account, in particular for the smaller countries, which could obtain a minimum of three members. We would thus have an assembly of 400 members, of which 320 would come from national parliaments and 80 from the European Parliament (see table 5).

It is also possible to consider the composition which a Eurozone Assembly might have in left-wing, right-wing political terms. Of course, this is rather artificial given that the "right," "left," and "radical left" political groupings presented in table 6 all exist, but the frontiers change from country to country, and they frequently have difficulty in surviving as such within European institutions. Our speculations do, however, show political regroupings and potential majorities, thus revealing the possible shape of a genuinely transnational politics. This highlights what a transnational parliamentary socialization around partisan identities and political divisions might possibly lead to, and the manner in which national lefts and rights might find themselves redefined in this assembly. This would in particular be the case if this assembly were to effectively exercise powers (as is provided for by the T-Dem, in particular with the voting of the eurozone budget and of a common tax on corporate profits contributing to this budget; see articles 12–15) and not be reduced to rubber-stamping policies.

Whatever the solution adopted, it must be stressed that the composition of the Parliamentary Assembly could lean distinctly to the left, at least in the present state of the political groups in the various national parliaments (March 2017). For example, in the example of the restricted assembly, the 105 members from national parliaments would be divided into forty-four from the right and center-right (CDU/CSU, LR, PP, etc.), forty-seven from the left and the ecologists (SPD, Grünen, PS, PD, PSOE, etc.), nine from the so-called Radical Left (Die

Table 5. Assembly of the eurozone: Allocation of seats among countries

Country	Population (millions)[a]	Population (% of eurozone)	Number of seats in the Assembly of the eurozone	
			Version 1: Assembly with 130 seats[b]	Version 2: Assembly with 400 seats[c]
Germany	82	24	24	72
France	67	20	20	60
Italy	61	18	18	54
Spain	46	14	14	42
Netherlands	17	5	5	15
Belgium	11	3	3	9
Greece	11	3	3	9
Portugal	10	3	3	9
Austria	9	3	3	9
Finland	5	2	2	6
Slovakia	5	2	2	6
Ireland	5	1	1	6
Lithuania	3	1	1	5
Slovenia	2	1	1	3
Lettonia	2	1	1	3
Estonia	1	0	1	3
Cyprus	1	0	1	3
Luxembourg	1	0	1	3
Malta	0	0	1	3
	340	100	105	320
Representatives of the European Parliament			25	80
Total number of seats in the Assembly			130	400

[a] *Eurostat estimates as of January 1, 2016.*
[b] *In proportion to population on the basis of 100 seats, with the addition of at least one seat for the smallest countries, hence a total of 105 seats.*
[c] *Numbers of seats multiplied by three as compared to previous version.*

Linke, Podemos, Syriza, etc.), and five who are unclassified (Five Star Movement, etc.) (see table 6). Taking into account the twenty-five members from the European Parliament, in proportion to the various groups, only makes marginal changes to this balance (detailed data are available in table 6).

It is also important to remember that on questions of budgetary policy, the relaunching of the European economy, the restructuring of the debt and so forth, the positions of the French, Spanish, or Italian right wing are frequently quite significantly different from the German right, which only has twelve seats (of the 105 members from national parliaments) in the Eurozone Parliamentary Assembly.

To recap: the Eurozone Parliamentary Assembly is not a cure-all. Our proposal of a treaty for democratization can and must be improved and completed, and we in no way claim that the decisions which will be taken by this assembly will always be in keeping with our desires or will enable the resolution as if by magic of all the problems of Europe. But it does seem to us reasonable to state that this Parliamentary Assembly would provide a democratic framework which would enable austerity to be outvoted, or at least to very substantially modify the present balance of power and to finally ensure that a rationale of public, pluralist, and democratic debate will prevail over the cult of diplomacy behind closed doors and opaque decision-making. Ask everyone—and in particular, Jean-Luc Mélenchon, Emmanuel Macron, and François Fillon—to say how they propose to amend and modify this proposal for the composition of the Parliamentary Assembly, or whether they intend to govern the eurozone permanently without a Parliamentary Assembly and to stick to the present intergovernmental status quo.

Finally, it may be worthwhile stressing that the results would not be very different if we distributed the seats in

Table 6. Assembly of the eurozone: Allocation of seats among political groups (members coming from national parliaments)

	Number of seats in the Assembly of the eurozone	Allocation of seats in proportion to the political groups present in National Parliaments (highest average) (February 2017)			
		Right (CDU, LR, PP, etc.)	Left (SPD, Grünen, PS, PD, PSOE, etc.)	Radical left (Die Linke, Podemos, Syriza, etc.)	Other (M5S)
Germany	24	12	10	2	0
France	20	9	11	0	0
Italy	18	3	12	0	3
Spain	14	7	4	3	0
Netherlands	5	2	2	1	0
Belgium	3	2	1	0	0
Greece	3	1	0	2	0
Portugal	3	1	1	1	0
Austria	3	1	1	0	1
Finland	2	1	0	0	1
Slovakia	2	1	1	0	0
Ireland	1	1	0	0	0
Lithuania	1	0	1	0	0
Slovenia	1	0	1	0	0
Lettonia	1	0	1	0	0
Estonia	1	1	0	0	0
Cyprus	1	1	0	0	0
Luxembourg	1	1	0	0	0
Malta	1	0	1	0	0
Total	105	44	47	9	5

Note: The seats are allotted in proportion to population on the basis of 100 seats, with the addition of at least one seat for the smallest countries, hence a total of 105 seats.

proportion to the GDPs of the various countries, and to their populations. This type of electoral system, which would amount to applying a rule of "one euro, one vote" between countries (a system which moreover currently exists for the voting in the Council of Governors of the European Stability Mechanism as well as in the European Central Bank for the votes related to the restructuring of its capital) would obviously be less satisfactory from a democratic point of view, and in our opinion, is totally unacceptable. (Why not extend it to the regions and between individuals?) But the fact is that it would lead to results that would not be very different for the composition of the Parliamentary Assembly, quite simply because the GDP per capita is actually fairly similar in the eurozone countries. In real terms, Germany represents 24% of the population of the eurozone, compared with 51% for France, Italy, and Spain combined and 25% for the other countries. As a proportion of the GDP, the distribution is 28% for Germany; 48% for France, Italy, and Spain; and 24% for the other countries. In other words, if we applied this distribution key, the number of seats allocated to Germany would rise slightly, but the political balance would be only marginally affected: for example the German right would have fourteen seats instead of twelve (of the 105 members from the national parliaments).

Now let's deal with the difficult question: What happens if some of our partners refuse to discuss the treaty for the democratization of the eurozone? Let's take a textbook case: What happens if the German political decisionmakers, frightened that they might be outvoted in a democratic Eurozone Parliamentary Assembly, close the door on any negotiation? We can suggest three sets of answers to this question.

In the first instance, even for the bleakest assumption in which some of our partners were to refuse any discussion, we

Table 7. Eurozone: Allocation of population vs. allocation of GDP

	Population (millions)[a]	Population (1% eurozone)	GDP (billions euros)[b]	GDP (% eurozone)
Germany	82	24	2,791	28
France	67	20	2,095	21
Italy	61	18	1,554	16
Spain	46	14	1,068	11
Netherlands	17	5	656	7
Belgium	11	3	384	4
Greece	11	3	184	2
Portugal	10	3	172	2
Austria	9	3	310	3
Finland	5	2	187	2
Slovakia	5	2	76	1
Ireland	5	1	229	2
Lithuania	3	1	34	0
Slovenia	2	1	37	0
Lettonia	2	1	1	0
Estonia	1	0	17	0
Cyprus	1	0	18	0
Luxembourg	1	0	46	0
Malta	0	0	8	0
Total	340	100	9,888	100
Incl. Germany	82	24	2,791	28
France-Italy-Spain	174	51	4,717	48
Other countries	84	25	2,380	24

[a] Eurostat, estimates to January 2016.
[b] 2015, SEC 2010, market prices; Eurostat, last updated 2/21/2017.

believe it is essential to put a possible alternative on the table. To date, the French political leaders have never proposed a genuine project for parliamentary and political union to their partners in the eurozone. France regularly complains about Brussels, Germany, and sometimes the whole world, but we have rarely seen her make a public and specific suggestion enabling the implementation of a more democratic and social Europe. Even for the bleakest hypothesis in which these proposals would be purely and simply rejected by our partners, this stage of proposal and explanation of disagreements seems to me to be fundamental from a political and historical standpoint. If France were to publicly propose a parliamentary democracy to the eurozone and to Germany, on a basis of one person, one vote, and Germany were to stubbornly refuse any discussion of such a proposal, then it is probable that the outcome would be a climate of suspicion and exasperation which would ultimately destroy the eurozone. It is probable that other votes, in other elections in France or elsewhere, would lead to other countries leaving and an implosion of the European project. But even in this extremely pessimistic scenario, I consider it is crucially important that a plausible democratic alternative first be explicitly debated.

Second, this extremely pessimistic scenario does not seem to me to be the most realistic—far from it. Our partners, especially our German partners, are at least as attached as we are to the values of parliamentary democracy, and are often much more advanced in their thinking about political union. In addition to the fact that political power might very well change hands and swing to the left in the near future in Germany, there are a very considerable number of German citizens and political decisionmakers, including of course on the right, who would very warmly welcome a French proposal for a eurozone parliamentary union. At the very least, there is not the slightest doubt that a negotiation would open and a compromise could be found, the nature of which nobody can foretell. The pressure of peoples and opinions, in particular in Italy and in Spain, is pushing toward the democratization of Europe.

Third, the T-Dem project itself, in its conditions for ratification (article 20) provides for a possible way out of the crisis. If ten countries out of the nineteen in the eurozone, representing at least 70% of the population, ratify the T-Dem, this is sufficient for it to enter into force. In absolute terms, it is possible to envisage the entry into force without one of the major countries, for example, without Germany. This path does not seem desirable, nor is it the most likely—far from it. But there is at least a path enabling countries which so desire to show their goodwill by launching a process of partial ratification, which would enable increased pressure to be put on the countries which might refuse any discussion. The issue at stake today is not to fix deadlines beyond which countries would start to play Brexit. The issue is one of taking specific actions to show that there is a democratic path leading out of the contradictions in which our continent is ensnared at the moment.

Note: The detailed data tables on national parliaments used to construct the above tables were collected with the help of Manon Bouju.

What Reforms for France?
2017–2018

Inequality in France
April 18, 2017

A longstanding legend has it that France is a profoundly egalitarian country which has miraculously escaped the sharp rise in inequality observed elsewhere. If so, how can we explain the anxiety provoked by globalization and by Europe, which is expressed so forcefully in this presidential campaign? First, by recognizing that this great national myth of France as egalitarian and an exception to the rule is grossly exaggerated, and second, by acknowledging that this myth is too often used by the dominant groups to justify our own national hypocrisy.

There is nothing new here. France was the last country to adopt a progressive income tax, and did so under the law of July 15, 1914, voted in extremis to finance the war. In contrast, this tax had already been introduced in Germany, the United Kingdom, Sweden, the United States, and Japan, sometimes decades previously, to finance schools and public services. Until 1914, the political and economic elites in the Third Republic had stubbornly refused this type of reform, declaring that France had already become egalitarian, thanks to the Revolution, and therefore had no need of an intrusive and predatory tax, more suited to the aristocratic and authoritarian societies which surrounded us. In reality, the inheritance archives demonstrate that the concentration of property and income was as extreme in France during that period as in other European societies (and greater than in the United States).

Today we find the same hypocrisy when confronted with the glaring inequalities in our educational system. In France, in all good republican conscience, we choose to devote three times more public resources to the selective "grandes ecoles" than is spent on those university courses in which young people from socially underprivileged backgrounds are concentrated. Now this elitist and austere tendency which has already led to a fall of 10% in expenditure per student between 2007 and 2017 (even though we all talk of the "knowledge society," "innovation," etc.) may well get worse in the next five years, if we judge by some of the electoral programs. France is also the country in which private primary and secondary schools are almost entirely financed by the taxpayers, while these schools reserve the right to choose the pupils who suit them. This contributes to unacceptable levels of social segregation. There again the status quo is breezing ahead.

As far as the development of monetary inequalities is concerned, a new study carried out with Bertrand Garbinti and Jonathan Goupille-Lebret[1] clearly shows the limits of the French myth of egalitarianism. True, the rise in inequality has been less widespread than in the United States, where the share of the poorest 50% in the national income has literally collapsed. The fact remains that France has also experienced a

1. Bertrand Garbinti, Jonathan Goupille-Lebret, and Thomas Piketty, "Income Inequality in France 1900–2014: Evidence from Distributional National Accounts," WID.world Working Paper 2017/04, https://wid.world /news-article/new-paper-income-inequality-dynamics-france/.

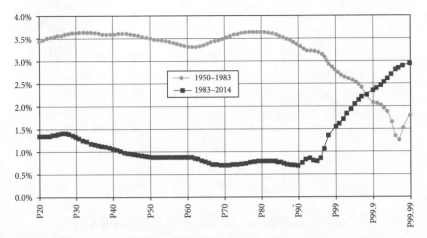

Figure 14. The Thirty Glorious Years are not over for everyone. Average annual real growth rates of pre-tax per adult income by percentiles (growth incidence curves). Equal-split-adults series (income of married couples divided by two). *Source:* Bertrand Garbinti, Jonathan Goupille-Lebret, and Thomas Piketty, "Income Inequality in France 1900–2014: Evidence from Distributional National Accounts," WID.world 2017.

sharp rise in inequality. Between 1983 and 2015, the average income of the richest 1% has risen by 100% (above inflation) and that of the 0.1% richest by 150%, compared with barely 25% for the rest of the population (or less than 1% per year). The richest 1% alone have siphoned off 21% of total growth, compared with 20% for the poorest 50%. The break with the *Trente Glorieuses* (the thirty-year postwar boom) is striking: Between 1950 and 1983, incomes were rising steadily by almost 4% per year for the immense majority of the population. On the contrary, it was the highest incomes which had to settle for a growth of barely 1% per year. The fact that the *Trente Glorieuses* is not over for everyone has not gone unnoticed: You only have to read the weekly magazines with the salaries of executives and the ranking of fortunes to realize this.

The study also confirms the strong growth of the highest assets, 90% of which are held in financial portfolios, when above 10 million euros. These have risen, not only much faster than GDP since the years 1980–1990, but also faster than the average assets (driven upward by property assets). We find this prosperity in the number and amounts of assets declared year after year in the wealth tax. There is no problem of outflow here: On the contrary, we see a very dynamic basis for fiscal purposes.

In these conditions, it is difficult to understand why some candidates think it opportune to abolish the wealth tax on financial assets or to impose a lower tax on financial incomes than on income from employment. To promote mobility, it would be more judicious to lower the property tax (which is by far the principal tax on wealth: It generates 30 billion euros as compared with 5 billion euros for the wealth tax) for the households who have borrowed to buy property.

Some may consider this a kickback in return for the political financing observed. One can also see in these fiscal choices the effects of a sincere but false ideology, whereby subjecting people and territories to whole scale competition would spontaneously result in social harmony and prosperity for all. What is sure is that it is dangerous to address first and foremost those who have gained from globalization and to invent a new French passion for the regressive tax, while the most vulnerable social groups have the impression they have been abandoned and are increasingly attracted by the sirens of xenophobia. It is urgent to face up to the fact that inequality does exist in France.

What Reforms for France?

May 16, 2017

Will the election of Emmanuel Macron enable France to relaunch itself and revive Europe? We would like to think so, but this is not guaranteed. The new president does have some good insights, but the overall impression is of a program in draft version that is somewhat opportunist.

The most promising project is the modernization and unification of our social protection. In France more than elsewhere, our social system has been constructed in stages with layers of reform stacked one on top of the other. The result is considerable complexity and illegibility. The most extreme example is the retirement pension schemes. The system is well financed, but the multitude of schemes and rules means that nobody understands anything about his or her future rights. A consolidation exercise is required, in particular for the young generations whose career paths often include several jobs in the public sector, the private sector, and as entrepreneurs, which should entitle people to the same rights. There is as yet no agreement on new common rules, on how to deal with fragmented careers, or with arduous or strenuous jobs, and so forth. This will be quite a challenge, particularly as we are starting from practically zero (there is only one line in Macron's program dealing with the consolidation of retirement schemes).

Another major project is unemployment insurance. Once again, it is important not to miss the target. The tightening of the rules imposed on the unemployed is supposed to lead to enormous (and barely credible) economies, and the extension of rights for voluntary departures and the self-employed is not well thought out. Instead, the system should be extended to the public sector, where ultraprecarious contracts have been allowed to develop with the utmost hypocrisy, and workers are being totally excluded from unemployment insurance. In the Labour Code, the conditions for balanced reform are clear: clarification and possibly an easing in the conditions for terminating a permanent contract can only be developed if recruitment on a permanent basis becomes the norm and the use of temporary contracts is restricted. We should furthermore bear in mind that the extreme decentralization of wage negotiations has contributed to the enormous surplus in Germany and is not the best recipe for balanced development in Europe.

The Macron program has good ideas on education: finally giving real additional means to disadvantaged schools which to date have merely been stigmatized. However, the proposed measure seems to focus on the first grades in primary schools (inequality of opportunity must be tackled at least until middle school), and it is not consistent with the cuts in spending announced, except if the numbers in classes in the other schools are considerably increased. The intended return to the four-day week, which is harmful and does not exist anywhere else, is also an indication of the ambiguities of the Macron system: a pinch of reform and a large dose of conservatism.

More broadly, it is difficult to see an overall vision for a real strategy of investment in vocational training. This is, however, crucial. At the moment, France has the most productive labor force in the world (on a par with Germany, and with a model which is much more equalitarian than in the United States), but this position is far from being guaranteed.[1] The country is emerging from a ten-year recession (the GDP per capita in 2017 is 5% lower than it was in 2007); the catastrophic consequence is a drop of almost 10% in the investment per student in higher education. We should always remember that the French population is still increasing (contrary to the German population), and the student population is growing even more quickly. This is an excellent thing as long as adequate means are provided.

Macron is extremely conservative in matters of financing social protection and taxation. He focuses exclusively on the increase in the general social security contribution (the CSG) whereas today, what is urgent is the deduction of income tax at source. France is preparing to implement this reform in January 2018, half a century after all the other countries, but now Macron wishes to postpone it—a rather odd decision on the part of someone who claims to be modernizing the country. This reform would finally enable the convergence of income tax and the CSG, which must become progressive and not proportional for salaried employees, retired people, and those with other incomes. Macron obviously has a problem with the very concept of a progressive tax, since he proposes capping at 30% the taxation on the highest financial incomes (as compared with 55% for the equivalent highest labor incomes), and eliminating the wealth tax on financial portfolios

1. Thomas Piketty, "Of Productivity in France and in Germany," *Le Monde,* January 9, 2017, https://www.lemonde.fr/blog/piketty/2017/01/09/of-productivity-in-france-and-in-germany/.

(for some strange reason, Macron considers that financial investment is necessarily more productive than real estate investment).

Finally, let's turn to the reform of Europe. The central issue is to endow the eurozone with solid democratic institutions enabling it to deal with crises in the future.[2] When the interest rates begin to rise again, when strong democratic legitimacy will be required to make the difficult decisions on rescheduling the debts, it is not behind the closed doors of meetings of heads of states and ministers of finance that the problems will be resolved. We will need the support of broad public deliberation and the plurality of views expressed in each country and therefore the support of a eurozone assembly based on members of the national and the European parliaments. The absence of strong democratic institutions is the most serious danger threatening Europe. Unfortunately, there is nothing to suggest that the French and German elections this year will enable us to overcome this.

2. "What Would a Democratic Eurozone Assembly Look Like?" March 22, 2017.

Reagan to the Power of Ten

June 13, 2017

I s Trump a UFO in American history or can he be seen as the continuation of long-term trends? While we have no desire to deny "Donald's" obvious specificities, including his inimitable art of the tweet, we do have to admit that elements of continuity prevail.

The tax agenda which he has just tabled in Congress is eloquent. It can be summed up in two central measures: reduction of federal income tax on corporate profits from 35% to 15% (a rate which Trump would also like to see applied to individual entrepreneurs like himself); and a total end to inheritance tax. This is clearly a direct prolongation of the program for "scrapping" the progressive tax launched by Reagan in the 1980s.

Let's go back a bit. To counter the rise in inequality and the excessive concentration of wealth (at the time, considered as contrary to the democratic spirit in America) and also to avoid any resemblance with Old Europe one day (considered across the Atlantic in the nineteenth century and at the Belle Epoque as aristocratic and oligarchic, and rightly so), between 1910 and 1920, the United States set up a level of progressive taxation hitherto unknown in history. This major movement of compression of inequalities implied both taxing income (the rate applied to the highest incomes was on average 82% between 1930 and 1980) and estates (with rates rising to 70% on the transmission of the largest estates).

All this changed with the election of Reagan in 1980: In 1986, the reform reduced the top rate of income tax and ignored the social policies set up by the New Deal under Franklin D. Roosevelt. These policies were accused of having "softened" America and of having helped those who lost out during the war to "catch up." But Reagan left a high corporate tax in place and high progressive rates of taxation on estates. Thirty years after Reagan and ten years after the first attempt by Bush junior to abolish so-called death duties, in 2017 Trump has launched a new wave of presents to the biggest and wealthiest fortunes, and all this after abolishing Obamacare.

There is a fair chance that he will be supported by Congress. The Republicans will, of course, attempt to add a "border adjustment mechanism" consisting of authorizing the deduction from exports of the taxable profit and, conversely, of forbidding the deduction from imports (the well-known Ryan plan). This unprecedented blend of corporate tax and of European-style value-added tax (VAT) has already aroused the anger of the WTO (something which pleases Trump) but also of importers (for example, Walmart supermarkets) which is more problematic. Theoretically the measure could be neutralized by a rise in the dollar, but in practice the exchange rates are determined by many other factors, and nobody wants to take the risk.

It is likely that those concerned will settle for targeting specific imports and exports (with the intention of getting the message out that the Republicans defend American industry better than the Democrats do, who are described as covert free traders and always ready to give everything to the Mexicans and all those other jealous people who surround America) and that a compromise will be found both for estate duties and for a massive reduction in the rate of corporate company profits, doubtless in the range of 15% to 20%, which may relaunch fiscal dumping in Europe and around the world.

The main question remains: How does a program which is so clearly pro-rich and antisocial succeed in appealing to a majority of Americans as it did in 1980 and again in 2016? The classical answer is that globalization and cut-throat competition between countries leads to the reign of every man for himself. But that is not sufficient: We have to add the skill of the Republicans in using nationalist rhetoric; in cultivating a degree of anti-intellectualism; and, above all, in dividing the working classes by exacerbating ethnic, cultural, and religious divisions.

As early as the 1960s, the Republicans began to benefit from the gradual transfer of part of the vote of the white and southern working classes, unhappy with the civil rights movement and the social policies, accused of benefiting primarily the Black population. This long and in-depth movement continued with the crucial victory of Nixon in 1972 (faced with the Democrat, McGovern, who suggested implementing a universal basic income at the federal level, financed by a new increase in estate duties: This was the summit of the Roosevelt Program), Reagan in 1980, and finally Trump in 2016 (who had no hesitation in racially stigmatizing Obamacare, as Nixon and Reagan had done previously).

In the meantime, the Democratic electorate focused increasingly on the most highly educated and the minorities, and in the end, in some ways resembled the Republican electorate at the end of the nineteenth century (upscale whites and Blacks emancipated), as if the wheel had turned full circle and the Roosevelt coalition uniting the working classes over and above racial differences had ultimately only been an aside.

Let's hope that Europe—which in some ways is threatened by a similar development with the working classes having greater faith for their defense in the anti-immigrant forces than in those who describe themselves as progressive—will be capable of learning the lessons of history. And that the inevitable social failure of Trumpism will not lead our "Donald" into a headlong nationalist and military rush, as it has done others before him.

Will Macron's Marchers Take Power?

June 26, 2017

With over 350 seats, the members of Parliament (MPs) elected on the *La république en marche* (LREM) ticket will have an overwhelming majority in the Assemblée Nationale (Parliament). Will they use it to be in the forefront of reform and renewal of French politics? Or will they simply play a passive role, rubber stamping and obediently voting the texts that the government sends them?

It happens that they will shortly be faced with their first real-life test with the question of deduction of income tax at its source. The government wishes to postpone the implementation until 2019, perhaps forever, for reasons that are totally opportunist and unjustified. This big step backward is bad news for the alleged intention to reform and modernize the French fiscal and social system proclaimed by the new government (a general intention that is unfortunately rather vague once we enter into the details)[1] and leads us to fear the worst

---

1. See "What Reforms for France?" May 16, 2017.

for what is to come. Now, contrary to what has been stated, the government cannot take this sort of decision without a vote in Parliament, which should therefore take place in the coming days or weeks.

There are two possibilities. Either the LREM MPs force the government to maintain this crucial reform and its application as from January 2018, as was already voted by the outgoing Parliament in the autumn of 2016 in the context of the 2017 Finance Act. It will then be clear that the new MPs are ready to play their role fully in future reforms and oppose the executive when necessary. The other option is to follow in the steps of the conservatism of the government, which, unfortunately, seems to be the most likely outcome. This would alert us to the fact that with this new majority and this new authority, we are dealing with reformers who are mere paper tigers.

What are we talking about? The deduction of income tax at source was implemented in 1920 in Germany and Sweden; during World War II in the United States, the United Kingdom, and the Netherlands; and in the 1960s–1970s in Italy and Spain. France is the only developed country which has not introduced this. This is one of the most archaic aspects of our tax system and our administration. In this respect, we are between 50 and 100 years behind all other countries.

This is all the more regrettable as tax deduction at source would enable a considerable gain in efficiency for all parties concerned. In the first instance, for taxpayers, who in the present system find themselves paying their taxes one year after receiving the income, when their professional and financial system may well have completely changed. On the contrary, the new system would enable tax payment to be adjusted in real time to the situation of each individual.

In matters of tax administration, this would enable tax officials to focus on more important tasks, in particular on tax inspection and combating tax evasion.

Finally, for businesses, some business leaders, noted for their conservatism, claim that this reform will mean more work for them (the same line of argument has always been used in all the countries in which this reform has been implemented over the past century). The truth is that deduction at source has already been established in France since 1945 for social contributions. In total, income deducted at source amounts to more than 20% of GDP, if one includes all social contributions (including CSG), whereas income tax represents less than 4% of GDP. The extension to deduction at source of income tax will be a source of simplification for our tax system which will ultimately be to the advantage of businesses and all social and economic stakeholders.

In fact, the constant postponement of this reform has led to bureaucratic nonsense of an incredible complexity. A blatant example is the employment allowance, recently renamed the "activity bonus." At the moment, after deduction at source of social contributions, the wages of a full-time worker earning the statutory minimum wage are reduced by approximately 300 euros per month (1,450 euros before tax to 1,150 euros net). Then, if he or she applies for it, several months later, the employee will receive the equivalent of 130 euros per month as an activity bonus from the family allowance benefits fund (*caisses d'allocations familiales*). It would obviously be preferable to deduct less at source, to ensure that each worker receives a higher net wage on his or her monthly payslip and thus be able to organize their lives as a function of resources of which he or she is assured, instead of wasting time on uncertain procedures that are random and stigmatizing. Why have we ended up with such an absurd system? Because income tax is not deducted at source. The result is that it has never been possible to pay the employment allowance—which was part of income tax when it was introduced—automatically on the payslip. This is one of many concrete situations which could be cleared up if the reform were implemented.

Over and above these practical aspects, which are essential, there is a much broader democratic, political, and philosophical dimension at stake in the establishment of tax deduction at source. It is one of the key elements in the clarification of the relation between the state and the tax-paying citizen. It enables the question of taxes and that of transfer payments, the issue of fiscal justice and of social justice, the question of a fair income and that of a fair wage to be considered at one and the same time.

Generally speaking, it would be a grave error to deal with these questions of taxation and mode of deduction as purely technical questions. In the absence of a fair and accepted system of deduction, without consent to taxation, there can be no collective capacity to act. Fiscal revolutions are central to all the major political revolutions. Without deduction at source, the social security system could not have been established. Just imagine each wage-earner writing a check to the social security fund one year late, for sums amounting to over 20% of GNP! The fact that deduction at source has never been extended to the state taxes conveys a distinct limit to our collective capacity to construct a relationship of trust between the taxpayer citizen and the central state in France. This is an issue which involves our social contract in its totality.

Unfortunately, the issue of generalizing deduction at source has been a subject for discussion for decades now in France. On each occasion, this reform has been rejected. In 1999, confronted with the protests of some of the tax officials

and businesses, the Jospin government finally decided to sacrifice M. Sautter, the minister who introduced the reform. At
the time, it was postponed for one year. That was eighteen
years ago.

After considerable hesitation, the socialist governments
in power between 2012 and 2017 finally decided to introduce a
very well-thought-out project which was voted by Parliament
in the autumn of 2016, enabling the reform to be introduced
in January 2018. It is of course regrettable that this new system was not implemented earlier, before the elections and not
after, to ensure that the reform could no longer be challenged.
Doubtless it can be considered a desperate attempt by François
Hollande in support of his campaign for re-election and we all
know how that ended.

The fact remains that it is a good reform, undoubtedly the
most important for decades in the field of taxation. The system formally adopted by the MPs in autumn 2016 in the context of the Finance Act for 2017 is a good system. In particular,
it is based on modern information technologies (which the
German, Swedish, American, and British reformers did not
have in the interwar years or during World War II) that enable the transmission in real time and anonymously of all the
information required for businesses to apply the correct rate
of deduction. All the relevant consultations with tax officials
and businesses had taken place, there were no further challenges to the reform, everything was ready for its implementation in January 2018.

Following the productive discussion in Parliament in autumn 2016, it had even been suggested that taxpayers who so
desired could easily choose the application of a neutral rate
(which would not take into account any other income they
might have, or their family situation) or a customized rate
(enabling the spouse who earns less, often the woman, to be

deducted at a lower rate than that applied to the other spouse). No other country in history has been able to provide as many guarantees and choices for the implementation of tax deduction at source (this is the advantage of later reforms: We have better technical support).

In May 2017, along comes a new president, Emmanuel Macron, self-proclaimed "head reformer" of the country. What did he announce in a press release dated June 7, a few days before the first round of the parliamentary elections? That the implementation of deduction at source had been postponed indefinitely. True, an implementation in 2019 is mentioned. But given that the last postponement for one year dates back to 1999, concern is legitimate. The historical experience of these issues suggests that this type of reform must be implemented at the beginning of the five-year term (*quinquennat*) especially when they are already fully operational, otherwise there is a high risk of permanent postponement.

All this is particularly worrisome in that the official excuse—that it would place too great a burden on businesses and that the reform was not yet ready—is quite simply not credible.

The German, Swedish, American, British, Dutch, Spanish, Italian, etc., businesses have been ready for a century, or half a century (depending on the country) to apply tax deduction at source at a time when information technology did not even exist, and we are being made to believe that French businesses would not be ready to implement this system in 2018? None of these countries has ever reversed this reform, and we are still wondering whether France is ready to meet the challenge? The whole thing makes no sense.

The truth is that everyone knows that the real reasons for postponement are elsewhere. It is a question of pleasing the most conservative fringe of business leaders on one hand;

but primarily it guarantees maximum visibility for the micro fiscal reform that Macron wishes to implement in January 2018. This is the rise of 1.7% in the CSG enabling the financing of a reduction of 3% in regular social contributions for employees (at the expense of pensioners, in particular). This reform should result in a rise in net salary. Macron wishes this message to come over loud and clear. The implementation of tax deduction at source at the same time might confuse the issue, something which Macron wishes to avoid.

I want to be very clear: This is a particularly lame excuse. First, because taxpayers are perfectly capable of understanding that these two reforms are separate, provided that an effort is made to explain this to them.

Second, because "fiddling" with the CSG rate and social contributions is particularly untenable in substance. The fact is that retirement pensions of over 1,400 euros per month are to be cut to raise the monthly salaries of 5,000 euros, 10,000 euros, or 20,000 euros. Good luck to the LREM MPs who have to explain the logic of this type of redistribution to their electors. I only hope that when the time comes, they will have more common sense than the lead "reformer." In this situation, the correct solution would obviously be a reform based on progressive rates, that is, lower for the low-income groups and higher for the higher ones, whether it be salaries or retirement pensions.

In any case, it is extremely alarming to see a president take the risk of permanently compromising a reform as structural as the implementation of tax deduction at source, simply to ensure more visibility for a very small tax reform (which, no matter what one might think about the content, is only a minor parametric reform: The rate of an existing tax is being raised, to lower that of another).

The last totally dishonest excuse sometimes relayed by complacent or poorly informed media is that deduction at source would be impossible to implement in France due to the "familialization or family-based" aspect of income tax, that is, the fact that income tax depends on the family situation (dependent children and spouse). In reality, the same applies in all countries.

Throughout the world, in one way or another, income tax depends on the number of dependent children with different systems of taxable income or tax reductions. These systems are indeed different from the family quotient used in France, but the rate of deduction to be applied, in consequence, is also a function of the number of dependent children (sometimes in an even more specific way than in France, given that the family quotient is capped in France), and this in no way prevents tax deduction at source from being applied. It should also be borne in mind that in Germany and the United States, the calculation of income tax depends also on the income of the spouse, in accordance with a system which is close to the marital quotient in France and, there again, this has in no way prevented the deduction at source from being applied for almost a century now. On all these questions, the French reform offers in reality much more flexibility and confidentiality than all similar reforms applied in other countries.

In conclusion: the government communiqué dated June 7, 2017,[2] announced the postponement of the reform, as if everything had already been decided, discreetly specifying that "appropriate legislative and regulatory measures would soon be taken to organize the postponement." In fact, even if the new executive power would very much like to do without the checks and balances of parliamentary oversight, this is happily im-

2. Sarah Belouezzane and Bertrand Bissuel, "Code du travail: ce qu'il y a dans le projet de loi d'habilitation," *Le Monde*, June 21, 2017.

possible under our current laws. The reform of tax deduction at source with a clear timetable for implementation was formally adopted by Parliament (the Assemblée) in the autumn of 2016. This timetable can only be changed and the reform postponed by a new vote in the Assemblée. It is to be hoped that the LREM MPs will know how to seize this golden opportunity to assert their faith in the democratic renewal, the reform, and the modernization of our country.

The CICE Comedy
July 11, 2017

Y et another deferral! The government of Emmanuel Macron and Edouard Philippe had already announced the postponement of the deduction of income tax at source until 2019 for totally opportunistic reasons.[1] The risk is that this elementary reform in tax modernization, awaited in France for decades, may finally never see the light of day, even though the scheme was all ready to come into operation in January 2018. The government has now announced the postponement until 2019 of the replacement of the CICE (Tax Credit for Competitiveness and Employment/*Crédit d'Impôt pour la Compétitivité et l'Emploi*) by a long-term reduction in the employers' contributions. This is despite the promise of this reform during the electoral campaign—and the fact that it had also been promised by François Hollande since 2014.

Let me be clear: These two deferrals are extremely disturbing and demonstrate the lack of preparation of the new government in matters of reform in France; or perhaps instead

1. "Will Macron's Marchers Take Power?" June 26, 2017.

they are an indication of extensive preparation for a cynical approach to government with no real desire for reform.

Let's go back for a moment. When Hollande came into power in 2012, he began by suppressing—wrongly—the reductions in the employers' contributions which his predecessor had just set up. Then, a few months later, he invented the notorious CICE, a complex scheme which aimed to refund to corporations one year later, part of the employers' contributions paid one year before. The new system was totally incomprehensible for companies, who in most instances found they were receiving checks without understanding why. Furthermore, this type of scheme is always characterized by chronic instability and almost total unpredictability several years ahead, which does not augur well for long-term decisions, including for the best-informed corporations.

In reality the CICE only added a layer of complexity to a fiscal-social system which already had far too many. Nevertheless, the whole of François Hollande's technostructure—headed at the time by the present President of the Republic—was quite determined. It was considered a brilliant idea, because that enabled the budgetary cost to be deferred to 2014 (the tax credit is reimbursed one year later, unlike the reductions in contributions, which would have been imputed to the state budget as from 2013). This meant the government could have its cake and eat it: The European deficits would fall immediately, and jobs would be created. Unfortunately it was not their lucky day: We had neither one nor the other, partly because of this complex waste of public money.

As early as 2014, François Hollande therefore came to the obvious conclusion. The CICE should be abolished, and there should be a return to the long-term simplification of employers' contributions. The only problem is that apparently neither he, nor Emmanuel Macron today, had the slightest idea of how to get rid of this blot on the fiscal landscape which they themselves had created and which, in the meantime, had assumed considerable proportions (over 20 billion euros per year). The problem is that what constituted the attraction of the CICE in the eyes of its creators (the deferment of its cost in time) has now become a millstone around their necks. The cost in the year when the scheme is ended (let's assume, in 2018) will be double, since the contributions paid in 2017 will have to be reimbursed and those due in 2018 will be reduced. However, the political courage to do this is long overdue—otherwise this complex system will go on forever.

The most worrying aspect is that Macron—like Hollande in 2014–2015, moreover—seems to wish the employers to carry the can for the status quo. He has made an offer to employers: the replacement of 100 euros of CICE by a reduction of 100 euros in social contributions, knowing full well that the operation will automatically lead to an extra 30 euros of extra corporation tax (because the reductions lead to a rise in the taxable profits, unlike the CICE). Faced with a choice of this sort, it is quite obvious that corporations will always choose to maintain the CICE. This pathetic comedy will have to stop if the government really wants to right past wrongs. The 100 euros of CICE should be replaced by a reduction in contributions of 140 euros. The budgetary cost to the state would remain the same (given the extra income from corporation tax).

The saddest thing is that all this fiddling about prevents us from advancing the fundamental debate, namely, the reform in our system of financing social protection which is overly reliant on contributions. But we still need to clarify the alternative sources of income. Some people consider that a correct approach would be a social VAT. But the cost for more modest incomes would be high. The only real alternative is a progressive general social security contribution (CSG) tax: This should involve all incomes (salaries in the private sector, wages in the public sector, retirement pensions, income from property) using a progressive scale based on the level of total income. Instead of refusing, as a question of principle, any reduction in contributions, the rebels in the Socialist Party would have done well to take up this debate.

What conclusions can we draw from all this? First, it is not enough to declare oneself a reformer to really be one. Absolute power goes to the head and leads people to lose touch with reality. The French style of presidency, with its courts and courtiers, does not help. Next, it would be easier for the left to oppose the right and the center constructively if they began by making proposals. Finally, the time has come to say farewell to the present macromania and discuss fundamentals. This is the best contribution that could be made toward the success of the five-year mandate and the country.

Rethinking the Capital Code

September 12, 2017

What should we think of the reform of the Labour Code defended by the government? The key measure, and also the one which is most highly criticized, consists of capping the compensation payments for unfair dismissal at one month's salary per year per year of seniority (and half a month for each year worked beyond ten years). In other words, an employer can freely dismiss an employee who has spent over ten years at the firm, without having to establish the slightest "real and serious cause"; and without the judge being able to impose on the employer the payment of an indemnity greater than ten months' salary. The compensation for an employee who has been with the firm for thirty years cannot exceed twenty months' salary.

The problem is that the social cost of dismissal, in terms of the payment of unemployment benefits and reclassification, is often much higher. Intended to strengthen recruitment incentives, this amounts to a license to lay off workers and may well increase the arbitrary power of the employer, developing a feeling of distrust which is not conducive to long-term investment by employees. It may also increase the complaints for harassment or discrimination (which are not capped). It would have been more useful to speed up the judicial procedures and practice which are disgracefully slow in France.

What is really to be regretted is that the government has not even taken this opportunity to strengthen the involvement of the employees in the governance of firms. In particular, the reform would have been much more balanced if at the same time it had been decided to appreciably increase the number of seats for employees on the executive boards of companies, as the CFDT (Conféderation française de travail—one of the main trade unions) requested. This would have enabled the promotion of a genuine European model for economic democracy.

Let's go back for a moment. Sometimes people think that the rules defining the power of shareholders and employees in joint-stock companies were fixed for once and for all in the nineteenth century: one share, one vote, and that's it! In reality, this is not true. In the 1950s, the Nordic and German-speaking countries adopted legislation which completely changed this balance. The stated aim was to promote "code-termination," that is, genuine power sharing between capital and labor. These rules were consolidated over the decades. At the moment, the employees' representatives thus hold half of the seats on the executive boards of the major firms in Germany and one-third of these seats in Sweden, independently of any capital shareholding. There is a very broad consensus that these rules have contributed to an improvement in the involvement of the employees in the strategies of German and Swedish firms and, in the last resort, to greater economic and social efficiency.

Unfortunately, until recently, this movement toward democratization has not been adopted by other countries to the extent that one might have imagined. In particular, the role of workers has long been purely consultative in French, British, and American firms. In 2014, for the first time, a French law attributed one seat with a decisionmaking vote to the representatives of the employees on the executive board of companies (one seat in twelve, which remains very low). In the United States and the United Kingdom, shareholders still hold all the seats, even if the debate is becoming increasingly pressing in the United Kingdom, driven by the Labour Party, but also by some Conservatives.

Against this background, if the French government were to decide to broaden the scope of the movement by introducing an appreciable number of seats for employees (let's say, between one-third and one-half, so as to converge with the German-Nordic axis), this would be a major achievement. It would enable the promotion of a worldwide standard in corporate law and would, in more general terms, contribute to defining a genuine European doctrine in the economic and social sphere. This would be infinitely more interesting and imaginative than the sacrosanct consecration of the principle of free and fair competition characteristic of the European Union.

Recent work by European researchers has also demonstrated that consideration of the German-Nordic form of codetermination was far from finished and that this model could even go further and be improved. To get away from these role plays between workers and shareholders which are at times not very fruitful, Ewan McGaughey has suggested that the members of executive boards should be elected by a mix of shareholders and employees. This would thus lead to defending programs for action that combine multiple aspirations. Isabelle Ferreras for her part has defended the idea of genuine bicameralism in firms, with shareholders' councils and workers' councils being obliged to agree and to adopt the same strategic texts and decisions. Julia Cage has suggested that the voting rights of hegemonic shareholders should be capped, and conversely, that those of the small shareholders and other "crowdfunders" should be raised by the same amount. This model, originally intended for not-for-profit media firms, is based on a nonproportional relation between input in capital and voting rights and could be extended to other sectors.

All these studies have one thing in common: They demonstrate that reflection on power relationships and property, which for a moment was thought to have been annihilated after the Soviet disaster, in reality is only beginning. Europe and France must take their rightful place.

Suppression of the Wealth Tax: A Historical Error

October 10, 2017

L et it be said at once: The suppression of the wealth tax (Impôt sur la Fortune) constitutes a serious moral, economic, and historical mistake. This decision reveals a profound misunderstanding of the challenges of inequality posed by globalization.

Let's go back for a moment. During the first globalization period between 1870 and 1914, a strong international movement gradually took shape which sought to promote a new type of redistribution and taxation. Based on a progressive taxation system on income, wealth, and inheritance, this new model was aimed at a better distribution of productivity gains and the structural reduction of the concentration of property and economic power. It was successfully implemented in the period 1920 to 1970, partly as a result of the pressure of dramatic historical events, but equally thanks to a lengthy intellectual and political process.

We may perhaps today be witnessing the beginnings of a similar movement. Confronted with the rise in inequality, awareness is gaining momentum. Those who advocate withdrawal into some form of cultural identity are, of course, attempting to exploit the feeling of abandonment experienced by the working classes, at times successfully. But concomitantly, we see the rise of a new demand for democracy, equality, and redistribution. The United Kingdom might swing distinctly to the left in the years to come—and perhaps also the United States if the Democratic candidates who are preparing to run are anything to judge by.

In this type of context, the abolition of the wealth tax today in France, almost forty years after the arrival in power of Reagan and Thatcher, has totally missed the plot. There is absolutely no sense in making tax gifts to groups who are old and wealthy and have already done very well in recent decades. All the more so as the loss in revenue is anything but symbolic. If we add the gifts made to dividends and interests (which will in the future be taxed at a maximum rate of 30%, as opposed to 55% for salaries and incomes from non-wage activities), we come to a total cost of over 5 billion euros. This is the equivalent of 40% of the total budget allocated to the universities and higher education, which will remain static at 13.4 billion euros in 2018, whereas the number of students has risen steadily, and preference should be given to investment in training. I would like to bet that the students will remind the government of this when it endeavors to add selection to austerity in the coming months.

The government's argument is that the wealth tax would provoke a fiscal hemorrhage. The problem is that this assertion is totally false. If one examines all the data available calmly and objectively—the national accounts, declarations of income and of fortunes, surveys on wealth—then the conclusion is irrevocable. The biggest fortunes are doing very well in France, and there is no hemorrhaging to be seen.

Here are the main facts:[1] Between 1980 and 2016, average national income per adult, expressed in 2016 euros, rose from 25,000 euros to just over 33,000 euros, or a rise of approximately 30%. At the same time, the average wealth held derived from property per adult doubled, rising from 90,000 to 190,000 euros. Yet more striking: the wealth of the richest 1%, 70% of which is in financial assets, rose from 1.4 to 4.5 million euros, or increased more than threefold. As to the 0.1% of the wealthiest, 90% of whose wealth is held in financial assets, and who will be the main beneficiaries of the abolition of the wealth tax, their fortunes rose from 4 to 20 million euros, that is, they increased fivefold. In other words, the biggest fortunes in financial assets rose even more rapidly than property assets, whereas the opposite should have been the case if the hypothesis of a fiscal flight were true.

Moreover, this type of finding is a characteristic in the ranking of fortunes, in France as in all countries. According to Forbes, the top world fortunes, which are almost exclusively held in financial assets—have risen at a rate of 6% to 7% per year (on top of inflation) since the 1980s, or 3–4 times more rapidly than growth in GDP and of world per capita wealth. Some see therein an almost messianic sign of the benefits of entrepreneurial dynamics. In truth, we see the same rise in numerous inherited fortunes (like that of the late L'Oréal fortune). This evolution is also in large part due to commercially advantageous privatizations, and particularly profitable monopolies, in particular in energy, telecommunications, and

1. See, in particular, Bertrand Garbinti, Jonathan Goupille-Lebret, and Thomas Piketty, "Accounting for Wealth Inequality Dynamics: Methods, Estimates and Simulations for France (1800–2014)," WID.world, Working Paper Series 2016/5.

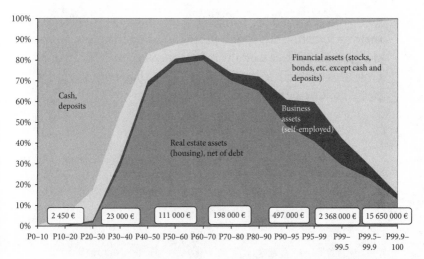

Figure 15. Composition of property (France 2015). In France in 2015 (as in most countries where data are available), small fortunes consist primarily of cash and bank deposits, medium fortunes of real estate, and large fortunes of financial assets (mainly stocks). The distribution shown here is per adult wealth (wealth of couples divided by two). *Sources and series:* see piketty.pse.ens.fr /ideology.e.

new technologies in Europe and the United States, as in Russia, Mexico, India, or China. In any event, whatever our individual opinions may be as to the importance of these various factors, we should be able to agree on the fact that a wealth tax at a rate of over 1.5% or 2% (or even more) is not a serious threat to a fiscal base which rises at a similar rate, and that there are other priorities to be addressed without making presents to those who are doing best.

The political strategy which consists of transforming the wealth tax into a property tax, to avoid a complete suppression of the wealth tax, quite frankly leaves me speechless. There is no logical reason to levy a higher tax on a person who invests their fortune in a house or a property rather than in a financial portfolio, a yacht, or any other type of good. We can only hope that elected members remember that they were not elected to be part of this kind of farce.

Budget 2018: French Youth Sacrificed

October 21, 2017

To date, the debate on the 2018 budget in France has concentrated on the question of tax gifts to the most wealthy. De facto, the abolition of the wealth tax and the measures in favor of top dividends and interests will cost the state budget over 5 billion euros.

But it is also important to insist on the other side of the coin, in other words, on the losers in the 2018 budget and, in particular, on the young people sacrificed as a consequence of the fall in student expenditure per capita in higher education. This will also enable me to clarify a number of issues raised by internauts about my last post.[1]

Officially, the draft 2018 Budget Bill which the government has just tabled shows a slight increase in expenditure on higher education. The budget for the program titled "Formations supérieures et recherche universitaire" ("Higher Education

---

1. See "Suppression of the Wealth Tax: A Historical Error," October 10, 2017.

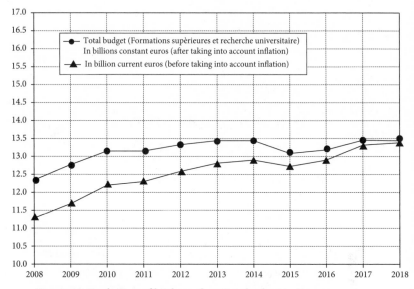

Figure 16. Evolution of higher education budget in France.
Source: author's calculations based on budget data from the
Ministry of Higher Education.

and University Research")—which covers all the operation and
equipment budgets allocated to the totality of French universities and institutions of higher education—will thus rise from
13.3 billion in 2017 to 13.4 billion in 2018.[2]

If we follow the path of the Finance Laws introduced
since 2008 by the Sarkozy and then the Hollande governments,
we observe a similar strategy in communication: The rise in
budgets allocated to higher education is minimal, but the governments usually manage to present these budgets as on the

2. See the official budgetary document proposed by the government,
p. 39: https://www.performance-publique.budget.gouv.fr/sites/performance
_publique/files/farandole/ressources/2018/pap/pdf/DBGPGMPGM150.pdf.

increase. In total, the nominal budget for the Higher Education and University Research program has thus risen from 11.3 billion euros in 2008 to 13.4 billion in 2018. Officially, honor has been saved and the university preserved.

The only thing is that all this is an illusion created by the government and a particularly unrefined one at that. To begin with, we have to allow for a rise in prices: even if this is gradual per year (it will be about 1% in 2017, and doubtless the same in 2018, which is already higher than the rise of 0.1 billion euros in the nominal higher education budget proposed for 2018). It nevertheless represents almost 10% over 10 years, which is enough to absorb a little over half of the nominal rise in the level between 2008 and 2018. If we talk in constant euros (that is, after taking inflation into account), we see that the budget for higher education has risen from 12.4 billion euros to 13.4 billion euros in ten years.

Furthermore, and above all, we have to take into consideration the considerable rise in the number of students, which rose from over 2.2 million in 2008, to almost 2.7 million in 2018, or an increase of roughly 20% (I am simply taking here the numbers of students published by the ministry and the forecasts for 2017–2018).

If we combine the evolution of the budget for higher education (barely 10% in constant euros) and that of the number of students (20%), then the inevitable conclusion is that between 2008 and 2018, the budget per student has fallen by almost 10% in France.

Let's put it plainly: This decline is totally anachronous and scandalous. Furthermore, it is in flagrant contradiction with the official European discourse, which proudly proclaims that the priority aim in Europe is to invest in training and innovation—except that there is no concern to take the appropriate measures to check whether the means have been

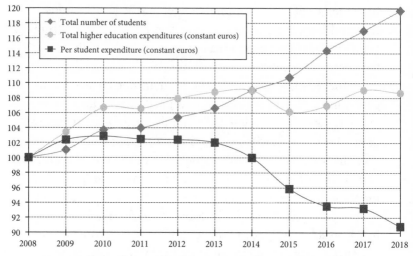

Figure 17. The fall in per student expenditure in France (base 100 in 2008). The number of students rose by about 20% in France between 2008 and 2018, while total higher education expenditures rose by less than 10% (in constant euros), hence there was a fall of about 10% of per student expenditure. *Sources and series:* see piketty.pse.ens.fr/ideology.

allocated to achieve these goals. This deafening silence contrasts strangely with the capacity of the European institutions to give lessons, awarding good marks and bad marks to all sorts of reforms. How are we going to become "the most competitive knowledge-based economy in the world" by 2020 (the aim proclaimed by the European leaders in Lisbon in 2000, with 2010 as the first target which has been regularly postponed since then) if we begin by reducing investment per student by 10% in France between 2008 and 2018?

It should also be pointed out that the rise in the number of students is obviously not a problem as such, quite the contrary. It conveys the dynamism of French demography and also the fact that young people are trying to get more and more qualifications, which is an excellent thing. The high level of training and education is what has enabled French society and the economy to become one of the most productive in the world,[3] and that trend must continue.

However, this is conditional on providing the means, which is absolutely not the case at the moment. The universities in particular were already very poorly provided for ten years ago, and the situation has distinctly deteriorated since. Does the government really think that this sort of policy is preparing the future of the country?

The responsibility for this sad state of affairs is of course shared by the successive governments over the past ten years and is to a large extent explained by the disastrous management by the eurozone countries of the crisis since 2008,[4] which has led to nothing less than the sacrifice of our youth. Their lot is one of high unemployment and low investment in the future.

The fact remains that the present government has a special responsibility: on the one hand because it is high time to adjust aims and recognize the numerous errors made since 2008; on the other hand because the 2018 budget chose to devote 5 billion euros immediately to lowering the taxes of the wealthiest, compared to 0.1 billion euros for the universities and higher education (immediately absorbed by inflation).

3. Thomas Piketty, "Of Productivity in France and in Germany," *Le Monde*, January 9, 2017, https://www.lemonde.fr/blog/piketty/2017/01/09/of-productivity-in-france-and-in-germany/.

4. Thomas Piketty, "2007–2015: Such a Long Recession," *Le Monde*, February 27, 2016, https://www.lemonde.fr/blog/piketty/2016/02/27/2007-2015-such-a-long-recession/.

Whatever one may think about the lowering of the wealth tax (and my personal opinion is that it is completely unjustified,[5] given the fact that the top financial assets are doing very well in France and show no signs of fiscal flight), one can only be struck by the comparison of these two figures, which convey a strange sense of priorities.

If the government had chosen to devote these 5 billion euros to higher education, it would have been able to increase the 2018 budget by almost 40% (very precisely, 37%: 5 billion/13.4 billion).

By simply devoting half of that amount, it would have been able to raise the budget for higher education by almost 20%, which would have been enough to cancel the fall observed between 2008 and 2017, and even to ensure expenditure per student in 2018 of roughly 10% higher than in 2008—a rise which over a period of 10 years would not be excessive, given the relative poverty of the French universities and the means observed elsewhere.

In sum, by choosing for ideological motives to devote everything to the wealthiest (who in practice often belong to the oldest groups), the 2018 budget turns its back on young people and the future, whereas the priority ought to be to invest in training and the future.

The saddest thing is that our higher education also needs in-depth reforms which have been put off for too long. We have to reduce the distance between the universities and the prestigious *grandes écoles,* and we must, at long last, ensure democratic transparency in the working of the admission and allocation system to higher education (the *admission post*

5. "Supression of the Wealth Tax: A Historical Error," October 10, 2017.

baccalauréat, or APB).[6] But reforms of this type can only be successfully implemented if at the outset there is an end to the reduction in means allocated to the universities. If the government endeavors to introduce selection over and above austerity (which is merely another form of selection based on means), then there is little doubt that it is heading for trouble.

6. Thomas Piketty, "APB Scandal," *Le Monde,* July 12, 2016, https://www.lemonde.fr/blog/piketty/2016/07/12/the-apb-scandal/.

The Catalan Syndrome
November 14, 2017

I s the crisis in Catalonia due to overcentralization and the intransigence of the authorities in Madrid? Or is it instead due to generalized competition between regions and countries in rivalry with one another, each pursuing their own interests, a process which has already gone much too far both in Spain and in Europe in general?

Let's take a step back. To explain the tougher pro-independence stand, reference is often made to the decision by the Spanish constitutional tribunal in 2010 to invalidate the new status of autonomy for Catalonia, following the high number of actions lodged by the elected members of the Popular Party. Even if some of the measures challenged by the judges did pose serious substantive issues (in particular concerning the regionalization of justice), the method used was indeed very likely to cause offense, in particular as the status had been adopted by the Spanish Parliament in 2006 (which at the time had a socialist majority), as well as by a referendum in Catalonia.

However, one should not forget that the new rules for fiscal decentralization were effectively validated in 2010, both for Catalonia and for the Spanish regions as a whole. Now these

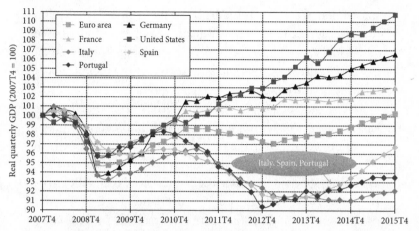

Figure 18. Level of economic activity (GDP), 2007–2015. The level of economic activity dropped by about 5% in the United States and in the eurozone between late 2007 and early 2009. Given the European setback in 2011–2012 (particularly in Southern Europe), one needs to wait until late 2015 to see a recovery of economic activity to its 2007 level in the eurozone, at a time when U.S. GDP is 10% above its 2007 level. *Sources and series:* see piketty.pse.ens .fr/ideology.

rules, which have been in force since 2011, already make Spain one of the most decentralized countries in the world in budgetary and fiscal matters, including when compared with federal states much larger in size.

In particular, since 2011 the base for income tax is split 50-50 between the federal and the regional governments. In practice, in 2017 the rates of the income tax contribution to the federal budget ranged from 9.5% (for annual taxable incomes below 12,450 euros) to 22.5% (above 60,000 euros). If a region decides to apply these same rates for its part of the income tax base, then the taxpayers in this region will pay in total income tax rates ranging from 19% to 45%, and the tax revenue will be shared equally between Madrid and the region. Each region can also decide to set its own income tax bands and its own additional rates, higher or lower than the federal rates. In all cases, the corresponding income accrues to the region, which no longer has to share it with other regions.[1]

This sort of system poses numerous problems. It challenges the very idea of solidarity within the country and comes down to playing the regions against one another, which is particularly problematic when the issue is one of income tax, as this is supposed to enable the reduction of inequalities between the richest and the poorest, over and above regional or professional identities. Since 2011, this system of internal competition has also led to dumping strategies and the fictitious fiscal domiciliation of the wealthiest households and firms, which in the long run may risk undermining the progression of the whole.[2]

By comparison, in the United States, a country with seven times the population of Spain, and well-known for its attachment to decentralization and the rights of the individual states, income tax has always been a tax that was almost exclusively federal. In particular, since its creation in 1913, it is the federal income tax which ensures the function of fiscal progressivity with rates applicable to the highest incomes that were set on average at over 80% between 1930 and 1980 and have stabilized

1. For the list of rates applied in 2017, see p. 505 in: https://www.agenci atributaria.es/static_files/AEAT/DIT/Contenidos_Publicos/CAT/AYUWEB /Biblioteca_Virtual/Manuales_practicos/Renta/ManualRentaPatrimonio 2016_es_es.pdf.

2. For example, see David R. Agrawal and Dirk Foremny, "Relocation of the Rich: Migration in Response to Top Tax Rate Changes from Spanish Reforms (April 1, 2018)." Available at https://ssrn.com/abstract=2796472 or http://dx.doi.org/10.2139/ssrn.2796472.

at a little below 40% since the 1980–1990s. The individual states can vote additional rates, but in practice, these are very low rates, usually between 5% and 10%. Doubtless, taxpayers in California (the state with a population that by itself is almost as big as Spain and is six times more populous than Catalonia) would have been very happy to keep half of the income from the federal tax for themselves and their children; but the fact is that they have never succeeded in so doing (if truth be told, they have never really tried).

In the Federal Republic of Germany, an example closer to Spain, income tax is exclusively federal; the Länder do not have the right to vote additional taxes. Nor do they have the right to keep the least part of the revenue for themselves, whatever the taxpayers in Bavaria may think. We would like to make it clear that the rationale for additional tax rates at the regional or local level is not necessarily a bad thing (in France it could enable the replacement of the local poll tax or *taxe d'habitation*) on the condition that they remain moderate. By choosing to split income tax 50-50 between state and regional governments, Spain has gone too far and now finds itself in a situation where some of the Catalans would like to keep 100% of the revenue from income tax on becoming independent.

Europe also bears a great deal of responsibility in this crisis. Apart from the catastrophic management of the crisis in the eurozone, in particular at the expense of Spain,[3] for decades now Europe has been promoting a model of civilization based on the idea that it is possible to have everything at the same time: integration in a large European and world market,

3. Thomas Piketty, "2007–2015: Such a Long Recession," *Le Monde*, February 27, 2016, https://www.lemonde.fr/blog/piketty/2016/02/27/2007-2015 -such-a-long-recession/.

without any real obligation to ensure fiscal solidarity and the financing of the public good. In these circumstances, why not try one's luck by making Catalonia a tax haven along the lines of Luxembourg? To be sure, there is a federal European budget, but it is very small. Above all, it should logically be based on those who benefit most from economic integration, with a common European tax on corporate profits and the highest incomes, as is the case in the United States (one could also endeavor to do better, but we are far from this). It is only by ensuring that solidarity and fiscal justice are at long last central to its practices that Europe will successfully tackle separatism.

Trump, Macron: Same Fight

December 12, 2017

I t is customary to contrast Trump and Macron: on the one hand, the vulgar American businessman with his xenophobic tweets and global warming skepticism; and on the other, the well-educated, enlightened European with his concern for dialogue between different cultures and sustainable development. All this is not entirely false and rather pleasing to French ears. But if we take a closer look at the policies being implemented, one is struck by the similarities.

In particular, Trump, like Macron, has just had very similar tax reforms adopted. In both cases, these constitute an incredible flight in the direction of fiscal dumping in favor of the richest and most mobile.

Let me recap recent events. In the United States, the Senate has approved the main lines of the Trump plan; the rate of federal tax on corporate profits will be reduced from 35% to 20% (with, moreover, an almost total amnesty for the profits repatriated by multinationals); a reduced tax of approximately 25% will be instituted for the pass-through income of company owners (as an alternative to the higher rate of income tax at 40% applicable to the highest salaries); and inheritance tax will be considerably reduced for the richest (and even totally eliminated in the version adopted by the House).

Now, here is what Macron has proposed in France. The rate of corporation tax will gradually be reduced from 33% to 25%; a lower rate of 30% will be introduced for dividends and interest (as an alternative to the 55% income tax rate applicable to the highest salaries); the wealth tax will be abolished for the largest financial and business wealth holders (while the real estate tax has never been as high for the less wealthy).

For the first time since the ancien régime, it has thus been decided in both countries to set up an explicitly derogatory system of taxation for the benefit of the categories of income and wealth held by the most affluent social groups. In each case the argument is presumed to be irrefutable; the bulk of taxpayers are neither free nor mobile and have no other option than to treat the rich with respect, otherwise the rich will up and leave the country and they will no longer be able to share in their benefits (jobs, investments, and other wonderful things that ordinary people cannot easily access). Trump refers to them as "job creators," while Macron refers to "lead climbers": the terms used to describe these new benefactors which the masses should cherish vary, but basically, they are similar.

Both Trump and Macron are probably sincere. The fact remains that they both reveal a profound lack of understanding of the inegalitarian challenges posed by globalization. They refuse to take into account facts which are now well established, namely, that the groups to which they give preference are those who have already acquired a disproportionate share of the growth in recent decades.

By denying this reality, they expose us to three major risks. The first is that in the richest countries, the working classes have a feeling of abandonment which sustains an attitude of rejection toward globalization and immigration in particular. Trump deals with this by flattering the xenophobia of his electors, while Macron hopes to remain in power by counting on the attachment of the majority of French public opinion to tolerance and open-mindedness and by rejecting his critics as being antiglobalization. But in reality, this development is a threat to the future, in Ohio and Louisiana, as it is also in France and in Sweden.

The second risk is that the refusal to tackle inequalities complicates considerably the challenge of addressing climate change. As Lucas Chancel has clearly demonstrated, the considerable adjustment in lifestyles to deal with global warming will only be acceptable if a fair distribution of the effort is guaranteed.[1] If the richest continue to pollute the planet with their SUVs and their yachts registered in Malta (tax-free, including no VAT, as the Paradise Papers has just revealed), then why should the poor accept the rise in the carbon tax, which is likely to be inevitable?

And the third risk is that the refusal to correct the inegalitarian tendencies of globalization has extremely negative consequences for our capacity to reduce global poverty. The new perspectives, which will be published on December 14 in the World Inequality Report,[2] are clear: The pursuit of the inegalitarian policies and trajectories chosen will result in the standards of living of the most disadvantaged half of the planet developing in a totally different manner between now and 2050.

Let's end on a more optimistic note: On paper, Macron defends an approach of international and European cooperation which is obviously more promising than Trump's unilateralism. The question is to know when we will leave theory and hypocrisy behind. For example, the Comprehensive

1. Lucas Chancel, *Unsustainable Inequalities: Social Justice and the Environment* (Cambridge, MA: Belknap Press, 2020).
2. World Inequality Report 2018, https://wir2018.wid.world/.

Economic Trade Agreement treaty between the European Union and Canada a few months after the UN Paris Climate Change Conference has no legally binding measures on climate and fair taxation. As to the French proposals purporting to reform Europe which are as music to our proud French ears, the truth is that they are extremely vague. We still do not know how the Eurozone Parliament will be formed nor what its powers will be (doubtless these are considered mere details). There is a real risk of all this leading to nothing. If Macron's dream is not to lead to a Trump nightmare, it is time to abandon minor nationalist satisfactions and to face the facts.

2018: The Year of Europe
January 16, 2018

Ten years after the financial crisis, will the year 2018 see Europe making a great leap forward? Several factors contribute to this view, but the outcome is far from certain.

The crisis in 2008, which triggered the sharpest global recession since the 1929 crisis, clearly originated in the increasingly obvious weaknesses of the American system: excessive deregulation, an explosion in inequalities, indebtedness of the poorest. Supported by a more egalitarian and inclusive model of development, Europe could have seized the opportunity to promote a better system of regulating global capitalism. However, the lack of trust among the members of the European Union, confined within rigid rules applied inappropriately, led them to provoke a further recession in 2011–2013,[1] from which they are just recovering.

The coming to power of Trump in 2017 is indicative of further considerable shortcomings in the American model.

1. See Thomas Piketty, "2007–2015: Such a Long Recession," *Le Monde*, February 27, 2016, https://www.lemonde.fr/blog/piketty/2016/02/27/2007 -2015-such-a-long-recession/.

This stimulates the demand for Europe, particularly as the development of the alternative models (China, Russia) is not reassuring, to say the least.

In response to these expectations, Europe will nevertheless have to overcome numerous challenges. To begin with, a general challenge: the global drift toward inequality. Europe will not reassure its citizens by explaining to them that they are better off than people in the United States or Brazil. Inequality is rising in all countries, encouraged by exacerbated fiscal competiveness in favor of the most mobile, with Europe continuing to feed the flames. The risk of cultural isolationism and of scapegoating will only be successfully dealt with if we succeed in offering the working classes and the younger generations a genuine strategy for reducing inequality and investing in the future.

The second challenge is the North-South divide, which has dramatically deepened in the eurozone and is based on contradictory versions of events. In Germany and France, people continue to think that the European Union helped the Greeks, since it loaned them money at a lower rate of interest than the rate they would have had to pay on the financial markets, but higher than the rate the European Union paid to borrow on these same markets. In Greece, the version is quite different: They see it as a large financial profit. The truth is that the purge imposed on the countries in the Europe of the South, with the dramatic secessionist consequences in Catalonia, is the direct outcome of a shortsighted Franco-German self-centered vision.

The third challenge is the East-West divide. In Paris, Berlin, or Brussels, people cannot understand the lack of gratitude on the part of countries which have benefited from huge public transfers. But in Warsaw or Prague, events are inter-

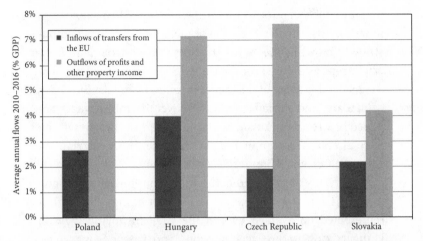

Figure 19. Inflows vs. outflows in Eastern Europe, 2010–2016. Between 2010 and 2016, the annual flow of net transfers from the European Union (difference between total expenditure received and contributions paid to the EU budget) amounted to 2.7% of GDP per year on average in Poland; over the same period, the outflow of profits and other property income (net of the corresponding outflows) amounted to 4.7% of GDP. For Hungary, these same figures were 4% and 7.2%. *Sources:* see piketty.pse.ens.fr/ideology.

preted quite differently. They point out that the rate of return on private investment from the West was high and that the flows of profits paid today to the owners of the firms far exceed the European transfers going in the other direction.

In fact, if we examine the figures, they do have a case. After the collapse of communism, Western investors (especially Germans) have gradually become the owners of a considerable proportion of the capital of Eastern European countries. This amounts to roughly a quarter if we consider the complete stock of fixed capital (including housing), and over half if we restrict ourselves to the ownership of firms (and even more for large firms). Filip Novokmet's research[2] has demonstrated that while inequality has not risen as strongly in Eastern Europe as in Russia or the United States, it is simply because a considerable share of the higher incomes from East European capital are paid abroad (which moreover resembles what happened before communism, with the owners of the capital who were already German or French, or sometimes Austrians or from the Ottoman Empire).

Between 2010 and 2016, the annual outflow of profits and incomes from property (net of the corresponding inflows) thus represented on average 4.7% of the GDP in Poland, 7.2% in Hungary, 7.6% in the Czech Republic, and 4.2% in Slovakia, reducing commensurately the national income of these countries

By comparison, over the same period, the annual net transfers from the European Union (that is, the difference between the totality of expenditure received and the contributions paid to the EU budget) were appreciably lower: 2.7% of the GDP in Poland, 4.0% in Hungary, 1.9% in the Czech Republic, and 2.2% in Slovakia (as a reminder, France, Germany, and the United Kingdom are net contributors to the EU budget of an amount equivalent to 0.3–0.4% of their GDPs).

Of course, one might reasonably argue that Western investment enabled the productivity of the economies concerned to increase and therefore, everyone benefited. But the East European leaders never miss an opportunity to recall that

2. Filip Novokmet, "Between Communism and Capitalism: Essays on the Evolution of Income and Wealth Inequality in Eastern Europe, 1890–2015," PhD thesis, Ecole des Hautes Etudes en Sciences Sociales. Prepared and defended at the Paris School of Economics on December 11, 2017.

investors take advantage of their positions of strength to keep wages low and maintain excessive margins.[3]

In the same way as for Greece, the leading economic powers tend on the contrary to consider inequality as natural. They work on the assumption that the market and "free competition" contribute to a fair distribution of wealth and consider the transfers resulting from this "natural" balance as an act of generosity on the part of the winners in the system. In reality, property relations are always complex, particularly in large-scale political communities like the European Union and cannot be regulated uniquely by the goodwill of the market.

These contradictions can only be resolved by a full-scale intellectual and political "refounding" of the European institutions along with their genuine democratization.[4] Let's hope that the year 2018 will make a contribution.

3. See, for example, this interview with the Czech Prime Minister Andrej Babis, "L'Europe à deux vitesses, ça me fait rigoler," *Le Monde,* December 6, 2017, https://www.lemonde.fr/europe/article/2017/12/06/andrej-babis-l-europe-a-deux-vitesses-ca-me-fait-rigoler_5225468_3214.html.

4. See Thomas Piketty, "Reconstructing Europe after Brexit," *Le Monde,* June 30, 2016, https://www.lemonde.fr/blog/piketty/2016/06/30/reconstructing-europe-after-brexit/.

Parcoursup: Could Do Better

February 13, 2018

A ll societies need a grand narrative to justify their inequalities. In contemporary societies, the focus is on the meritocratic narrative. Modern inequality is just because it is the outcome of a process which is freely chosen in which each individual has the same opportunities. The problem is that there is a yawning gap between official meritocratic declarations and reality.

In the United States, the chances of accessing higher education are almost entirely determined by the income of one's parents; barely 20% for the poorest 10%, and over 90% for the richest 10%.[1] We should moreover make it clear that we are in no way talking about the same quality of higher education in the two cases. Possibly, the situation is not quite as extreme in France. But the truth is that we do not really know, because it is impossible to access the same data.

In this context, the reform of the student university entry admission system with the move from the APB (or *admis-*

---

1. See Raj Chetty, John N. Friedman, Emmanuel Saez, Nicholas Turner, and Danny Yagan, "Mobility Report Cards: The Role of Colleges in Intergenerational Mobility," The Equality of Opportunity Project, 2017.

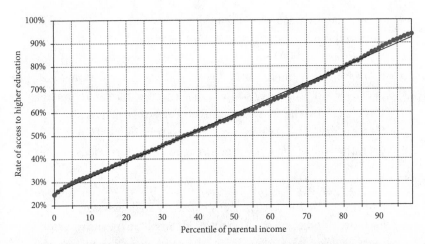

Figure 20. Parental income and access to university, United States, 2014. In 2014, the rate of access to higher education (percentage of individuals aged 19–21 enrolled in a university, college, or any other institution of higher education) was barely 30% among the bottom 10% poorest children in the United States and over 90% among the top 10% richest children. *Sources and series:* see piketty .pse.ens.fr/ideology.

sion post baccalauréat) to the *Parcoursup* platform is potentially very promising.[2] Unfortunately, it is to be feared that all this will only reinforce the inequality and opacity of the system.

It should be said at the outset that taking into account the marks, the tracks, and the student records in the university entrance admission procedure (the main innovation in *Parcoursup*) is not necessarily a bad thing as such. Given that

2. The bill introduced by the government can be found at: http://www .assemblee-nationale.fr/dyn/15/textes/l15b0391_projet-loi.pdf; the version adopted in December 2017 by the National Assembly is available at: http:// www.assemblee-nationale.fr/dyn/15/textes/l15t0061_texte-adopte-provisoire .pdf.

marks have always been taken into consideration for admission to the preparatory classes for the *grandes écoles* (both in the former APB system and in the new *Parcoursup*), which nobody seems to quarrel with, it is not clear why they should not play a role in university admission. True, the marks are not always just, and the marking system needs to be rethought. But they do nevertheless contain some useful information, a priori rather more than the random drawing of lots used to date (hopefully).

To address the obvious risk of a drift toward inequality and the academic hyper-stratification of such a system, however, two conditions must be fulfilled. First, the means invested must enable each student with a baccalaureate degree to have access to quality education. This is all the more urgent as the French system is characterized by a particularly extreme and hypocritical form of dualism: on the one hand, we have selective sectors which are richly endowed (the preparatory classes and the *grandes écoles*), and on the other, we have universities which have been neglected and in which massive investment is required. Unfortunately the government has chosen to prolong the decline in public investment observed since 2008 and to devote all available resources to reducing the taxes of the better off. One should keep in mind that budget per student has fallen by 10% in ten years and the 5 billion euros in tax gifts to the richest would have enabled a 40% increase in the per capita expenditure.[3]

Second, over and above the question of the means, taking marks into account must imperatively be moderated by other criteria; this poses basic questions which to date have not

3. See "Budget 2018: French Youth Sacrificed," October 21, 2017.

been resolved. The law, adopted at its first reading in the National Assembly, stipulates that in each higher-education track (both the universities and in the preparatory classes), there must be a minimal percentage of low-income students. In other words, for the same marks, a state-aided holder of the baccalaureate degree (*élèves boursiers,* i.e., roughly 20% of secondary school students) could be accepted while another whose parental income is slightly higher than threshold level will be refused. The idea is not necessarily bad in itself, though it would undoubtedly have been preferable to limit the threshold effect by using a points system taking into account in a more continuous and gradual fashion the family origin (as is the case in some of the Indian universities).

In any event, the problem is that the way in which this potentially explosive system will be set up in *Parcoursup* remains totally obscure. The law states that the percentage of low-income students per academic track will be fixed "by the academic authorities" (therefore, the rector) by taking into consideration "the relation between the number of state-aided students and the total number of candidates" but also "in conjunction and negotiation with the heads of the establishments concerned," with no further details. It has been announced on countless occasions that the source code of *Parcoursup* will be made available to the public in its entirety (as, moreover, the previous government had announced), but no date has been fixed. Secondary school students have until March 13 to choose their preferred tracks. Will the rules of the game be made public before this date, or afterward? Nobody knows.

The law also stipulates that the "best pupils in each stream in each school will have priority access to all the courses" (in particular the preparatory classes for the *grandes écoles*). But there again, we have no further information: "the percentage

of secondary school students who will have the right to benefit from this priority access will be fixed by decree." In reality,
this is simply a reworking of an article adopted in 2013 which
in practice was applied in a totally opaque and purely symbolic
manner at the very end of the allocation process, in the context of the final chances provided for in the system (therefore
much too late for the secondary pupils concerned to genuinely
benefit from them). Has any consideration been given to revealing the source code intended for the application of this article to secondary school pupils in the *Parcoursup* procedure,
and if so, at what date? It's something of a mystery.

Let's be clear: these are complex questions which no
country has resolved in a totally satisfactory manner. But once
the government states a policy of transparency, it cannot afford to maintain such an opaque process, all this plus inequality and austerity for the less well off.

Toward a Union in the Union

March 13, 2018

After the Italian elections and Trump's commercial antics, one might well feel depressed and be tempted to use Europe to play the same silly game of introverted assertion of identity—strengthening immigration laws and ramping up protectionist measures. In so doing, we would be forgetting two key points.

One: contrary to what we sometimes hear, the rise of European populism is not explained by any flood of immigrants. The truth is that the number of migrants entering the European Union was much higher before the financial crisis (1.2 million per year between 2000 and 2008). The numbers then collapsed (500,000 per year between 2008 and 2016), whereas the geopolitical situation would have demanded greater openness.[1] If we had not made serious mistakes in managing the economy, provoking a further recession in 2011–2013, and an explosion of unemployment in Southern Europe, then Europe could have been—and still could be—more open, and we could

---

1. See Thomas Piketty, "On the Migratory Situation in Europe," *Le Monde,* May 22, 2016, https://www.lemonde.fr/blog/piketty/2016/05/22/on -the-migratory-situation-in-europe/.

have avoided the abandoning of our responsibilities and relying on the camps in Turkey to manage the refugee crisis. Those
responsible for the rise in populism are those who implement
these ill-timed austerity policies and not the migrants and the
people who support them.

Two: the American trade sanctions, stupid as they are,
are merely symbolic gestures enabling Trump to differentiate
himself from the Democrats and to surf the nationalist wave
at little cost. At the core of Trump's program are the hundreds
of billions of dollars spent on the tax reform adopted in December, and which aim to considerably reduce the taxation on
company profits and the income and wealth of the richest taxpayers. The threat to the world today is not a trade war but a
social war, conducted by means of aggressive policies of fiscal
dumping that benefit the wealthiest and the most mobile. This
nurtures the sense of abandonment felt by the working classes
and leads to the impoverishment of the public sector: Public
capital is becoming negative in all the rich countries, which
means that the holders of private assets not only own all the
public assets (schools, hospitals, etc.) through their holdings
in financial assets, but they also have drawing rights on future
tax revenues.

A good example of this type of transfer is demonstrated
by recent events in France. The government began by giving
the wealthiest a fiscal bonus worth 6 billion euros per year, and
then offered to sell them *Aéroports de Paris* for 8 billion euros.
It would have been simpler just to transfer the property free
of charge.

This development in inequality is far from new; it began with the policies of liberalization in finance and trade
introduced as from the 1980s with no coordinated implementation of new instruments of regulation and taxation.
On paper, the solution is simple: The current path of global-

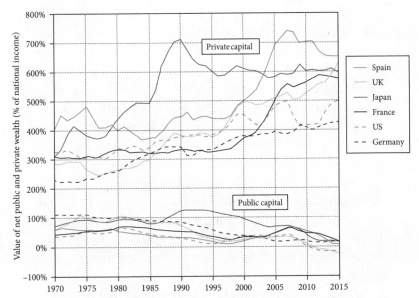

Figure 21. The rise of private capital and the fall of public capital in rich countries, 1970–2016. In 2015, the value of net public wealth (or public capital) in the United States was negative (–17% of net national income), while the value of net private wealth (or private capital) was 500% of national income. In 1970, net public wealth amounted to 36% of national income, while the figure was 326% for net private wealth. Net private wealth is equal to new private assets minus net private debt. Net public wealth is equal to public assets minus public debt. *Source:* WID.world (2017).

ization has to be changed by stipulating that all international treaties should contain, and be conditional on, binding rules for the promotion of equitable and sustainable development (minimal rates of taxation, limits on carbon emission, etc.). This raises no technical problem; the only difficulty is that each individual country felt too small to denounce the treaties in force on its own.

Confronted with this global challenge, Europe has a special responsibility: it has been constructed as a free trade area with no fiscal rules in common, and it has made an appreciable contribution in the race to the lowering of corporate taxation (which the United States is simply following today). Everything flows from the European requirement of unanimity rule in the area of taxation, which nothing seems to be able to shake.

The only solution is that France, Germany, Italy, and Spain (which together represent more than 75% of the population and the GDP of the eurozone) finally set up a strengthened political and fiscal union within the European Union, open of course to all the members, but one which nobody can block. The problem with Macron's proposals is that they are vague: There is talk of the eurozone budget, without any mention of the composition either of the parliament responsible for voting this budget, or of the taxes capable of funding it.

Along with Stéphanie Hennette, Guillaume Sacriste, and Antoine Vauchez, we have suggested the creation of a new European Assembly by the countries who wish to join, based on elected members of national parliaments, in proportion to their respective population and groups.[2] This European Assembly would be responsible for adopting a budget for investment in the future (training and research, renewable energy), sustained by a common corporate tax (to which could be added a common tax on the highest incomes and fortunes).

The proposal is not perfect but does have the virtue of existing. By choosing to rely on national parliaments, we recognize the fact that the French National Assembly and the German Bundestag are not ready to surrender their fiscal

2. See "What Would a Democratic Eurozone Assembly Look Like?" March 22, 2017.

power. Above all, we de facto transform national parliamentary elections into European elections. National elected members will have to state what they intend to do in the European Assembly and will no longer be able to complain about Europe and shift problems onto Brussels.

In order to reassure German opinion, we could add a clause guaranteeing that each country would benefit from expenditure equivalent to its contribution in tax. The aim is not to organize transfers between countries but to build a social and democratic public body which will enable the regulation of globalization.

Let's put everything on the table and advance! Our collective incapacity to discuss the Europe which we would like could mean that the populists and Trump supporters of all kinds win their biggest victory.

Capital in Russia
April 10, 2018

Next month Karl Marx will be 200 years old. What would he have thought of the sad state Russia is in today? This is a country which never ceased claiming to be "Marxist Leninist" throughout the Soviet period. Doubtless he would have denied any responsibility for a regime which appeared long after his death. Marx grew up in a world of censitory oppression and private property sacralization, where even the owners of slaves could be handsomely compensated if their property was violated (for "liberals" like de Tocqueville, this was a matter of course). It would have been difficult for him to anticipate the success of social democracy and the welfare state in the twentieth century. Marx was thirty years old at the time of the 1848 revolutions, and he died in 1883, the year of Keynes' birth. Both were acute commentators on their times; we were doubtless wrong to take them for consummate theoreticians of the future.

The fact remains that when the Bolsheviks took power in 1917, their action plans were far from being as "scientific" as they claimed. Private property was to be abolished, that was agreed. But how would the relations of production be organized, and who would be the new masters? What would be the mechanisms for decision-making and distribution of

wealth in the huge state planning apparatus? For lack of a solution, resort was made to the hyper-personalization of power
and for lack of results, scapegoats were quickly found and imprisoned, with purges being the order of the day. When Stalin
died, 4% of the Soviet population was in prison, more than half
for "theft of socialist property" and other petty crimes that
helped to improve one's lot. This is the "society of thieves" described by Juliette Cadiot, and it signals the dramatic failure
of a regime that wished to emancipate. To exceed this level of
incarceration, we have to take the situation of Black American
men today (5% of Black adult men are in prison).

Soviet investments in infrastructure, education, and
health do indeed enable a certain amount of catching up; per
capita national income stagnated before the Revolution at
about 30–40% of the level in Western Europe; it rose to over
60% in the 1950s. But the lag increased in the 1960s–1970s, life
expectancy even began to fall (a unique phenomenon in time
of peace), and the regime was on the brink of implosion. The
dismantling of the USSR and its productive apparatus led to a
fall in its citizens' standard of living in 1992–1995. Income per
capita rose as from 2000, and in 2018 stands at approximately
70% of the West European level in terms of purchasing power
parity (but is twice as low if one uses the prevailing rate of exchange, given the weakness of the rouble). Unfortunately, inequalities have risen much more rapidly than the official
statistics claim, as is demonstrated in a recent study carried out
with Filip Novokmet and Gabriel Zucman.[1]

1. See Filip Novokmet, Thomas Piketty, and Gabriel Zucman, "From
Soviets to Oligarchs: Inequality and Property in Russia, 1905–2016," National Bureau of Economic Research, August 2017, Working Paper 23712,
https://www.nber.org/papers/w23712.

More generally, the Soviet disaster led to the abandonment of any ambition of redistribution. Since 2001, income tax
is 13%, whether your income is 1,000 roubles or 100 billion roubles. Even Reagan and Trump have not gone as far in the destruction of progressive taxation. There is no tax on inheritance
in Russia, nor in the People's Republic of China. If you want
to pass on your fortune in peace in Asia, it is better to die in
the ex-communist countries and definitely not in the capitalist countries, such as Taiwan, South Korea, or Japan, where the
tax rate on inheritance on the largest estates has just risen from
50% to 55%.

But while China has succeeded in conserving a degree of
control on capital outflows and private accumulation, the characteristic of Putin's Russia is an unbounded drift into kleptocracy. Between 1993 and 2018, Russia had massive trade
surpluses: approximately 10% of GDP per year on average for
twenty-five years, or a total in the range of 250% of GDP (two
and a half years of national production). In principle that
should have enabled the accumulation of the equivalent in financial reserves. This is almost the size of the sovereign public fund accumulated by Norway under the watchful gaze of
the voters. The official Russian reserves are ten times lower—
barely 25% of GDP.

Where has the money gone? According to our estimates,
the offshore assets alone held by wealthy Russians exceed one
year of GDP, or the equivalent of the entirety of the official financial assets held by Russian households. In other words,
the natural wealth of the country (which, let it be said in passing, would have done better to remain in the ground to limit
global warming) has been massively exported abroad to sus-
tain opaque structures enabling a minority to hold huge Russian and international financial assets. These rich Russians live
between London, Monaco, and Moscow: some have never left

Russia and control their country via offshore entities. Numerous intermediaries and Western firms have also recouped large crumbs on the way and continue to do so today in sport and the media (sometimes this is referred to as "philanthropy"). The extent of the misappropriation of funds has no equal in history.

Rather than apply commercial sanctions, Europe would do better to finally go for these assets and to address Russian public opinion. Today postcommunism has become the worst ally of hypercapitalism: Marx would have appreciated the irony, but this is not a reason for putting up with it.

May 1968 and Inequality

May 8, 2018

S hould we burn May '68? Critics claim that the spirit of May '68 has contributed to the rise of individualism, even to ultra-liberalism. In truth, these assertions do not stand up to close scrutiny. On the contrary, the May '68 Movement was the start of a historical period of considerable reduction in social inequalities in France which ran out of steam later for quite different reasons.

Let's go back for a moment. In France the years 1945–1967 are marked by high rates of growth but also by a movement of reconstitution of inequalities, with, at one and the same time, a steep rise in the share of profits in national income and the reconstitution of highly ranked salary scales. The share of the 10% highest incomes, which was barely 31% of total income in 1945, gradually rose to 38% in 1967. The whole country was focused on reconstruction, and the reduction of inequalities was not a priority, particularly as everyone was well aware that they had been considerably reduced after the war (destruction, inflation) and the political upheavals of the Liberation (Social Security, nationalizations, and tighter pay structures).

In this new context, the salaries of executives and engineers rose structurally faster than the low- and medium-range salaries in the 1950s–1960s and at first, nobody seemed to be worried. A minimum wage had been created in 1950, but it was almost never revised thereafter, with the result that there was a wide gap in comparison with the evolution of the average wage. Society had never been so patriarchal; in the 1980s, 80% of the total payroll was paid to men. Women were entrusted with numerous tasks (in particular, childcare and the provision of tender loving care in the industrial era), but the control of the wallet was clearly not in their domain. Society was also massively geared toward production; the 40-hour week, promised in 1936, still did not apply, because the trade unions had accepted working a maximum number of hours overtime to accelerate the country's economic recovery.

The break came in 1968. As a way out of the crisis, General de Gaulle's government signed the Grenelle Agreements which included, in particular, a rise of 20% in the minimum wage. The minimum wage was officially indexed on average wage gains in 1970, and most importantly, all successive governments from 1968 to 1983 felt obliged to grant very high "special hikes" almost every year in a social and political climate that was far from stable. The result was that the purchasing power of the minimum wage rose in all by over 130% between 1968 and 1983, whereas at the same time, the average salary only rose by about 50%, whence a very strong compression of pay inequalities. The break with the previous period was clean and wide-ranging; the purchasing power of the minimum wage had risen by barely 25% between 1950 and 1968, whereas the average salary had more than doubled. Driven by the strong rise in low salaries, throughout the years 1968–1983, the total payroll rose significantly faster than did production; as a result there was a considerable fall in the share of capital in the national income. All this took place at the same time as a reduction in the number of hours worked and an increase in paid holidays.

The movement reversed again in 1982–1983. The new socialist government, originating in the May 1981 elections, would doubtless have liked to continue in this direction indefinitely. Unfortunately for them, social movements had already imposed the major catch-up of low wages on right-wing governments, thus beating electoral democracy to the post. To prolong the movement of reduction in inequalities, it would have been necessary to invent other tools: real powers for employees in firms, wide-ranging investment and equality in education, the implementation of a universal system of health insurance and retirement, the development of a social and fiscal Europe. Instead, the government used Europe as a scapegoat when it resorted to austerity in 1983, although Europe was in no way responsible for blocking wage rises: the minimum wage cannot go on rising three times faster than production forever, whether the economy is open or closed.

Worse still: as from 1988, French governments have contributed considerably to the movement at the European level of fiscal dumping of corporate tax then, with the Maastricht Treaty in 1992, to setting up a fully fledged monetary and commercial union with no joint budget or tax system and no political governance. A currency without a state, democracy, or sovereignty: a model whose fragility we witnessed after the crisis in 2008 and which contributed to the 10-year recession from which we are only just emerging.

Today throughout Europe, social democracy is in crisis. This is primarily the consequence of an incomplete internationalism. During the twentieth century and particularly from the 1950s to the 1980s, the implementation of a new capital-labor compromise was re-thought and implemented within the nation-states. This was an undeniable success, but at the same time this process involved considerable weaknesses, because national policies were caught in the increasing competition between countries. The answer is not to turn our backs on the spirit of May 1968 and social movements. On the contrary, we must turn to them to develop a new internationalist program to reduce inequalities.[1]

1. For more information, see Thomas Piketty, *Top Incomes in France in the Twentieth Century: Inequality and Redistribution* (Cambridge, MA: Harvard University Press, 2018).

The Transferunion Fantasy

June 12, 2018

While the political crisis deepens in Italy and in Spain, France and Germany are still demonstrably incapable of formulating precise and ambitious proposals for reforming Europe. All that is required, however, is for these four countries, who alone account for three quarters of the GDP and the population of the eurozone, to agree on a common approach, and the way to reform would be open. How can we explain such extraordinary inertia, and why is it so serious?

In France, there is a tendency to lay the blame on other people. The official view is that our young and dynamic president has made innovative proposals for the reform of the eurozone, its budget, and its Parliament. But the unfortunate thing is that our neighbors are incapable of taking these into account and responding with the same Gallic audacity!

The problem with this superficial theory is that these notorious French proposals are quite simply nonexistent. Nobody is capable of writing three simple sentences explaining which common taxes will fund this budget, who will be the members of the Eurozone Assembly who will exercise this new fiscal sovereignty, etc. If you want to make sure, just ask your favorite pro-Macron friend, or, if you do not have any—nobody is perfect—write to your favorite newspapers!

It is almost as if the revolutionaries in 1789, instead of setting up a National Assembly enabling all privileges to be abolished immediately and a new fiscal system to be set up, had only announced that it would be a good idea to pause to reflect on the setting up of a commission to consider a long-term plan to save the ancien régime. It is the difference between doing something and empty rhetoric.

The truth is that the French proposals are so vague that they are open to almost any interpretation. This is precisely the problem: all the nationalist and anti-European discourses can easily oppose them by putting what they want in it. Today, it is easy to criticize the reluctance of Angela Merkel, and the fact is that her reply to the "French proposals" is more than hesitant. The latest version is that she would apparently agree to an investment budget for the eurozone on condition, however, that it be ridiculously small (less than 1% of the GDP of the zone).

Obviously, in all this there is no mention of the common taxation system capable of financing it (so much so that there is a strong risk of finding ourselves recycling investments which have already been made or announced, with considerable "creative accounting," as with the Juncker plan).

And of course, there is no mention of the all-important democratization of the eurozone. The single proposal made by Merkel is to rename the European Stability Mechanism which would become the "European Monetary Fund"; this expresses fairly clearly the hyper-conservative vision. It is a question of applying the IMF model to the government of Europe, in other words, government behind closed doors, piloted by the ministers of finance and the technostructure.

This is the antithesis of the public, democratic, parliamentary, and contradictory discussion which should always have the last word. It is extremely sad to see that Merkel and Germany have ended up here, thirty years after the end of communism and the certainties of its bureaucratic closed-door procedures.

But it is too easy to criticize Merkel's reluctance. It is time that the French media understand that she is only responding to Macron's timidity. The fact is they share the same conservatism. Ultimately, these two leaders do not wish to make any fundamental changes in present-day Europe, because they suffer from the same form of blindness. Both consider that their two countries are doing quite well, and they are in no way responsible for the ups and downs of Southern Europe.

By so doing, they run the risk of undermining the whole endeavor. After having humiliated Greece in 2015, whose "extreme left" government was perhaps not perfect, but did at least have the virtue of promoting values of solidarity with the poorest and the migrants, France and Germany now find themselves in 2018 with the extreme right in power in Italy. The only thing that holds this government together is hostility to, and active pursuit of, foreigners, all of which has been enabled by the effect of European rulings.

The difficulty now is: How to get out of this impasse? The dilemma is that a fair number of the German and North European leaders have for years explained to their voters that all the problems in Europe were caused by the lazy people in the South. These populations were said to be jealous of their money, and all that was required was to get them to start working and exporting like the Germans or the Dutch, and all would be well.

From the economic point of view, these speeches are as ridiculous as those made by the *Front National* in France or the League in Italy (since no country in the world could ever absorb a German trade surplus generalized at the level of the eurozone). The fact remains that this fear of the transfer union—(or as the Germans say, "Transferunion")—prevents any debate.

To overcome this problem, one would probably need to guarantee that the future budget of the eurozone, funded by a common corporate income tax on the profits of companies and on the highest incomes and property holders, voted by a genuinely democratic assembly, should benefit each country in proportion to its fiscal contribution (with net transfers limited to 0.1% or 0.5% of GDP).

This intrinsically national vision of solidarity is not satisfactory, but ultimately, this is not the most important aspect: The aim is primarily to enable a European public power to tax the most powerful economic actors at least as much as the poorest, in order to invest in the future and to reduce inequality within each country. Let's discuss Europe at last and forge ahead!

Europe, Migrants, and Trade

July 10, 2018

While European leaders are preparing to tighten the conditions of entry into the European Union, it is worth trying to get a clearer picture of the current patterns of migration and more broadly of Europe's positioning in the globalization process.

The data available are incomplete but are sufficient to establish the main orders of magnitude. The most comprehensive data are those gathered by the United Nations Population Division on the basis of demographic statistics provided by each country and a patient labor of homogenization. They serve to indicate the trend of the migratory flows entering and leaving the different countries of the world; they also include the sensitive issue of the World Population Prospects established for the decades to come.[1] If we consider the most recent data available, two observations clearly stand out.

---

1. World Population Prospects 2019, United Nations Department of Economic and Social Affairs Population Dynamics, https://population.un .org/wpp/.

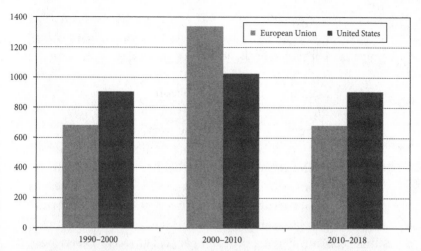

Figure 22. Average migration flow entering the European Union and United States (net of outflows, in thousands of individuals per year). The migration flow entering the European Union (net of outflows) was close to 1.4 million individuals per year between 2000 and 2010, and about 0.7 million between 2010 and 2018. *Source:* United Nations, World Population Prospects 2018.

The first observation is that the migratory flows entering the rich countries (net of outflows) have fallen since 2010. From 1990 to 1995 they stood at approximately 2 million persons per year, from 1995 to 2000 at 2.5 million, and subsequently from 2000 to 2010 exceeded 3 million; the numbers then fell to around 2 million persons per year between 2010 and 2018, the level at which the United Nations bases its forecasts for the years to come. The population of the rich countries is roughly 1 billion persons (500 million in the European Union, 350 million in the United States and Canada, and 150 million in Japan/ Oceania). This means that the migratory flow was below 0.2% per year in the 1990s, before rising to almost 0.2% per year since 2010. These flows may seem minuscule and, in a way, they are: The globalization of the years 1990–2018 is primarily financial and commercial and has never reached the levels of migration observed in the 1870–1914 period.

The difference however is that the new migratory flows lead to greater multicultural exchanges involving people of different cultural origins (whereas in the past, the migratory flows were primarily internal to the North Atlantic) and that these migratory flows take place in a context of demographic stagnation: The annual number of births is now less than 1% of the population in a number of rich countries. This means that an annual contribution of 0.2 or 0.3% leads in the long run to an appreciable change in the composition of the population. This is obviously not a problem per se, but recent experience demonstrates that this may unfortunately generate successful bids for the political exploitation of issues of identity, particularly if adequate policies have not been set up to promote the creation of jobs, housing, and the requisite infrastructure.

The second striking observation which emerges from the United Nations' data is that the fall in the migratory flows is mainly due to the situation in Europe. The number of migrants entering the European Union (net of outflows) has been halved, falling from almost 1.4 million persons per year between 2000 and 2010 to less than 0.7 million per year between 2010 and 2018, despite the influx of refugees and the peak in 2015. In the United States, where the recovery from the recession in 2008 was easier than in Europe, the flow remained stable (1 million per year between 2000 and 2010, and 0.9 million between 2010 and 2018).

There is a third observation that is worth bearing in mind alongside the first two. According to the most recent ECB (European Central Bank) data, the trade surplus of the eurozone stood at 530 billion euros in 2017, or almost 5% of the GDP of the eurozone (11,200 billion euros), and the trend is the same in 2018.[2] In other words, each time the countries in the euro-zone produce 100 units of goods and services, they only consume and invest 95 units in their own country. The gap may seem narrow, but repeated year after year, it is in reality considerable. Never in economic history, or at least never since the existence of trade statistics (that is, since the beginning of the nineteenth century), have we found evidence of such a huge trade surplus for an economy of this size.

Some oil-producing countries have sometimes had surpluses greater than 5% or 10% of their GNPs, but these are much smaller economies relative to the world economy and are often countries with very small populations (with the result that the happy owners of these resources do not really know what to do with them, apart from accumulating them abroad). This highly abnormal situation, or in any case totally unprecedented, is driven to a large extent by Germany, but Germany is not alone: Italy for example has had a trade surplus in excess of 3% of its GNP since 2015.

For those advocates of the market as being all-knowing and ever efficient, this situation is the rational consequence of aging; European countries anticipate the future scarcity of labor and production to come—possibly even their total disappearance—and are simply saving for their old age. The truth is that we must above all see there the consequences of exacerbated competition with no political guidance and excessive wage stagnation which has led to compressing growth and boosting trade surpluses.

We should also bear in mind that at the moment, the eurozone has a primary budgetary surplus. Taxpayers pay more

2. See European Central Bank, *Economic Bulletin,* no. 4, 2018, Table 3.1, p. S8, https://www.ecb.europa.eu/pub/pdf/ecbu/eb201804.en.pdf.

in taxes than they receive in expenditure, with a gap greater than 1% of GNP. Just as Trump's budgetary deficits only make the American trade deficit worse, the European budgetary surpluses exacerbate our trading surplus.

If there does come a time when Europe wishes to revive the policies for integration, it will have to begin by learning how to invest and how to consume once again.

Social-Nativism:
The Italian Nightmare
September 11, 2018

Since spring 2018, Italy has been governed by a strange social-nativist coalition of the Five Star Movement (M5S) and the Lega (the former Northern League). The Five Star Movement (M5S) is an antisystem and anti-establishment party, which is unclassifiable in the usual left-right typologies, but one of its leitmotifs is a guaranteed basic income. The Lega is a regionalist and anti-tax movement, now converted into a nationalist party specializing in hunting foreigners. It would be an error to attribute this astonishing partnership to an Italian taste for exoticism. In reality, all the European governments have a share in the responsibility for the emergence of this type of coalition, as desperate as it is incoherent. If we are not careful, the Italian social-nativist nightmare could rapidly be of concern to us, to begin with because of its European consequences and subsequently because there is a risk that similar coalitions could one day become widespread in other countries, including in France.

To recap: the Five Star Movement obtains its highest scores in the working-class categories in the south of Italy and from the disappointed in all the parties, attracted by the

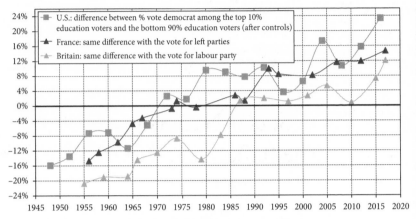

Figure 23. Electoral left in Europe and the United States, 1945–
2020: from the workers' party to the party of the highly educated.
Author's computations using French, U.S., and British post-electoral
surveys. In the 1950–1970 period, the vote for the Democrats in the
United States, left-wing parties (socialists-communists-radicals-
greens) in France, and the Labour Party in Britain was associated
with voters with the lowest education; in the 1990–2010 period, it
became associated with the voters with the highest education.
Sources and series: see piketty.pse.ens.fr/ideology.

promises of new social policies and the development of the
backward regions. The Lega attracts the anti-immigrant vote,
particularly in the north, where the party has also retained a
base of anti-tax independents and managers.

At one point, the Five Star Movement did consider a coalition with the (Italian) Democratic Party, including the former left-wing parties and now located somewhere between the
center-left and the center-right, nobody knows exactly where),
but the Democratic Party finally refused, preferring to count
on the failure of the populists.

The Five Star Movement and the Lega then agreed on a program based on the implementation of a guaranteed basic income, advocated by the Five Star Movement (which could be comparable to the French-style basic income scheme, *revenu de solidarité active*), and the "flat tax" defended by the Lega. This is a tax levied at the same rate on all incomes, which implies the total dismantling of the progressive tax system (with the highest rates on the biggest incomes) and a huge loss of fiscal revenue. The Five Star Movement—Lega alliance is also, and primarily, based on a violent anti-refugee policy typified by the Minister for Home Affairs, Salvini, the leader of the Lega, who spent his summer preventing rescue ships from landing, thus disregarding the rules, but which enabled his scores to soar in the opinion polls. Both parties have also come to an agreement on a number of unexpected issues; for example, they oppose vaccinations, which are associated with elitist know-alls and profit-seeking pharmaceutical laboratories.

How can an ideological cocktail of this sort survive? In the French context, we can see all the elements which would separate Melenchon's *La France insoumise* ("France Unbowed") party from an alliance of this sort: central to their values are solidarity with the migrants and the defense of progressive taxation (even if Melenchon's recent Poujadist remarks about the "torments" of deduction of tax at source are a cause for alarm). The fact that the Five Star Movement agreed to the "flat tax" speaks volumes about the lack of backbone in their program, the debilitating effects of the gradual decomposition of Italian politics (ongoing since 1992 and the collapse of the post–World War II political parties), and also on the damage resulting from decades of anti-tax rhetoric and fiscal dumping (since the wealthiest elude taxation and nobody seems to do anything about it, then why not publicly lower taxation for everyone?).

But if the cocktail works, it is primarily because the Italian leaders excel in criticizing the selfishness of the French government, which preaches about the refugees but closes its own ports and borders, and, more generally the hypocrisy of Europe, which imposes rigid budgetary rules on Italy, preventing the country from investing and from recovering from the crisis in 2008 and the ensuing purge. The main thing learned from the Orbán-Salvini meeting was the display of anti-migrant solidarity: "We have proved that immigration can be stopped on land which proves that it can be stopped at sea" declared Orbán. We should also bear in mind Salvini's words: "Today we are setting out on a path which we shall tread together and which will be followed by many other steps in the next few months to bring to the fore the right to employment, health and security. We will ensure everything which the European establishment has refused us."

What makes Salvini so dangerous is precisely his capacity to link nativist discourse with the social, and migratory discourse with the debt. This is all rolled into the accusation of the establishment as being hypocritical everywhere. Since the ECB printed billions to save the banks, why could it not help Italy by postponing the debt to more favorable times? This commonsense discourse will appeal until Europe replaces it with something better. In Poland and in Hungary, the far-from-liberal governments have also had an eye to public opinion by financing social welfare measures, family allowances, and retirement benefits which the pro-European governments refused.

We can of course consider that Italian public opinion will always be opposed to the final clash and the return of the lira and inflation. One might also consider that it is time for Europe to demonstrate to the working classes that it is best suited to defend them by finally implementing a policy to re-launch the economy and for a just form of taxation. As long as the centrists on all sides practice a similar form of antisocial liberalism, social-nativism will have a promising future.

Brazil: The First Republic under Threat

October 16, 2018

I n the United States, it was not until the mid-1960s that the former slaves finally obtained the right to sit in the same buses as whites, to go to the same schools, and at the same time, gained the right to vote. In Brazil, the right to vote for the poor dates from the 1988 constitution, just a few years before the first multiracial elections in South Africa in 1994.

The comparison may shock: The population in Brazil is much more mixed than in the other two countries. In 2010, in the last census, 48% of the population declared themselves to be "white," 43% "mixed," 8% "Black," and 1% "Asian" or "natives." In reality, more than 90% of Brazilians are of mixed origin. The fact remains that social and racial divisions are closely linked. While Brazil is not a country devoid of racism, it is sometimes described as the country of "cordial racism." This is also a country where democracy is recent and fragile and at the moment is faced with a very serious crisis.

Brazil abolished slavery in 1888, at a time when the slaves still represented 30% of the population in some provinces, particularly in the sugar-growing regions in the northeast. Apart from the extreme case of slavery, this is a country where labor relations have long been extremely difficult, in particular between the landowners and agricultural laborers or landless peasants. On the political level, the 1891 constitution was careful to specify that nonliterate people would not have the right to vote, a rule that was also incorporated into the constitutions of 1934 and 1946. This permitted the exclusion of 70% of the adult population from participation in the electoral process in 1890, and still over 50% in 1950 and 20% in 1980. In practice, these were not only former slaves but more generally the poor, who were thus excluded from the political scene for a century. In comparison, India had no hesitation in implementing genuine universal suffrage beginning in 1947, despite the huge social and status divisions inherited from the past and the immense poverty of the country.

In Brazil, despite the political exclusion of the illiterate, no proactive education policy was implemented. The reason inequality has remained so widespread in the country is primarily because the property-owning classes have never really attempted to reverse the heavy historical legacy. The quality of the public services and schools open to the majority has long remained extremely inadequate and is still insufficient today.

It was not until the end of the military dictatorship (1964–1985) and the 1988 constitution that voting rights were extended to all, with no educational stipulations. The first universal suffrage presidential election took place in 1989 and Lula, a former lathe operator, reached the second round and obtained 47% of the votes. His electoral success in 2002 with 61% of the votes in the second ballot, then his reelection in 2006 with the same score—the candidate who had been ridiculed because of his lack of education and who was said not to be capable of representing the country abroad appropriately—

marked the symbolic entry of Brazil into the era of universal suffrage. On the contrary, the election of Bolsonaro would signify a terrible regression and would go beyond the normal changeover following the new victories obtained by the Workers' Party (PT) and Dilma Roussef (56% in 2010, 52% in 2014) with an electorate increasingly divided socially, racially, and geographically.[1]

The representative from Rio is a militarist, a macho, and homophobic; he is also antisocial and anti-poor, as witnessed by his ultraliberal economic program. He also rides the wave of nostalgia for the reign of the white man, in a country where the "whites" have now ceased to be the majority (they still accounted for 54% in the 2000 census). Given the questionable circumstances of the deposition of Roussef in 2016 and the obstruction of Lula in 2018, this election runs the risk of leaving dreadful traces.

When in power, the PT put in a credible performance. Thanks to the rise in minimum wage and the new system of family allowances (Bolsa Familia), economic growth was accompanied by an unexpected fall in poverty. The PT also set up schemes for preferential access to the universities for the working classes and the Black and mixed populations. But for lack of reform in the electoral system, the PT never succeeded in attacking the structural fiscal backwardness of the country (indirect taxes rise to 30% on electricity bills, whereas top inherited wealth is taxed at 4%). The result is that the reduction

1. See the research on the evolution of electoral cleavages in Brazil by Amory Gethin, "Cleavage Structures and Distributive Politics: Party Competition, Voter Alignment and Economic Inequality in Comparative Perspective," Paris School of Economics, Master Analysis and Policy in Economics, June 2018, http://piketty.pse.ens.fr/files/Gethin2018.pdf.

in inequality has been made at the expense of the middle classes and not the richest categories.[2]

When the progressive forces have succeeded in reducing inequalities in the twentieth century, it is because they fought for an ambitious, egalitarian agenda based on political reforms while at the same time implementing fiscal and social reforms. In the United States, the 1913 constitution had to be amended to create a federal income and inheritance tax, which became the most progressive of its kind in history and enabled the financing of the New Deal. In the United Kingdom, the veto of the House of Lords had to be ended, and in France that of the Senate, failing which the social reforms in 1945 would never have seen the light of day. Today, the progressive forces refuse any sort of ambitious discussion on the democratization of American, European, or Brazilian institutions. However, it is not by leaving the monopoly of breaking with the past to the nativists or the reactionaries that equality and democracy will be saved.

2. See this research on the evolution of inequities in Brazil by Marc Morgan, "Falling Inequality beneath Extreme and Persistent Concentration: New Evidence for Brazil Combining National Accounts, Surveys and Fiscal Data, 2001–2015," WID.world, Working Paper Series no. 2017/12.

Le Monde and the Billionaires
November 13, 2018

So, the share ownership of the newspaper *Le Monde* is going to change. A French investment banker is going to sell his shares to a Czech billionaire, who himself made a fortune in coal mining and frequently used tax havens. Should we acquiesce in this situation or is it not time to consider the legal and fiscal regime which would enable us to reshape the model of the media?

Let us be very clear: We in no way wish to question the journalists or the management of the press. They campaign with courage and integrity to obtain from their shareholders all possible guarantees of independence both at *Le Monde* and in the other daily papers. The fact remains that one cannot avoid thinking about the laws which would have to be changed to avoid this type of situation.

It should be specified that in France, as elsewhere, there are rules governing the concentration of ownership of the media. But apart from the fact that they are insufficient and seldom applied, and that they have not been updated and adapted for the digital age, these laws have never sought to redefine the legal form of the media. We still believe that a joint stock company constitutes the normal way for the media to be organized with, as a basis, the principle of "one euro, one vote": The investor who brings a billion euros will always have a billion more votes than those who provide one euro.

However, there are many sectors of activity which are organized in a quite different fashion. Think, for example, of education, culture, and health, which together, employ incomparably more workers than the media or the car industry. In these sectors, when they take the form of private establishments, the actors usually resort to associations or foundations, as do many major U.S. and international universities. The laws applicable usually forbid the use of joint stock companies to create primary or secondary schools, and when they do authorize them, for universities, the few experiments which have been made have led to such disasters (as, for example, Trump University) that they have not been followed.

Let's take, for example, Harvard University. Its endowment of $37 billion was accumulated thanks to the gifts of former students and billionaires, and above all, thanks to the financial yields obtained on past gifts; in addition numerous research programs are financed from public funds, and in reality the university itself could not actually exist without the public infrastructures and schools. When a generous donor gives money to Harvard, he does accede to some advantages, like in some cases being appointed to the board of directors, and sometimes even obtaining the admission of one of his children whose grades are insufficient. These advantages would actually deserve to be more strictly limited. It would be normal for public authorities to play a much bigger role in the admission procedures as in the governance of these universities, which was the case moreover in the past, and will perhaps be the case again in the future: It all depends on the lawmakers. The fact remains that this generous donor is in a more precarious situation than a shareholder: There is no guarantee that the board of directors will renew him indefinitely, and above all, he can in no way threaten to pull out and withdraw his donation. His gift has been definitively incorporated into the endowment of the university; however, this has not prevented him from giving it.

On the contrary, our generous donors-shareholders in the media can at any time threaten to pull out of the business and to resell their shares, as is the case today with *Le Monde,* and this is where it hurts. As regards the media, given the need for permanent renewal of the structures, the correct solution would doubtless be an intermediary form between the foundation and the corporation or joint stock company. For example, with nonprofit media organizations (NMO), which were suggested by Julia Cage,[1] the contributions of journalists, readers, and donors would be treated differentially according to size. Below a specified threshold they would be associated with high voting rights and could possibly be refunded (without profit). Beyond this threshold, the contributions would be treated as permanent gifts (nonrefundable, as at Harvard), and lead to capped voting rights (which is more favorable than Harvard). For example, one could imagine that only a third of the contributions above 10% of the capital give voting rights, and that the votes of smaller contributions would be revised upward accordingly. If the billionaires pouring into the media at the moment are as disinterested as they say, then sharing power with journalists, readers, and donors who are not as rich as they are should not be a problem.

What is preventing the present majority from adopting a reform of this sort? Perhaps the fear of displeasing the billionaires, and further still, the need to provide the requisite fi-

---

1. Julia Cage, *Saving the Media: Capitalism, Crowdfunding, and Democracy* (Cambridge, MA: Harvard University Press, 2016).

nancial means. For, as soon as it is a question of nonrefundable gifts, it would be logical to extend to the media the tax reductions applicable to gifts in the educational or medical sector, which has always been refused. However, it would be money well invested, and it could easily be obtained by restoring the wealth tax on financial assets. Until the government shows some contrition for this original sin, it will have considerable difficulty convincing the country that it is concerned about fiscal justice and combating populism.

To Love Europe Is to Change It, 2018–2020

Manifesto for the
Democratization of Europe
December 10, 2018

Threquired T

he Manifesto reproduced below has been open to signature by over 120 intellectuals, legal scholars, historians, economists, and politicians from all over Europe.[1]

We, European citizens, from different backgrounds and countries, are today launching this appeal for the in-depth transformation of the European institutions and policies. This Manifesto contains concrete proposals, in particular a project for a Democratization Treaty and a Budget Project which can be adopted and applied as it stands by the countries who so wish, with no single country being able to block those who want to advance. It can be signed online by all European citizens who identify with it. It can be amended and improved by any political movement.

Following Brexit and the election of anti-European governments at the head of several member countries, it is no

---

1. Manifesto for the Democratization of Europe, https://www.tdem.edu /en/manifesto.

longer possible to continue as before. We cannot simply wait for the next departures, or further dismantling without making fundamental changes to present-day Europe.

Today, our continent is caught between political movements whose program is confined to hunting down foreigners and refugees, a program which they have now begun to put into action, on one hand. On the other, we have parties which claim to be European but which in reality continue to consider that hard core liberalism and the spread of competition to all (states, firms, territories, and individuals) are enough to define a political project. They in no way recognize that it is precisely this lack of social ambition which leads to the feeling of abandonment.

There are some social and political movements which do attempt to end this fatal dialogue by moving in the direction of a new political, social, and environmental foundation for Europe. After a decade of economic crisis, there is no lack of these specifically European critical situations: structural underinvestment in the public sector, particularly in the fields of training and research, a rise in social inequality, acceleration of global warming, and a crisis in the reception of migrants and refugees. But these movements often have difficulty in formulating an alternative project, and in describing precisely how they would like to organize the Europe of the future and the decisionmaking infrastructure specific to it.

We, European citizens, by publishing this Manifesto, Treaty, and Budget, are making specific proposals publicly available to all. They are not perfect, but they do have the merit of existing. The public can access them and improve them. They are based on a simple conviction. Europe must build an original model to ensure the fair and lasting social development of its citizens. The only way to convince them is to abandon vague and theoretical promises. If Europe wants to restore solidarity with its citizens, it can only do so by providing con-

crete proof that it is capable of establishing cooperation between Europeans and by making those who have gained from
globalization contribute to the financing of the public goods
which are cruelly lacking in Europe today. This means making large firms contribute more than small and medium businesses, and the richest taxpayers paying more than poorer
taxpayers. This is not the case today.

Our proposals are based on the creation of a Budget for
democratization which would be debated and voted by a sovereign European Assembly. This will at last enable Europe to equip
itself with a public institution which is both capable of dealing
with crises in Europe immediately and of producing a set of fundamental public and social goods and services in the framework
of a lasting and solidarity-based economy. In this way, the promise made as far back as the Treaty of Rome of "improving living and working conditions" will finally become meaningful.

This Budget, if the European Assembly so desires, will be
financed by four major European taxes, the tangible markers
of this European solidarity. These will apply to the profits of
major firms, the top incomes (over 200,000 euros per year), the
highest wealth owners (over 1 million euros), and the carbon
emissions (with a minimum price of 30 euros per ton). If it is
fixed at 4% of GDP, as we propose, this budget could finance
research, training, and the European universities, an ambitious
investment program to transform our model of economic
growth, the financing of the reception and integration of migrants, and the support of those involved in operating the
transformation. It could also give some budgetary leeway to
member states to reduce the regressive taxation which weighs
on salaries or consumption.

The issue here is not one of creating a "transfer payments
Europe" which would endeavor to take money from the "virtuous" countries to give it to those who are less so. The project

for a Treaty of Democratization states this explicitly by limiting the gap between expenditure deducted and income paid by a country to a threshold of 0.1% of its GDP. This threshold can be raised in case there is a consensus to do so, but the real issue is elsewhere: it is primarily a question of reducing the inequality *within* the different countries and of investing in the future of *all* Europeans, beginning of course with the youngest among them, with no *single* country having preference. This computation does exclude spending that benefits equally all countries, such as policies to curb global warming. Because it will finance European public goods benefiting all countries, the Budget for democratization will de facto also foster convergence between countries.

Because we must act quickly but we must also get Europe out of the present technocratic impasse, we propose the creation of a European Assembly. This will enable these new European taxes to be debated and voted and also the budget for democratization. This European Assembly can be created without changing the existing European treaties.

This European Assembly would of course have to communicate with the present decisionmaking institutions (in particular the Eurogroup, in which the Ministers for Finance in the eurozone meet informally every month). But, in cases of disagreement, the Assembly would have the *final word*. If not, its capacity to be a locus for a new *transnational, political space* where parties, social movements, and NGOs would finally be able to express themselves, would be compromised. Equally its actual effectiveness, since the issue is one of finally extricating Europe from the eternal inertia of intergovernmental negotiations, would be at stake. We should bear in mind that the rule of fiscal unanimity in force in the European Union has for years blocked the adoption of any European tax and sustains the eternal evasion into fiscal dumping by the rich and most mobile, a practice which continues to this day despite all the speeches. This will go on if other decisionmaking rules are not set up.

Given that this European Assembly will have the ability to adopt taxes and to enter the very core of the democratic, fiscal, and social compact of member states, it is important to truly involve national and European parliamentarians. By granting national elected members a central role, the national, parliamentary elections will de facto be transformed into European elections. National elected members will no longer be able to simply shift responsibility on to Brussels and will have no other option than to explain to the voters the projects and budgets which they intend to defend in the European Assembly. By bringing together the national and European parliamentarians in one single Assembly, habits of co-governance will be created which at the moment only exist between heads of state and ministers of finance.

This is why we propose, in the Democratization Treaty available online, that 80% of the members of the European Assembly should be from members of the national parliaments of the countries which sign the Treaty (in proportion to the population of the countries and the political groups), and 20% from the present European parliament (in proportion to the political groups). This choice merits further discussion. In particular, our project could also function with a lower proportion of national parliamentarians (for instance 50%). But in our opinion, an excessive reduction of this proportion might detract from the legitimacy of the European Assembly in involving all European citizens in the direction of a new social and fiscal pact, and conflicts of democratic legitimacy between national and European elections could rapidly undermine the project.

We now have to act quickly. While it would be desirable for all European Union countries to join in this project without delay, and while it would be preferable that the four largest countries in the eurozone (which together represent over 70% of the GNP and the population in the zone) adopt it at the outset, the project in its totality has been designed for it to be legally and economically adopted and applied by any subset of countries who wish to do so. This point is important, because it enables countries and political movements who so desire to demonstrate their willingness to make very specific progress by adopting this project, or an improved version, right now. We call on every man and woman to assume his or her responsibilities and participate in a detailed and constructive discussion for the future of Europe.

Yellow Vests and Tax Justice
December 11, 2018

The crisis of the "yellow vests" raises a key issue both in France and in Europe,[1] namely, that of fiscal justice. Since his election, Emmanuel Macron has spent considerable time in explaining to the country that the "premiers de cordée" (i.e., the leading fortunes and industrialists) should be treated with care; the top priority was to grant tax cuts to the wealthiest, and as a start, the wealth tax was abolished. All this was done at top speed, in a spirit of invincibility and without the slightest qualm of conscience. Even Nicolas Sarkozy had been wiser in 2007 with his "tax shield," which he did nevertheless have to cancel in 2012. Inevitably all those who do not consider themselves to be "leading lights" have felt abandoned and humiliated by the Macron discourse, and this is how we now find ourselves in the present situation. The current leadership has committed a series of factual, historical, and political errors which it is urgent and possible to correct today.

1. See "Manifesto for the Democratization of Europe," December 10, 2018.

In the first instance, Macron attempted to justify the abolition of the wealth tax by stating that this tax was instrumental in wealth leaving France. The problem is that this statement is totally unfounded from a factual point of view. Since 1990 we have witnessed a spectacular and continuous rise in the number of estates and amounts of wealth declared to the wealth tax. This development has taken place in all bands of the wealth tax, in particular in the highest bands, where the number and amount of financial assets has risen even faster than the holdings in real estate, which in turn have risen more rapidly than the GDP and the total payroll. The falls in the stock exchange in 2001 and 2008 meant a temporary calm in this evolution, but as soon as the crises ended, the long-term trends picked up again.

In total, the income from the wealth tax (the ISF) more than quadrupled between 1990 and 2017, rising from 1 billion to over 4 billion euros, whereas the nominal GDP was only multiplied by two. All this despite the numerous reductions, exemptions, and capping granted over the years to the wealth-tax payers and despite the fact that the threshold for inclusion in the wealth tax has gradually been raised from 0.6 million euros of net wealth in 1990 to 1.3 million euros since 2012 (after deduction of 30% on the value of the main residence of the household). Furthermore, the fiscal control of this tax has always been inadequate.

We just have to consider, for example, that the preprepared returns have been in place for 10 years for income tax, but they have never been applied to the wealth tax, even though the banks could easily transmit all the information required to the tax authorities. In 2012, the detailed tax declaration above 3 million euros was even abolished (since then, all that is required is a global amount of wealth with no possibility of systematic control). With improved administration, the wealth

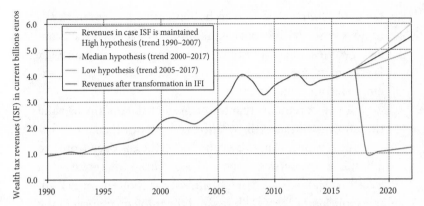

Figure 24. Wealth tax revenues in France, 1990–2022: fast growth
interrupted. Wealth tax revenues (ISF, impôt sur la fortune) have
more than quadrupled between 1990 and 2017 (from 1.0 to 4.2 billion
euros), while nominal GDP doubled in France. This reflects the
very fast growth of the number and size of wealth portfolios
reported to ISF, in all wealth brackets, in particular the highest
ones, where the highest financial assets have risen even faster
than real estate assets. This rapid rise of revenues occurred in spite
of numerous tax reductions and loopholes (in particular bouclier
fiscal in 2007), and in spite of the rise in exemption threshold
(from 0.6 million euros in 1990 to 1.3 million euros since 2012).
The revenue projections for 2018–2022 that are reported here
assume that household wealth keeps up with the same trends as
in previous periods (three variants), that wealth tax brackets are
indexed on average nominal wealth growth, and that high wealth
levels rise at the same speed as average wealth. These should
therefore be viewed as lower-bound projections, especially given
that tax audit on ISF could greatly be improved (e.g., via
preprepared wealth declarations, etc.). *Sources and series:*
see piketty.pse.ens.fr/ideology.

tax could today yield over 10 billion euros. Moreover, this is in no way surprising, bearing in mind the fact that the property tax yields over 40 billion euros and that the wealth tax is extremely concentrated (especially the financial assets, exempted from property tax).[2]

The fact remains that in the present state of the law and the administration of the wealth tax, both of which are defective, the revenue from this tax has nevertheless risen from 1 to 4 billion euros between 1990 and 2017. Given the evolution in wealth, it should have risen to almost 6 billion in 2022. With the abolition of the wealth tax and the implementation of the *Ipôt sur le fortune immobilière* (IFI, i.e., tax on real estate wealth, excluding all financial assets), the revenue has fallen to just over 1 billion euros in 2018. Between now and 2022 we will have lost 5 billion euros per year and find ourselves back at the level we were at thirty years ago.

The government's second mistake is historical: They are in the wrong time period. It is undeniable that the United States and the United Kingdom launched a process of dismantling fiscal progressivity in the 1980s and that this movement was partly followed in Europe in the 1990s and at the beginning of the years 2000—for example, with the suspension of the wealth tax in Germany and Sweden (and as a bonus, that of the inheritance tax in the latter case).

But are we really so sure that these policies produced the effects expected? Since the crisis in 2008, and even more so since Trump, Brexit, and the explosion of the xenophobe vote

---

2. See "Suppression of the Wealth Tax: A Historic Mistake," October 10, 2017; and Bertrand Garbinti, Jonathan Goupille-Lebret, and Thomas Piketty, "Accounting for Wealth Inequality Dynamics: Methods, Estimates and Simulations for France (1800–2014)," December 2016, WID. world Working Paper Series no. 2016/5.

all over Europe, there is a better appreciation of the dangers posed by the rise in inequality and the sense of abandonment in the working classes, so that many now understand the need for a new social regulation of capitalism. In these conditions, adding a further measure in favor of the richest in 2018 was not really very clever. If Macron wants to be the president of the 2020s and not the 1990s, he is going to have to adapt quickly.

The saddest thing is the appalling wastage and mess concerning global warming. If a carbon tax is to succeed, it is imperative that the totality of the net proceeds be allocated to the social measures associated with the ecological transition. The government has done just the opposite: only 10% of the 4 billion–euro rise in fuel duty in 2018, and the extra 4 billion expected in 2019, were earmarked for social measures, while the remainder financed, de facto, the abolition of the wealth tax and the flat tax on income from capital.

If Macron wants to save his five-year period in power, he must immediately reinstate the wealth tax and allocate the revenue to compensate those who are the most affected by the rises in the carbon tax, which must continue.

If he does not do so, that will mean that he will have opted for an outdated pro-rich ideology at the expense of the campaign against global warming.

1789: The Return of the Debt

January 15, 2019

One of the ideas raised by the yellow vests is the possibility of a referendum on the cancellation of the public debt. For some, this type of proposal, already heard in Italy, demonstrates the extent of the "populist" danger: How can one possibly imagine not repaying a debt? In reality, history shows that it is customary to resort to exceptional solutions when the debt reaches this level of magnitude. However, a referendum would not enable us to solve such a complex problem. There are numerous ways of cancelling a debt, with very different social effects. This is what should be discussed instead of leaving these decisions to others and to the forthcoming crises.

To ensure that everyone can make up their minds, I am going to give two sets of information here. The first concerns the present European regulations; then I will turn to the way in which debts of this size have been dealt with in history.

Let's begin with the European regulations, which are not well known and have generated a certain amount of confusion. Many people continue to refer to the "3% rule" and do not understand why Italy, which was considering a deficit of 2.5% of GDP, before agreeing to a compromise of 2%, has been blacklisted. The explanation is that the Maastricht Treaty (1992) was amended by the new budgetary treaty adopted in 2012. Its real name is the Treaty for Stability, Coordination and Governance (TSCG).[1] This text stipulates that henceforth the deficit must not exceed 0.5% of GDP (Article 3), with the exception however of the countries whose debt is "significantly less than 60% of GDP," in which case the deficit can rise to 1%. Barring "exceptional circumstances," the violation of these rules leads to automatic penalties.

We should point out that the deficit targeted by these texts is always the secondary deficit, that is, after payment of interest on the debt. If a country has a debt equal to 100% of GDP and the interest rate is 4%, then the interest will be 4% of GDP. To achieve a secondary deficit limited to 0.5%, a primary surplus of 3.5% of GDP is required. In other words, taxpayers will have to pay taxes which are higher than the expenditures benefiting them, with a difference of 3.5% of GDP possibly for decades.

The TSCG approach is not illogical: If we choose not to cancel the debt, and if we have almost zero inflation and limited growth, then only huge primary surpluses can reduce debts in the range of 100% of GDP. However, the social and political consequences of this type of choice have to be considered.

Although they have been reduced by the unusually low rates which will perhaps not last forever, at the moment, interest payments stand at 2% of GDP in the eurozone (the average deficit is 1% and the primary surplus 1%). This amounts to over 200 billion euros per year, which one can compare for example with the miserable 2 billion per year invested in the

1. Treaty for Stability, Coordination and Governance, https://www .consilium.europa.eu/media/20399/stootscg26_en12.pdf.

Erasmus program. This is a possible choice, but are we sure that it is the best one to prepare for the future? If similar amounts were devoted to training and research, then Europe could become the leading center of innovation at world level, ahead of the United States. In Italy, the interest payments represent 3% of GDP, or six times the budget for higher education.[2]

What is certain is that history shows that there are other ways of proceeding.[3] One example often quoted is the big debts of the twentieth century. Germany, France, and the United Kingdom all found themselves with debts ranging from 200% to 300% of GDP post–World War II, which have never been repaid. Their debts were written off in a few years by a mix of cancellation pure and simple, inflation, and exceptional taxation of private property (which is the same thing as inflation, but is more civilized: The rich can be made to pay more, and the middle class protected). The German external debt was frozen by the London Debt Agreement in 1953, and then definitively written off in 1991. This is how Germany and France found themselves with no public debt and able to invest in growth in the years 1950–1960.

However, the most relevant comparison is the Revolution in 1789. The ancien régime was unable to force its privileged classes to pay taxes and had accumulated a debt of approxi-

2. On interest maturities in Italy, see European Central Bank, Statistical Data Warehouse, "Italy. Government Debt Securities: Debt Service," http://sdw.ecb.europa.eu/reports.do?node=1000003919.

3. On the history of debts in the eighteenth to twentieth centuries, see, for example, Thomas Piketty, *Capital in the Twenty-First Century* (Cambridge, MA: Harvard University Press, 2014), chapters 3–5. For the complete series, see Thomas Piketty and Gabriel Zucman, "Capital Is Back: Wealth-Income Ratios in Rich Countries, 1700–2010," *Quarterly Journal of Economics* 129, no. 3 (2014): 1155–1210.

mately one year of national income, even a year and a half if the sale of *charges* and *offices* (official posts and functions) are included (these were a way for the state to obtain money immediately in exchange for the future revenue to be collected from the population). In 1790, the Assembly obtained the publication of the list of names in the *Grand livre des pensions,* which contained both annuities to courtiers, as well as payments to former senior officials, with payments ten or twenty times higher than the average income, which created a scandal (the comparison with the salary of the President of the National Commission for Public Debate springs to mind). It all ended with the setting up of a somewhat fairer form of taxation and above all, the bankruptcy of two-thirds of those named and a major inflation of the *assignats* or promissory notes.

In comparison, the present situation is both more complex (each country holds a part of the debt of the others) and more simple: We have, with the European Central Bank (ECB), an institution which enables us to freeze debts, and we could adopt a fairer European tax system by finally setting up a sovereign assembly. But if we continue to explain that it is impossible to make the richest Europeans pay and that only the immobile classes have to pay, then inevitably we run the risk of facing serious rebellions in the future.

Wealth Tax in America

February 12, 2019

What if the final blow for Emmanuel Macron came from the Massachusetts State senator and not from the yellow vests? Elizabeth Warren, Harvard University law professor, not really an adept of Chavism or urban guerrilla warfare, a declared candidate in the Democratic primaries in 2020, has just made public what will doubtless be one of the key points in the coming campaign, namely, the creation for the first time in the United States of a genuine federal progressive wealth tax. Carefully calculated by Emmanuel Saez and Gabriel Zucman, supported by the best constitutionalists, the Warren proposal sets a rate of 2% on fortunes valued at between $50 million and $1 billion, and 3% above $1 billion.[1] The

---

1. See Elizabeth Warren, "Senator Warren Unveils Proposal to Tax Wealth of Ultra-Rich Americans," January 24, 2019, https://www.warren .senate.gov/newsroom/press-releases/senator-warren-unveils-proposal-to -tax-wealth-of-ultra-rich-americans. See also Emmanuel Saez and Gabriel Zucman, "How Would a Progressive Wealth Tax Work? Evidence from the Economics Literature," February 5, 2019, https://www.icrict.com/you -should-also-read/2019/6/17/how-would-a-progressive-wealth-tax-work -evidence-from-the-economics-literature.

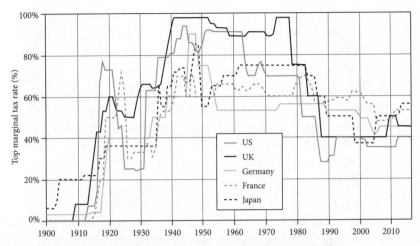

Figure 25. Top income tax rates in rich countries, 1900–2017.
Source: World Inequality Report, 2018, wir2018.wid.world.

proposal also provides for an exit tax equal to 40% of total wealth for those who choose to leave the country and to relinquish American citizenship. The tax would apply to all assets, with no exemptions, with dissuasive sanctions for persons and governments who do not transmit appropriate information on assets held abroad.

The debate has only just begun, and the schedule proposed could still be extended and made more progressive with rates rising for example to 5–10% per year for multibillionaires. What is certain is that the issue of fiscal justice will be central to the presidential campaign in 2020. The representative from New York, Alexandria Ocasio-Cortez, has suggested a rate of 70% on the highest incomes, while Bernie Sanders defends a tax rate of 77% on the highest inherited estates. While the Warren proposal is the most innovative, the three approaches are complementary and should be mutually beneficial.

To understand this, let's look back. Between 1880 and 1910, while the concentration of industrial and financial wealth was gaining momentum in the United States and the country was threatening to become almost as unequal as old Europe, a powerful political movement in favor of an improved distribution in wealth was developing. This led to the creation of a federal tax on income in 1913 and on inheritances in 1916.

Between 1930 and 1980, the rate applied on the highest incomes was on average 81% in the United States, and the rate applied to the highest inherited estates was 74%. Clearly, this did not destroy American capitalism, far from it. It made it more egalitarian and more productive, at a time when the voters in the United States had not forgotten that it was their level of educational advancement and their investment in training and skills that was the backbone of their prosperity, and not the religion of property and inequality.

Reagan, then Bush and Trump subsequently endeavored to destroy this heritage. They turned their backs on the egalitarian origins of the country, by counting on historical amnesia and by fueling identity-based divisions. With the hindsight we have today, it is obvious that the outcome of this policy is disastrous. Between 1980 and 2020, the rise in per capita national income was halved in comparison with the period 1930–1980. What little growth there was, has been swept up by the richest, the consequence being a complete stagnation in income for the poorest 50%. There is something obvious about the movement of return to progressive taxation and greater justice which is emerging today and which is long overdue.

The innovation is that it is now a question of creating an annual wealth tax, in addition to the income and inherited estate taxes. This is a crucial innovation in terms of justice and efficiency. Numerous one-shot capital levies have been successfully applied to real estate and professional and financial assets

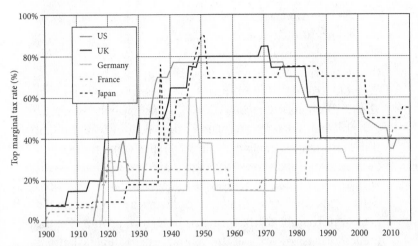

Figure 26. Top inheritance tax rates in rich countries, 1900–2017.
Source: World Inequality Report, 2018, wir2018.wid.world.

subsequent to the world wars to pay off public debts, in particular in Japan, Germany, Italy, France, and in many other European countries. Collected only once, the rates applied to the largest private estates often rose to 40% or 50%, or even more. With an annual wealth tax designed to be applied on a permanent basis, the rates are of necessity more restricted. However, they must be high enough to enable genuine mobility of wealth. From this point of view, the tax on inherited wealth comes much too late. We are not going to wait until Bezos or Zuckerberg reach the age of 90 before they begin to pay taxes. With the 3% annual rate proposed by Elizabeth Warren, a static estate worth $100 billion would return to the community in thirty years. This is a good beginning, but given the average rate of progression of the highest financial assets, the aim should undoubtedly be higher (5–10% or more).

It is also crucial to allocate all the revenue to the reduction of inequalities. In particular, the American property tax, like the French real estate tax (*taxe foncière*), weighs heavily on those with limited resources. Those two venerable property taxes which, contrary to what is sometimes stated, tax not only the ownership of housing (independent of any income, which everyone readily admits, at least for the biggest owners), but also tax business assets (offices, plots of land, warehouses, etc.). The problem is that they have never been genuinely re-thought since the eighteenth century. The time has come for them to become progressive taxes with graduated rates on net assets, with the key element being strong reductions for indebted households who are seeking to accede to property ownership. Let's hope that the forthcoming American campaign, like the French discussion around the yellow vests, will at last afford the opportunity for an in-depth discussion on the taxation of property and fiscal justice.

To Love Europe Is to Change It
March 12, 2019

To love Europe is to want to change it. The French and German governments which have been in power for the past ten years claim to be Europhiles, but the truth is that they are first and foremost Euroconservatives. They do not wish to make any fundamental changes to present-day Europe, for fear of losing their power and their illusory hold over Brussels affairs. By so doing, they are digging Europe's grave. Even Brexit does not seem to give them reason for doubt.

The most recent episode is the Franco-German Treaty, or the so-called Elysée Treaty, renegotiated in January, proposing the creation of a Franco-German Parliamentary Assembly to enable the elected members from both countries to discuss questions of defense or of company law together. This is an excellent initiative, except that this Assembly is purely consultative and will have no real power.

However, one could very well entrust it with the task of voting the urgent measures of fiscal justice which we need. For example, it is about time that we had a tax on carbon emissions which would tax major emitters more than the smaller ones.

At the moment, the exact opposite is happening; in the name of competition and European rules, those who take their cars to go to work are taxed full pelt, while the kerosene for those who take the plane to go on a weekend break is exonerated.

The Franco-German leaders claim to be concerned about global warming. But how do they intend to make these policies acceptable with such absurd policies?

More generally speaking, it is ridiculous to spend time explaining that it is impossible to tax the richest at national level, without proposing anything specific to coordinate action at a higher level. In this instance, the Franco-German Assembly could also be responsible for voting common taxes on the profits of major companies and on the highest incomes and wealth holders. This is a simple question of common sense. In a large-scale federal community, bound by agreements on the free movement of goods, people, and capital, it is logical to entrust a central government with the key role for the taxes, ensuring the greatest redistribution.

In the United States, progressive taxes on the top incomes and estates are managed primarily at the federal level, in the same way as are taxes on company profits, while U.S. states rely mainly on quasi-proportional forms of tax or indirect taxes.

In Europe, it is the reverse: the European Union regulates VAT but leaves individual states to deal with the damage of cutthroat competition in matters of taxation on company profits, incomes, and estates. The result is that Europe is the leader in the global movement of the race to lower rates on company profits and has concentrated the rises in taxation on the lowest incomes. All this derives from the fact that Europe and its institutions were built to manage a big market and have failed to respond to the new challenges.

The result is that the tax system is increasingly biased in favor of the most mobile, to the extent that the costs of fiscal competition are becoming increasingly heavy for the middle and working classes, potentially heavier than the gains from market integration. In other words, the growing distrust which Europe has evoked among the lower income groups for decades is not an irrational whim, but does, on the contrary, correspond to a profound reality, a fundamental mistake in conception that needs to be corrected as a matter of urgency before the situation becomes explosive.

Now the fact is that the creation of a Franco-German Assembly, open immediately to Italy, Spain, and all the countries that so desire, and qualified to adopt strong measures of fair taxation, is not a utopia. This could be set up immediately. This would permit a reduction in the tax burden on the lower income groups and the financing of the ecological transition. A detailed proposal, developed by lawyers and citizens from all over Europe, has received the support of over 100,000 signatures.[1] It can and should be improved. The main point is that each government and political movement should publicly defend specific proposals, and stop declaring that this is impossible and taking refuge behind the reluctance of the others.

Should it be impossible to convince the twenty-seven for the moment, then we must resolve to cut the Gordian knot and build separate political institutions for a small number of countries; these would complement the current EU institutions. The present institutions are blocked by the unanimity rule, and it has now been demonstrated that these do not enable the adoption of the slightest tax in common. We therefore have to build new institutions which the other countries will join when these have proved their efficiency.

1. Manifesto for the Democratization of Europe, https://www.tdem.edu /en/manifesto.

If the French and German governments refuse to change Europe, it is also because basically they remain convinced that the advantages of tax competition outweigh the disadvantages or that the benefits are not large enough to justify such a huge change. By so doing, they demonstrate that they are not in step with the times: They have not yet recognized the strong trend to increase inequalities. Their position was tenable in the 1990s. But ten years after the financial crisis in 2008 demonstrated the fragility of the euro and of Europe, this position is outdated. If Europe does not stand for fiscal justice, then the nationalists will win the day.

Basic Income in India

April 16, 2019

The biggest election in world history has just begun in India: There are over 900 million electors. It is often said that India learned the art of parliamentary democracy through contact with the British. The observation is not entirely false, provided that we add that India is now implementing this art on an unprecedented scale in a political community of 1.3 billion people, split along huge socio-cultural and linguistic divisions, which is a much more complex issue.

Meanwhile the United Kingdom has considerable difficulty remaining united at the level of the British Isles. Following in the steps of Ireland at the beginning of the twentieth century, it may just possibly be Scotland's turn to leave the United Kingdom and its Parliament at this start of the twenty-first century. For its part, the European Union and its 500 million inhabitants have still not succeeded in setting up democratic rules for the adoption of the slightest common tax and continue to grant a right of veto to Grand Duchies, in which barely 0.1% of its citizens reside. Instead of explaining in learned fashion that nothing in this fine system can be changed, European leaders would be well advised to look at

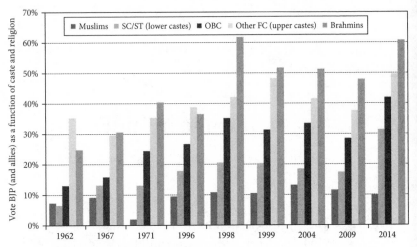

Figure 27. BJP vote by caste and religion: India, 1962–2014. In 2014, 10% of Muslim voters voted for the BJP (Hindu nationalists) and allied parties, vs. 31% among SC/ST (scheduled castes/scheduled tribes, lower castes), 42% among OBC (other backward classes, intermediate castes), 49% among other FC (forward castes, upper castes except Brahmins), and 61% among Brahmins. *Sources and series:* see piketty.pse.ens.fr/ideology.

the Indian union and its model of a federal and parliamentary republic.

Obviously, not everything in the garden is rosy in the biggest democracy in the world. The country's development is marred by huge inequalities and poverty which is too slow in its decline. One of the principal innovations of the electoral campaign which is ending is the proposal made by the party in Congress to introduce a system of basic income, the NYAY (*nyuntam aay yojana,* minimum guaranteed income). The amount announced is 6,000 rupees per month and per household, or the equivalent of about 250 euros in purchasing power parity (three times less at the current exchange rate), which is far from negligible in India (where the median income does not exceed 400 euros per household). This system would apply to the poorest 20% of Indians. The cost would be significant (a little over 1% of GDP) but not prohibitive.

As always with proposals of this type, it is important not to stop there and not to take the basic income as a miracle solution or a final settlement. Setting up a fair distribution of wealth and a model for sustainable and equitable development requires the backing of a total package of social, educational, and fiscal measures, the basic income being only one element therein. As Nitin Bharti and Lucas Chancel have shown,[1] public expenditure on health has stagnated at 1.3% of GDP between 2009–2013 and 2014–2018, and the investment in education even fell from 3.1% to 2.6%. A complex balance remains to be found between the reduction in monetary poverty and these social investments, which condition the closing of the gap between India and China. China has found a way to mobilize greater resources to raise the level of training and health of the population as a whole.

The fact remains that the proposal by Congress has the merit of stressing the questions of redistribution and of going beyond mechanisms of "quotas" and "reservations." True, these have enabled a fraction of the lower castes to access the university and public-sector jobs and to hold elective offices, but they are not sufficient.

1. Nitin Bharti and Lucas Chancel, "Tackling Inequality in India. Is the 2019 Election Campaign up to the Challenge?" WID.world Issue Brief 2019/2. On the transformations of political divisions in India, see Abhijit Banerjee, Amory Gethin, and Thomas Piketty, "Growing Cleavages in India? Evidence from the Changing Structure of Electorates, 1962–2014," WID.world, Working Paper Series no. 2019/05.

The biggest drawback of the proposal is that Congress has chosen to remain very discreet about its financing. This is a pity, because it afforded an opportunity to rehabilitate the role of progressive taxation and to definitely turn the page on its neoliberal moment in the 1980s and 1990s. Above all, it would have provided an occasion for more explicitly coming closer to the new alliance between the socialist parties and the lower castes (SP, BSP) who propose the creation of a federal tax of 2% on net worth over 25 million rupees (1 million euros in purchasing power parity), which would bring in the equivalent of the amounts required for the NYAY and strengthen the progressivity of the federal income tax.

Fundamentally, the real issue at stake in this election is the constitution in India of a left-wing coalition, both egalitarian and multicultural, the only coalition capable of beating the pro-business and anti-Muslim nationalism of the BJP. This time this may not be enough. The Congress, which was formerly the hegemonic party from the center, is still led by the far-from-popular Rahul Gandhi (from the Nehru-Gandhi family), whereas the BJP had the sense to adopt Modi, for the first time a leader from humble origins. Congress fears it may be outflanked and lose the control of the government if it were to launch into an overly explicit coalition with parties to its left.

Furthermore, Modi is massively funded by Indian big business, in a country which is well known for its total absence of regulation in this respect. In addition, he has skillfully exploited the Pulwama attack in Jammu and Kashmir and the air raids which followed to activate anti-Pakistan feelings and accuse the Congress and the left-wing parties of collusion with fundamentalist Islam (this does not only happen in France), in what may well remain the turning point in the campaign.

Whatever the case may be, the seeds sown will grow along with the politico-ideological changes ongoing all over the world. The decisions debated in India will increasingly affect us all. In this respect, this Indian election is indeed an election of global importance.

Europe and the Class Cleavage

May 14, 2019

Three years after the referendum on Brexit and on the eve of the new European elections, the skepticism about Europe is still as strong, particularly among the most disadvantaged sections of society.

The problem is deep and longstanding. In all the referendums for the last twenty-five years, the working classes have systematically expressed their disagreement with the Europe presented to them, whereas the richest and the most privileged classes supported it. During the French referendum on the Treaty of Maastricht in 1992, we observed that 60% of the voters with the lowest incomes, personal wealth, or qualifications voted against, whereas the 40% of the electorate with higher incomes voted in favor; the gap was big enough for the yes vote to win with a small majority (51%). The same thing happened with the Constitutional Treaty in 2005, except that this time, only the top 20% were in favor of the yes vote, whereas the lower 80% preferred to vote no, resulting in a clear victory for the latter (55%). Likewise for the referendum on Brexit in the United Kingdom in 2016: this time it was the top 30% who voted enthusiastically to remain in the European Union. But, as the bottom 70% preferred to leave, the leave vote won with 52% of the votes.

What is the explanation? Why are votes on the European Union always characterized by such a marked division of social class? This outcome is all the more puzzling as the structure of the vote for the different political parties has long since ceased to be so clearly marked by class structure, with the three dimensions of social division (qualifications, income, personal wealth) all pulling in the same direction. Since the 1970s–1980s, the most highly qualified have swung distinctly toward the left-wing parties in both countries, whereas those with the highest incomes and personal wealth continue to tend to support the right-wing parties, which are themselves undergoing change. In contrast, during the votes concerning Europe in 1992 (French referendum on the Maastricht Treaty), 2005 (French referendum on constitutional treaty), and 2016 (UK referendum on Brexit), the intellectual and economic elites in both instances found themselves supporting the European Union as it existed, whereas the less-privileged categories on the left and on the right rejected it.

The reason for this, according to those who are better off, is that the working classes are nationalist and xenophobic, perhaps even backward. However, the xenophobia of the less well off is no more natural than that of the elites. There is a much simpler explanation: The European Union, as built in recent decades, is based on widespread competition between countries, on fiscal and social dumping in favor of the most mobile economic actors, and it functions objectively to the benefit of the most privileged. Until the European Union takes strong symbolic measures for the reduction of inequalities, for example a common tax which impacts the richest, enabling the taxes of the poorest to be lowered, this situation will continue.

This opposition between several visions of Europe is not new, and it gains by being set in a historical perspective. In 1938, young militants launched the Federal Union movement in the United Kingdom.[1] They were soon joined by academics like Beveridge and Robbins; it was the inspiration for Churchill's proposal in June 1940 to create a Federal Franco-British Union; this was refused by the French government, in refuge in Bordeaux at the time, and which preferred to give full powers to Pétain. It is interesting to note that a group of British and French academics met in Paris in April 1940 to study the working of a possible federal union, in the first instance at Franco-British level, then enlarged to European level; they did not come to an agreement. Hayek defended the vision most permeated with economic liberalism. He wanted a purely commercial union based on competition, free markets, and monetary stability. Robbins defended a fairly similar approach, while at the same time envisaging the possibility of a federal budget and, in particular, a federal inheritance tax in situations where the free market and free movement of persons were not sufficient to spread prosperity and reduce inequalities.

Other members of the group had visions much closer to democratic socialism; in the first instance, Beveridge, an enthusiast for social insurance, along with the sociologist Barbara Wooton, who proposed a federal income tax and a federal inheritance tax at a rate of over 60%, along with a system of income limits and a maximum inheritance. The participants in the meeting separated in the acknowledgment of their disagreement on the social and economic content of the federal union envisaged. All these discussions concerning the Federal Union movement resonated throughout Europe. For example, in 1941, they inspired Altiero Spinelli, a militant

1. See Or Rosenboim, *The Emergence of Globalism. Visions of World Order in Britain and the United States, 1939–1950* (Princeton, NJ: Princeton University Press, 2017).

communist then imprisoned in the jails of Mussolini, to draw up his *Manifest for a Free and United Europe,* or *Manifeste de Ventotene* (the name of the island where he was imprisoned).

However, there is no reason why present-day Europe should remain imbued with a Hayek-type vision. Today the European banner serves the interests of those whose aim is to impose their class politics. But it is up to us to remind people that Europe could be organized in a different manner, as was already the opinion of Wooton, Beveridge, or even Robbins almost eighty years ago.

PS: For more about the Federal Union movement, see the fascinating book by Or Rosenboim, *The Emergence of Globalism,* cited above.

The Illusion of Centrist Ecology

June 11, 2019

Good news: Given the results of the European elections, it would seem that French and European citizens are becoming more concerned about global warming. The problem is that the election which has just taken place did little to further the basic issue. In real terms, which political forces do the ecologists intend to govern with, and what is their program for action? In France, the Greens achieved a respectable score, gaining 13% of the votes. But, given that they had already obtained 11% in the 1989 European elections, 10% in 1999, and 16% in 2009, there is nothing to show that an autonomous majority of the Greens is within reach. In the European Parliament the Greens will have almost 10% of the seats (seventy-four out of 751). This is better than in the outgoing parliament, where their share was only 7% (fifty-one seats) but this does force us to ask the question concerning alliances. Now the decisionmakers in the Greens, intoxicated by their success, particularly in France, refuse to say whether they would like to govern with the left or with the right.

However, it is increasingly clear that the resolution of the climate challenge will not be possible without a strong move-

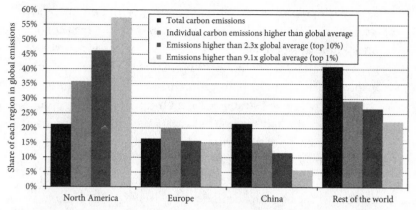

Figure 28. Global distribution of carbon emissions, 2010–2018. The share of the United States plus Canada in total global emissions (direct and indirect) was 21% on average in 2010–2018; this share rises to 36% if one looks at emissions greater than global average (6.2 tons of CO_2 per year), 46% for emissions above 2.3 times the global average (i.e., the top 10% of world emitters, accounting for 45% of total emissions, compared to 13% for the bottom 50% of world emitters), and 57% of those emitting over 9.1 times the global average (i.e., the top 1% of world emitters, accounting for 14% of total emissions). *Sources and series:* see piketty.pse.ens.fr/ideology.

ment in the direction of the reduction of social inequalities at all levels. With the present magnitude of inequality, the advance toward austerity of energy will be wishful thinking, because carbon emissions are strongly concentrated among the rich. At the global level, the richest 10% are responsible for almost half the emissions, and the top 1% alone emit more carbon than the poorest half of the planet. A drastic reduction in purchasing power of the richest would therefore in itself have a substantial impact on the reduction of emissions at the global level.

Furthermore, it is difficult to see how the middle and working classes in the rich countries as in the emerging economies would accept to change their lifestyle (which is nevertheless essential) if they do not have proof that the richest are also involved. The chain of political events observed in France in 2017–2019, which was strangely absent from the campaign, provides a dramatic and symbolic illustration of this need for justice. The principle of the carbon tax was relatively well accepted in France in 2017, and it was intended to increase the tax regularly until 2030 to enable the country to reduce its emissions in keeping with pledges made under the Paris Accords.

But if a progression of this sort is to be acceptable, it is essential that it affect the biggest polluters at least as much as those with more modest incomes, and that the totality of the product of the tax be allocated to the energy transition and used to assist those households most affected. The Macron government has done just the opposite. The taxes on fuels paid by the lowest incomes have been used to finance other priorities, beginning with the abolition of the wealth tax (ISF) and the progressive tax on incomes from capital. As the IPP (Institut des Politiques Publiques) has shown, between 2017 and 2019, the result has been an increase in 6% of the purchasing power of the top 1% and of 20% of the top 0.1% of the richest.[1]

Given the social unrest, the government could have decided to cancel its gifts to the richest and to devote the money at long last to the climate and to compensating the poorest. On

1. Mahdi Ben Jelloul, Antoine Bozio, Thomas Douenne, Brice Fabre, and Claire Leroy, "The 2019 French Budget: Impacts on Households," Institut des Politiques Publiques, 2019, https://halshs.archives-ouvertes.fr/halshs-02520775.

the contrary: Being as stubborn as Sarkozy was between 2007 and 2012, with his pro-rich tax shield, Macron has decided to stick with his gifts to the rich and to cancel the increases in the carbon tax in complete disregard for the Paris Accords— today nobody knows when the carbon tax will be reinstated. By choosing to make the abolition of the wealth tax the symbol of his policy, the party of the president has confirmed that he is indeed the heir to the liberal and pro-business right wing. The sociological structure of his electorate, focused on top incomes and wealth, in 2017 and even more so in 2019, means there can be no doubt about this.

In these conditions, one might wonder why the French or German Greens envisage governing with the liberals and the conservatives. The desire to acquire responsibilities is only human. But can we be sure that this is really in the interest of the planet? If the left-wing and the ecologists were to have allied in France, they would have overtaken the liberals and the nationalists. If they were to unite in the European Parliament, they would form by far the biggest group and could have more influence. If a social-federal and ecological alliance of this sort were to come into existence, the various left-wing parties would also have to go some of the way. *Les Insoumis* in France and *Die Linke* in Germany cannot just say that they want to change the present version of Europe or to get out of the treaties. They have to explain which new treaties they would like to sign. As far as the socialists and social-democrats are concerned, their practice of power does mean that they bear considerable responsibility for the breakdown of the political system, and they have a central role to play in enabling its reconstruction. They will have to recognize past errors: They are largely responsible for forging the present European framework, in particular by organizing the free circulation of capital without taxation, and by leading us to believe that they were going to renegotiate the treaties, whereas, in reality, they have no precise plan.

It is possible to build a model for equitable and sustainable development in Europe, but this demands discussion and difficult choices: all the more reason to get down to work with no more ado.

Will Money Creation Save Us?

July 9, 2019

Before the 2007–2008 crisis, the balance sheet of the European Central Bank (that is, the totality of securities owned and loans granted by the ECB) was approximately 1,000 billion euros, or barely 10% of the GDP of the eurozone. In 2019 it had risen to 4,700 billion euros, or 40% of the GDP of the zone. Thus between 2008 and 2018, the ECB has implemented a monetary creation equivalent to over one and a half years of the French GDP, one year of German GDP, or 30% of the GDP of the eurozone (or 3% of GDP in additional monetary creation each year for ten years). These considerable resources are for example three times higher than the total budget of the European Union during the same period (1% of GDP per year, all categories of expenditure taken together, from agriculture to Erasmus to the regional funds and research). These resources have enabled the ECB to intervene massively in the financial markets, to buy public and private debt securities, and to make loans to the banking sector to guarantee solvency.

These policies have probably prevented the "Great Recession" in 2008 from becoming the "Great Depression," as was the case between 1929 and 1935. At the time, the central banks were shaped by a liberal orthodoxy based on nonintervention

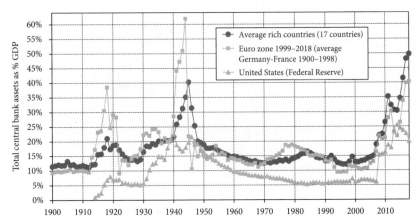

Figure 29. Size of central bank balance sheets, 1900–2018. Total assets of the European Central Bank (ECB) rose from 11% of eurozone GDP on December 31, 2004 to 41% on December 31, 2018. The evolution from 1900 to 1998 indicates the average obtained for the balance sheets of the German and French central banks (with peaks equal to 39% in 1918 and 62% in 1944). Total assets of the Federal Reserve (created in 1913) rose from 6% of GDP in 2007 to 26% at the end of 2014. *Note:* The average of rich countries is the arithmetic average of the following seventeen countries: Australia, Belgium, Britain, Canada, Denmark, France, Finland, Germany, Holland, Italy, Japan, Norway, Portugal, Spain, Sweden, Switzerland, and the United States. *Sources and series:* see piketty.pse.ens.fr /ideology.

and had allowed a wave of bank failures to take place. This precipitated the collapse of the economy, the explosion of unemployment, the rise of Nazism, and the march toward war. The fact that on this point at least, history has taught us a lesson and that in 2008 (almost) nobody suggested a repetition of this "liquidationist" experience is obviously a good thing. Confronted with the extreme weaknesses of global financial capitalism, the central banks were in fact the only public institutions capable of avoiding a cascade of bank failures in the emergency.

The problem is that not all problems can be settled by monetary creation and the boards of directors of central banks, and these episodes have profoundly and permanently disrupted the collective representations in this respect. Before 2008, the prevailing opinion was that it was forbidden (or at least highly inadvisable) to carry out a monetary creation of such magnitude. This conception had been imposed in the 1980s following the "stagflation" of the 1970s (a mix of slow growth and high inflation). This was the climate in which the Maastricht Treaty (1992), which was to give birth to the euro in 1999–2002, was conceived. The huge monetary creation which has taken place since 2008 has shattered this consensus. Following the creation in the click of a mouse, by the ECB of 30% of the GDP to save the banks, in Europe today, many voices clamor (for example, with the project of the finance-climate pact) for a repetition of the same thing to finance the energy transition, to reduce inequalities, or invest in research and training. Similar demands are also being expressed in the United States and in other regions of the world. They are natural and legitimate, and it will not be possible to simply dismiss them.

Several points must however be clarified. It is very possible that the central banks may again increase the size of their balance sheets (these have already risen to 100% of GDP in Japan and in Switzerland[1]) in order to deal with financial crises to come, or simply to follow the evolution of the balance sheets in the private sector (over 1,000% of GDP at present, compared to 300% in the 1970s). There is nothing in the slightest reassuring about this rationale of a never-ending high-speed chase: It would be better to set up the regulations

---

1. See "The Age of Green Money," May 12, 2020.

required to end this hyper-financialization and to reduce private balance sheets.

Furthermore, in a context of sluggish growth, of near-zero interest rates, and nonexistent inflation, it is legitimate for the public authorities to take on more debt to invest in the climate and in training, with the support of central banks. It is particularly paradoxical to observe that the total public expenditure in education (primary, secondary, and higher) has been stagnating in the richer countries at around 5% of GDP since the 1980s, whereas the proportion of an age group entering higher education has risen from less than 20% to over 50%. In the European context, this will however demand an in-depth intellectual and political reform. The questions of investment, debt, and money must be discussed openly in the context of a parliamentary body in place of the automatic budgetary rules (constantly circumvented) and the usual closed doors. These discussions involve the whole of society and cannot be left to councils of ministers of finance or governors of central banks.

Finally, and above all, the monetary expansion which took place in the period 2008–2018 must not lead to a new form of monetarist illusion. The considerable challenges which are ours (global warming, the rise of inequalities) do not simply demand that we mobilize adequate resources. They also demand that we build new norms of justice in the distribution of effort, which involves the adoption by elected assemblies of progressive taxes on income, financial assets, and carbon emissions and the implementation of a new system of financial transparency. The creation of money can help, provided that it is not a fetish and remains in its proper place: namely, a tool within a collective system in which taxes and parliaments must retain the main role.

What Is a Fair Pension System?

September 10, 2019

Even if the timing remains vague and the conditions uncertain, the government does seem to have decided to launch a vast reform of the retirement pensions system, with the key element being the unification of the rules applied at the moment in the various systems operating (civil servants, private sector employees, local authority employees, self-employed, special schemes, etc.).

Let's make it clear: Setting up a universal system is in itself an excellent thing, and a reform of this type is long overdue in France. The young generations, particularly those who have gone through multiple changes in status (private and public employees, self-employed, working abroad, etc.), frequently have no idea of the retirement rights which they have accumulated. This situation is a source of unbearable uncertainties and economic anxiety, whereas our retirement system is globally well financed.

But, having announced this aim of clarification and unification of rights, the truth is that we have not said very much. There are in effect many ways of unifying the rules. Now there is no guarantee that those in power are capable of generating a viable consensus in this respect. The principle of justice invoked by the government seems simple and plausible: One euro contributed should give rise to the same rights to retirement, no matter what the scheme and the level of salary or of earned income. The problem is that this principle amounts to making the inequalities in income as they exist at present sacrosanct, including when they are of mammoth proportions (underpaid piece work for some, excessive salaries for others), and to perpetuating them at the age of retirement and dependency which is in no way particularly "fair."

Aware of the difficulty, High Commissioner Jean-Paul Delevoye's plan stipulates that a quarter of the contributions will continue to be allocated to "solidarity," that is to say, for example, to subsidies for children and interruptions of career, or to finance a minimum retirement pension for the lowest salaries. The difficulty is that the way this calculation has been made is highly controversial. In particular, this estimate purely and simply takes no account of social inequalities in life expectancy. For example, if a low-wage earner spends ten years in retirement while a highly paid manager spends twenty years, we have forgotten to take into account the fact that a large share of the contributions of the low-wage earner serves in practice to pay the retirement of the highly paid manager (which is in no way compensated for by the allowance for strenuous and tedious work).

More generally, there are naturally multiple parameters to be fixed to define what one considers to be "solidarity." The government's proposals are respectable, but they are far from being the only ones possible. It is essential that a broad public debate take place and that alternative proposals should emerge. The Delevoye Plan, for example, provides for a replacement rate equal to 85% for a full career (forty-three years of contributions) at the minimum wage level. This rate would then very rapidly fall to 70%, to only 1.5 SMIC (minimum wage) before stabilizing at this precise level of 70% until approximately

7 SMIC (120,000 euros gross annual salary). This is one possible choice, but there are others. One could thus imagine that the replacement rate would go gradually from 85% of the SMIC to 75–80% around 1.5–2 SMIC, before gradually falling to around 50–60%, or approximately 5–7 SMIC.

Similarly, the government's project provides for a financing of the system by a retirement contribution of which the global rate would be fixed at 28.1% on all the gross incomes below 120,000 euros per year, before falling suddenly to only 2.8% beyond this threshold. The official justification is that retirement rights in the new system would be capped at this wage level. The Delevoye Report goes as far as congratulating themselves because the supermanagers will nevertheless be subject to this contribution (which will not be capped) of 2.8%, to mark their solidarity with the older generations. In passing, once again no account is taken of the salaries between 100,000 euros and 200,000 euros, which usually correspond to very long life expectancies and which benefit greatly from the contributions paid by the lower-waged workers with shorter life expectancies. In any event, this contribution of 2.8% to solidarity by those earning over 120,000 euros is much too low, particularly given the levels of remuneration; their very legitimacy is open to challenge.

More generally, it is perhaps time to abandon the old idea according to which reduction of inequalities should be left to income tax, while the retirement schemes should content themselves with reproducing them. In a world in which fabulous salaries and questions of retirement and dependency have taken on a new importance, the most transparent norms of justice could be that all levels of salary (including the highest) should finance the retirement scheme at the same rates (even if the pensions themselves are capped) while leaving to income tax the task of applying higher rates to the top incomes.

To be clear: The present government has a big problem with the very concept of social justice. As everyone knows, it has chosen from the outset to grant huge fiscal gifts to the richest (suppression of the wealth tax; the flat tax on dividends and incomes). If today it does not demand a significant effort from the most privileged, it will have considerable difficulty in convincing the public that its pension reform is well founded.

Toward a Circular Economy

October 15, 2019

T he idea of the circular economy frequently brings to mind issues of recycling waste and materials and making moderate use of natural resources. But if a new system is to emerge which is sustainable and equitable, the whole economic model will have to be re-thought. With the differences in wealth which exist at the moment, no ecological ambition is possible. Energy saving can only come from economic and social restraint and not from excessive fortunes and lifestyles. We will have to construct new norms of social, educational, fiscal, and climate justice through democratic discussion. These norms will have to say "no" to the present hyper-concentration of economic power. On the contrary, the economy of the twenty-first century must be based on the permanent circulation of power, wealth, and knowledge.

It is the spread of property ownership and education which enabled social and human progress to become a reality in the twentieth century. A powerful movement of reduction in social inequality and increased mobility (the first intellectual signs of which were already visible in the eighteenth and nineteenth centuries) gained momentum from 1900–1910 and into the years 1970–1980, thanks to an unprecedented level of

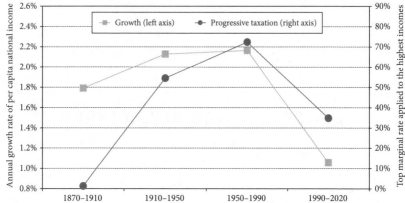

Figure 30. Growth and progression taxation in the United States, 1870–2020. The U.S. growth rate of per capita national income dropped from 2.2% per year between 1950 and 1990 to 1.1% between 1990 and 2020, while the top marginal tax rate applied to the highest incomes dropped from 72% to 35% over the same period. *Sources and series:* see piketty.pse.ens.fr/ideology.

investment in education. A new equilibrium was established with the rights of shareholders being matched by those of the wage earners (particularly in Northern Europe)—the circulation of incomes and wealth was accompanied by progressive taxation (in particular in the United States), and so on.

This movement was interrupted in the decade 1980–1990 following the change in direction in the wake of the postcommunist disillusion and lapse into the Reagan approach. Postcommunism then became hypercapitalism's best ally. Natural resources were overexploited and privatized to the advantage of a minority, legal systems were systematically circumvented via fiscal paradises, and any form of progressive taxation was completely eliminated. In Putin's Russia, income tax is 13% whether your income is 1,000 roubles or 1 billion roubles. The same excesses can be seen in China, where individuals close to those in power have carved out empires for themselves which they transmit to their heirs with no inheritance tax. Hong Kong is thus an astonishing example of a country which has become even more unequal by submitting to the authority of a supposedly communist regime.

The Reagan approach in the 1980s was less radical: It lowered the rate of taxation applied to the wealthiest from 70% to 30%. Reagan intended to put an end to what he exposed as excessive redistribution and egalitarianism resulting from the New Deal and which, in his opinion, had weakened America's entrepreneurial spirit and anticommunist crusade. By liberating the energies of the entrepreneur, Reagan promised a new phase of unprecedented growth. Of course, the inequalities were going to increase, the number of millionaires would rise, and they would be wealthier, but all that would provide a degree of innovation which would benefit the masses, meaning that everyone would gain thereby. In fact, the hold of billionaires over the American economy has grown considerably since the 1980s, with a concentration of property approaching the levels witnessed in Europe at the beginning of the twentieth century.

The problem is that the dynamic increase in growth has not taken place: The national per capita income has witnessed its progression divided by 2 (2.2% per year between 1980 and 1990; 1.1% between 1990 and 2020). Salaries have stagnated, and a growing percentage of the population is beginning to doubt the benefits of globalization. The hardening of Trump's nationalism is directly linked to this failure in Reaganism: Since economic liberalism is not enough, the Mexicans and the Chinese are now accused of stealing the hard labor of white America.

In reality, the failure of Reaganism mainly demonstrates that the hyperconcentration of property and power does not correspond to the requirements of a modern and circular economy. It is not because a person has made a fortune at the age of 30 that they should continue to concentrate power as a shareholder at the age of 50, 70, or 90 years. The decrease in growth is also explained by a worrying stagnation in educational investment since the 1990s as well as by the immense inequalities in access to education and training in both the United States and Europe.

The challenge of global warming and the international awareness of the growing inequalities do act as leverage for change, but we are still far from the goal. The Organisation for Economic Co-operation and Development (OECD) projects for the taxation of the profits of multinationals only concerns a small fraction of the latter, and the scale of the contribution proposed is much more favorable to the rich countries than to the poor ones.[1] *The Triumph of Injustice,* a book published in the United States by Emmanuel Saez and Gabriel Zucman, demonstrates that there are more ambitious solutions with the key element being financial transparency and the return to fiscal progressivity in order to finance health and education for all, and the ecological transition.[2] The success of these ideas among the American Democrats (in particular, Warren and Sanders) does allow for optimism.

1. As is demonstrated by the work of the Independent Commission for the Reform of International Corporate Taxation. See "ICRICT Response to the OECD Consultation on the Review of Country-by-Country Reporting (BEPS Action 13)," March 9, 2020, https://www.icrict.com/press -release/2020/3/9/icrict-response-to-the-oecd-consultation-on-the-review -of-country-by-country-reporting-beps-action-13.

2. Emmanuel Saez and Gabriel Zucman, *The Triumph of Injustice: How the Rich Dodge Taxes and How to Make Them Pay* (New York: W. W. Norton, 2019).

But Europe cannot simply stand by and wait for change to come from the United States. If we are to go beyond merely taking a stance and finally give substance to the Green New Deal, it is urgent that strong measures for social and fiscal justice be taken in Europe. This may also be the price to pay for the hope of bringing the British Labour Party back into the European orbit and avoiding a disastrous Conservative victory in the forthcoming elections. Thirty years after the fall of the Berlin Wall, it is time for the march toward equality, the circular economy, and participatory socialism to get back on track.

Surpassing Identity Conflict via Economic Justice

November 12, 2019

Europeans have long observed from a distance the mix of social and racial conflicts which structure political and electoral cleavages in the United States. Given the growing, and potentially destructive, importance taken by these identity conflicts in France and in Europe, they might do well to consider the lessons to be learned from foreign experiences.

Let's take a step backward. After having been the party of slavery during the American Civil War from 1861 to 1865, in the 1930s, the Democratic Party gradually became the party of Roosevelt and the New Deal. As far back as the 1870s, the Democratic Party had begun to reconstruct itself on the basis of an ideology which could be described as social-differentialist: it was violently inegalitarian and segregationist toward Black Americans, but more egalitarian than the Republicans toward the white population (in particular, the new immigrants from Italy and Ireland). The Democrats supported the creation of the federal income tax in 1913 and the development of social insurance after the crisis of 1929. It was not until the 1960s, under the pressure from Black militants, and in a transformed geopolitical context (Cold War, decolo-nization), that the Democratic Party was to turn its back on its segregationist past and to support the cause of civil rights and racial equality.

From this point on, it was the Republicans who were to gradually get the racist vote, or more precisely, the vote of those in the white population who considered that the main concern of the federal government and the educated white elites was to ensure that the minorities were given preference. The pro-cess began with Nixon in 1968 and Reagan in 1980; it then gained momentum under Trump in 2016, who hardened the identity and nationalist discourse in the wake of the economic failure of Reaganomics and its promises of prosperity. Given the open hostility of the Republicans (the stigmatization by Reagan of the "welfare queen," this "queen of social welfare," presumed to personify the laziness of unmarried Black mothers, until the support by Trump for the white suprema-cists during the riots in Charlottesville, Virginia), it is not sur-prising to learn that the vote of the Black electorate has been a consistent 90% for the Democrats since the 1960s.

This type of division on the basis of ethnic origin is in the process of being established in Europe. The hostility of the right in matters of extra-European immigration has led vot-ers who originate from these parts of the world to take refuge in the only parties who do not openly reject them (therefore, on the left), which in return leads to right-wing accusations of favoritism toward them on the part of the left. For example, during the second round of the presidential election in 2012, 77% of voters who stated they had at least one grandparent of extra-European origin (or 9% of the electorate) voted for the socialist candidate, compared with 49% for the voters of Eu-ropean origin (19% of the electorate) and for those with no stated foreign origin (72% of the electorate).

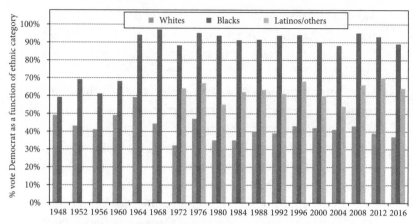

Figure 31. Political conflict and ethnic identity: United States, 1948–2016. In 2016, the Democratic candidate obtained 37% of the vote among white voters (70% of the electorate), 89% of the vote among Black voters (11% of the electorate), and 64% of the vote among Latinos and other non-whites (19% of the electorate, including 16% for Latinos). In 1972, the Democratic candidate obtained 32% of the vote among whites (89% of the electorate), 82% among Blacks (10% of the electorate), and 64% among Latinos and other categories (1% of the electorate). *Sources and series:* see piketty.pse.ens.fr/ideology.

In comparison, in the United States, the European "minorities" are characterized by a much higher percentage of mixed marriages (30% among first-generation North African immigrants, compared with little more than 10% for Black Americans), which should alleviate the divisions. Unfortunately the religious dimension and the question of Islam (almost totally absent in the United States) contribute on the contrary to hardening the situation.

From this point of view, the European situation is closer to that of India, where the Hindu nationalists in the BJP built their ideology on the rejection of the Muslim minority. In

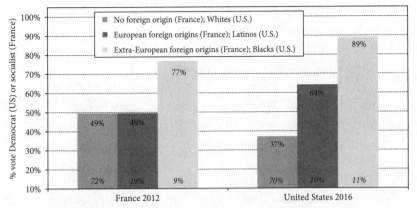

Figure 32. Political conflict and origins: France and the United States. In 2012, the socialist candidate in the second round of the French presidential election obtained 49% of the vote among voters with no foreign origin (no reported foreign grandparent) and among voters with European foreign origins (in practice mostly Spain, Italy, and Portugal) and 77% of the vote among voters with extra-European foreign origins (in practice mostly North Africa and sub-Saharan Africa). In 2016, the Democratic candidate in the U.S. presidential election obtained 37% of the vote among white voters, 64% among Latinos and other minority voters, and 89% among Black voters. *Sources and series:* see piketty.pse.ens.fr/ideology.

India the confrontation of identities concerns the consumption of beef and the vegetarian diet. In France, it focuses on the question of the headscarf and sometimes on the length of skirts and the wearing of leggings on the beach. In both cases, we witness a similar anti-Muslim obsession in the ranks of the supporters of Hinduism and the supporters of extremist secularism and the National Front. This also takes the form of an extremely violent discourse which extends to all those who defend the rights of minorities (who are almost accused of being pro-jihadi). In both cases, the latter sometimes run the risk of exacerbating the conflict, for example, by defending the legitimate right to wear a headscarf with more determination than the right not to do so, and not to be subjected to this somewhat retrograde form of pressure.

How can we escape this escalation of conflict? First, the discussion should be set in the context of economic justice and the fight against inequality and discrimination. Countless studies have demonstrated that for one and the same diploma, those whose names have an Arab-Muslim consonance are often not invited to a job interview. It is urgent to set up indicators and sanctions enabling us to monitor the development of these discriminatory practices and get them to resolve.

More generally speaking, it is the absence of any economic discussion which feeds identity-based no-win conflicts. Once we abandon any discussion of an alternative economic policy and we continue to explain that the state no longer controls anything, apart from its frontiers, there is no reason to be surprised that the political discussion focuses on questions of frontiers and identities.

It is time for all those who refuse to acquiesce to the clash forecast between identitarian nationalism and elitist globalism to get together and rally around a program for economic transformation. This involves educational justice, going beyond capitalist ownership, and an actual and ambitious project for the renegotiation of the European treaties. If we do not succeed in going beyond these petty squabbles and old hatreds, then hatred reminiscent of fascism may well win the day.

Several Universal Retirement Schemes Are Possible

December 10, 2019

Could we possibly have a reasoned debate about the several alternative retirement schemes? To judge from the government's attitude, one might well doubt it. The current government is endeavoring to restrict the discussion to the following schema: Either you support my project (which remains extremely vague) or you are an old-time defender of the privileges of the past and refuse any change.

The problem with this binary approach is that in reality, there are many ways of constructing a universal retirement scheme, depending on whether the focus is on social justice and the reduction of inequalities, ranging from the "common pension system" (maison commune des régimes de retraite) long defended by the CGT (General Confederation of Labour) to the project presented in the Delevoye Report. In 2008, Antoine Bozio and I published a short book outlining possible paths for unification of the schemes.[1] This publication had a

---

1. Antoine Bozio and Thomas Piketty, *For a New Pensions System* (Paris: CEPREMAP Booklets, 2008).

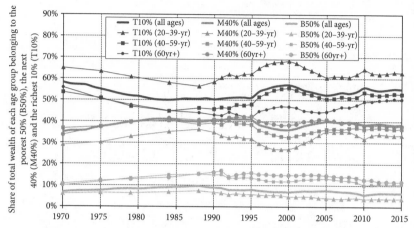

Figure 33. Inequality of property as a function of age: France. In 2015, among twenty- to thirty-nine-year-old individuals, the share of total wealth owned by the poorest 50% (B50%) was equal to 4%, vs. 34% for the next 40% (M40%) and 62% for the richest 10% (T10%). Among 60-year-old-and-older individuals, these shares were 10%, 38%, and 50%, respectively. The concentration of property is very high at all ages. *Sources and series:* see piketty.pse .ens.fr/ideology.

number of limitations, and the discussions which ensued enabled me to clarify several basic points.

In particular, this book referred to several possible solutions in order to take into consideration the social inequality of life expectancy: either directly on the basis of the length of life observed by profession (for example, to correct the fact that a specific category of worker spent on average ten years in retirement, compared with twenty years for a specific category of executive); or in indirect or approximate fashion by structurally increasing the rates of contribution applied to the highest salaries (which on average benefit from longer retirements) by raising the level of pensions open to the lowest salaries (which on average have shorter retirements).

The book merely listed these solutions, without clearly taking a position, with the risk that the question would be eluded, which is the case in the project of the present government.

On reflection, the direct method seems to me to be impracticable. It is better to clearly assume the indirect method, by introducing into the calculation of pensions more favorable treatment for low and medium salaries as compared with high salaries to correct the differences in life expectancy. This is not a perfect solution to a complex problem (these differences are determined by many other factors besides the level of salary, whence the need to also take into consideration the difficulty of certain professions), but it is nevertheless more satisfactory than the traditional solution, which consists of stating that the problem is enormous and complex, then doing nothing substantial to deal with it.

More generally, beyond the question of life expectancy, the old idea according to which the retirement system is only there to perpetuate into advanced old age the inequalities of working life does seem to me today to be outdated. Given the increasing inequality in the labor market (piece work for some, super-salaries for others), and the new human and social challenges posed by the high dependency of an aging population, it is time to take a more redistributive view of pension schemes. In material terms, we have to do our utmost to guarantee and to improve the lowest pensions (between one and three times the minimum wage), even if it means requesting a bigger effort from very high salaries and the very wealthy.

It is, after all, the absence of ambition in terms of social justice which poses a problem in the government's project, as is the case elsewhere in all of its actions. An attempt is being made to get low wage earners in the public sector to oppose low wage earners in the private sector when in both cases, their incomes are modest compared with those who have benefited from the fiscal generosity from the start of the government (abolition of the wealth tax, flat tax). Now, it is time to imagine a universal scheme which would be much more just in social terms, which would be in line with the ideas of the CGT on the "common pension system."

For example, the Delevoye project envisages a pension equal to 85% of the minimum wage (the SMIC) for a complete career (forty-three years of contributions) at this level. Then the replacement rate falls suddenly to only 70% at the level of 1.5 times the minimum wage, before stabilizing at this precise level of 70% until 7 times the minimum wage (120,000 euros gross annual salary). This is one possible choice, but there are others. One could imagine that the replacement rate falls from 85% at the level of the minimum wage to 80% at 2 times the minimum wage, 75% at 3 times the minimum wage, before gradually declining toward 50% at around 7 times the minimum wage. One could also choose to close the gaps in standard of living even further at retirement.

In any event, it is essential that the new universal scheme operates on "defined benefits," that is to say, with retirement benefits defined in advance in terms of the replacement rate applicable to the different levels of salaries, and not on a system of points. The latter can lead to concealing major cuts in the future, as witness the freezing of points in the civil service for the past ten years. The system of accounts in euros which we had imagined in our book in 2008 to get away from the approach in terms of points is, in the end, less transparent and more anxiety-provoking that that of defined benefits.

Finally, the financing of universal retirement pensions must be based on solidarity and involve the participation of everyone and, in particular, the wealthiest. It must at least be made clear that a contribution rate of 28% applies to all wage earners, including the highest, instead of falling to 2.8% on the salary bracket above 120,000 euros, as stated in the Delevoye Report. One could also imagine a progressive scale with a greater engagement from the highest incomes and the wealthiest, particularly as the inequalities in wealth are high in our society, both among the oldest and the wage earners. Several retirement schemes are possible: It is time to seize the opportunity for public discussion.

After the Climate Denial, the Inequality Denial

January 14, 2020

I n the wake of the denial of global warming, now on the wane, at least superficially, are we at present witnessing the denial of the rise in inequality?

This is obvious in the case of the French government, where all the efforts undertaken since 2017 appear to be guided by the idea that the country is suffering from a surfeit of equality. Hence the tax rewards for the wealthiest when the government came into office; hence similarly its inability to understand the demand for justice expressed in the social movement at the moment. In real terms, a universal retirement pension scheme is possible, but only on condition that everything is done to improve the small and medium pensions, even if this involves increased efforts on the part of the highest salaries and the wealthiest. Those who are at the top of the scale must understand that aging and the end of life mean new challenges in terms of dignity and equality.

More generally speaking, while the demand for justice is expressed in numerous protest mobilizations all over the world, in the media associated with business circles, we witness an attempt to relativize the rise in inequality over recent decades.

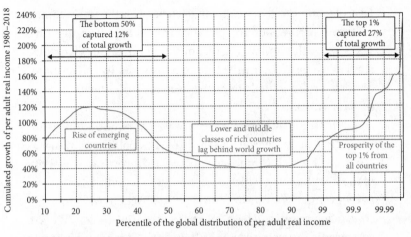

Figure 34. The elephant curve of global inequality, 1980–2018. The bottom 50% incomes of the world saw substantial growth in purchasing power between 1980 and 2018 (between +60% and +120%). The top 1% incomes saw even stronger growth (between +80% and +240%). Intermediate categories grew less. In sum, inequality decreased between the bottom and the middle of the global income distribution and increased between the middle and the top. *Sources and series:* see piketty.pse.ens.fr/ideology.

True, nobody expects the weekly publication, *The Economist,* to be in the lead in a campaign for equality. But this is no reason to manipulate the facts, once they have been established.

It is all the more regrettable, because the governments of the rich countries have not made any genuine attempt to promote transparency concerning the distribution of wealth since the crisis in 2008. Given all the declarations on tax havens, the automatic transmission of banking data, and so forth, one would have expected that financial opacity would have decreased. In theory, all countries should now be equipped to collect and publish banking and fiscal data, enabling them to follow the development of the distribution of wealth according to the level of income and of wealth, in particular for the top incomes. With the suppression in several countries of progressive-type taxes on wealth and on the income from capital, in several instances (in particular in France, but also equally in Germany, Sweden, or the United States), we even see a decline in the public data available.

Too frequently, researchers, as well as public administrations, find themselves using the rankings published in magazines, data which do indeed indicate the growing prosperity of the wealthiest but which do not fulfill the conditions of transparency and rigor one has the right to expect to inform a reasoned democratic debate on these essential issues. We are supposedly living in the age of "big data." This is undoubtedly true for the major private monopolies which have the right to unashamedly gain access to our personal data. But as far as public statistics on the distribution of wealth and its necessary redistribution are concerned, in reality we live in an age of considerable opacity which is perpetuated by all those who oppose the reduction of inequalities.

Furthermore we too often forget that we will not be able to resolve environmental challenges unless we make the reduction of inequality central to political action. We must undoubtedly fundamentally rethink the indicators enabling us to measure economic and social progress. To begin with, it is urgent for governments and the media to stop using the concept of "gross domestic product" (GDP) and concentrate on that of "national income." Let me remind you of the two main differences: national income is equal to GDP minus the incomes which go to foreign countries (or increased by the income entering from foreign countries, depending on the situation of the country), and minus the consumption of capital (which should, in principle, include the consumption of natural capital in all its forms).

To illustrate, let's take a simple example. If 100 billion euros of hydrocarbons are extracted from the ground (or of fish from the seas), then we have an additional 100 billion euros of GDP. But as the stock of hydrocarbons (or of fish) has decreased by an equal amount, then national income has not increased by one iota. If, furthermore, the fact of burning the hydrocarbons contributes to making the air unbreathable and the planet uninhabitable, then the national income produced in this manner is in reality negative, provided that the social cost of the carbon emissions have been taken into account correctly.

Using national income and national wealth rather than GDP and focusing on distribution and not on averages is not enough to solve all the problems—far from it. It is equally urgent to multiply the indicators specific to climate and the environment (for example, the volume of emissions, the quality of the air, or the diversity of the species). But it would be a mistake to imagine that one could conduct the forthcoming debates with these indicators alone, dispensing with any reference to income or wealth. To develop new standards of justice acceptable by the greatest number, it is essential to be able to measure the efforts demanded of various social groups. This requires the ability to compare levels of wealth within a given country as well as between countries and over the course of time. We will not save the environment by consigning all concepts of income or growth to the dustbin.

On the contrary, if ecological parties neglect social issues, they may well, on the contrary, find themselves confined to a privileged electorate and thus enable the maintenance in power of conservatives and nationalists. The challenges of climate change and the rise in inequalities can only be resolved simultaneously. All the more reason, I believe, to combat this dual denial by tackling them with a single voice.

Social-Federalism vs. National-Liberalism

February 11, 2020

The United Kingdom officially left the European Union a few days ago. So now, make no mistake; along with the election of Trump in the United States in 2016, this is a major upheaval in the history of globalization. The two countries which had the choice of ultra-liberalism with Reagan and Thatcher in the 1980s and which, since then, have witnessed the highest rise in inequalities, have decided three decades later to opt for nationalism and a form of return to frontiers and national identity.

This change in direction can be viewed from different angles. In its way, it expresses the failure of Reaganism and Thatcherism. The British and American middle and working classes have not experienced the affluence promised by absolute liberalism, laissez-faire policies, and economic deregulation. Over time they have felt themselves increasingly under pressure from international competition and the world economic system. Culprits had to be found. For Trump, it was the workers from Mexico, China, and all those cunning people in the rest of the world who are reputed to have stolen the hard work of white America. For the Brexiters, it was the Polish

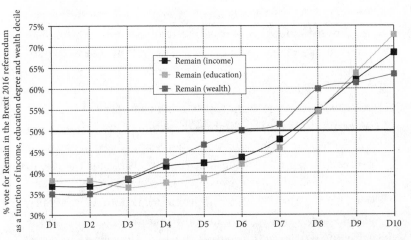

Figure 35. The European cleavage in Britain: the Brexit referendum in 2016. In the 2016 referendum over Brexit (victory of Leave with 52%), one observes a very strong social cleavage of the vote: the top deciles of income, education, and wealth vote strongly for Remain, while bottom deciles vote for Leave. *Note:* D1 refers to the bottom 10% (either for income, education, or wealth), D2 to the next 10%, etc., and D10 to the top 10%. *Sources and series:* see piketty.pse.ens .fr/ideology.

workers, the European Union, and all those who attack the grandeur of Great Britain. In the long run, withdrawing into nationalism and identity-based politics will in no way resolve any of the major challenges of our times which are associated with inequality and global warming. This is all the more true as the Trumpists and the Brexiters have added a new layer of fiscal and social dumping in favor of the wealthiest and the most mobile, which will only increase the inequalities and frustrations. But in the immediate future, the nationalist-liberal discourse often appears to those voters who do still vote as being the only new and credible answer to their sense of unease, for lack of any convincing alternative discourse.

De facto, this risk of ideological drift extends far beyond the English-speaking world. The temptation of nationalism and xenophobia exists in many places, in Italy and in Eastern Europe, in Brazil and in India. In Germany, in Thuringia, the "right-wing center" party has just elected a regional government with support from the extreme right for the first time since World War II. In France, the Arabophobic hysteria has grown to epic proportions. An increasing share of the press seems to imagine that the "left" is responsible for the rise in Islamism worldwide as a result of its permissiveness, its support for the Third World, and its electoral politics. In reality, if voters of North African or sub-Saharan origin vote for the left-wing parties, it is primarily due to the violent hostility expressed toward them by right-wing and extreme-right parties; the same applies to Black voters in the United States or Muslims in India.

Over and above national specificities, Brexit must be analyzed in the first instance for what it is: the consequence of a collective failure in the way in which economic globalization has been organized since the 1980s, particularly in the European Union. All the European leaders in turn, in particular, the French and the Germans, bear their share of responsibility. The free circulation of capital, goods, and services with no collective regulation or joint fiscal or social policy functions primarily to the benefit of the richest and the most mobile, and undermines the most disadvantaged and the most vulnerable. It is not possible to define a political project and a model for development by relying simply on free trade, everyone competing with everyone else, and market discipline.

True, the European Union has added two elements to this general scheme of organization of the world economy: free circulation of persons and a small joint budget (1% of European GDP) maintained by contributions from states and financed

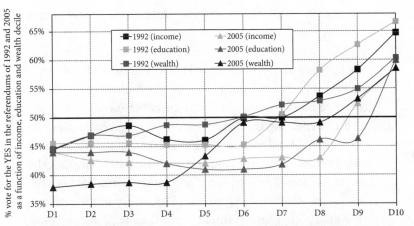

Figure 36. The European cleavage in France: the referenda of 1992 and 2005. In the 1992 referendum over the Maastricht treaty ("yes" won with 51%) as well as in the 2005 referendum on the European constitutional treaty ("yes" lost with 45%), one observes a very strong social cleavage: top deciles of income, educational degrees, and wealth vote strongly for "yes," while bottom deciles vote for "no." *Note:* D1 refers to the bottom 10% (for the distribution of income, education, or wealth), D2 to the next 10%, etc., and D10 the top 10%. *Sources and series:* see piketty.pse.ens.fr/ideology.

by small transfers from the richest countries (approximately 0.5% of their GDP) to the poorest ones. Along with the shared currency (which we also find in West Africa), this is what distinguishes the European Union from other free-trade areas in the world, for example, North America (Mexico, the United States, and Canada), where there is neither free circulation of persons nor a joint budget or joint regional structural funds.

The problem is that these two elements are not enough to bond these countries together. The Brexiters' gamble is simple: The present rate of globalization enables their access to free trade in goods, services, and capital, while at the same time, it allows them to maintain control over the flow of people and does not involve contributing to a joint budget.

This trap, which spells death to the European Union, can only be avoided by radically redefining the rules of globalization with a "social-federalist" type of approach. In other words, free trade must be conditional on the adoption of binding social aims, enabling the wealthiest and most mobile economic actors to be obliged to contribute to a model for sustainable and equitable development. To sum up: The nationalists attack the free circulation of people; social federalism must deal with the circulation of capital and the fiscal impunity of the wealthiest. Karl Polanyi and Hannah Arendt in 1944 and 1951 denounced the naiveté of the social democrats in the face of capital flows and their federal timidity—a lesson that still applies today. To go in this direction, a revision of the European and international treaties is required, beginning with a few countries. In the meantime, we can and must all take new unilateral and incentive measures, for example, by taxing imports from countries and firms which practice fiscal dumping. If we do not oppose national-liberalism with a resolute alternative, it will sweep aside everything in its path.

The Franco-German Assembly, a Unique Opportunity for Tax Justice in Europe

February 21, 2020

Written with Manon Bouju, Lucas Chancel, Anne-Laure Delatte, Stéphanie Hennette, Guillaume Sacriste, and Antoine Vauchez (initiators of the Manifesto for the Democratization of Europe).[1]

On February 5 and 6, 2020, the third meeting of the Franco-German Parliamentary Assembly (APFA) was held in the hemicycle of the European Parliament. This place was highly symbolic, because as Wolfgang Schaüble, the president of the Bundestag, pointed out, the new assembly, over and above its bilateral dimension, must act as an example for the European Union as a whole.

---

1. Manifesto for the Democratization of Europe, https://www.tdem.edu /en/manifesto.

This assembly, which has no equivalent, is composed of fifty French and fifty German elected parliamentarians; it was created to institutionalize the cooperation between the two most important states in the European Union by becoming the parliamentary equivalent of the Franco-German Council of Ministers, set up in the framework of the Elysée Treaty of January 22, 1963. Its purpose is to ensure the implementation of the 1963 treaty but also that of the Franco-German Cooperation Treaty signed in Aix-la-Chapelle by Emmanuel Macron and Angela Merkel on January 22, 2019. Article 1 of the latter states:

> The two states are deepening their cooperation on European policy . . . and are working to build a competitive European Union based on a strong industrial foundation, which serves as the basis for prosperity, promoting economic, fiscal and social convergence, as well as sustainability in all its dimensions.

We recognize here a rhetoric which is well established among the drafters of the European treaties: "competitive" first, followed by "economic, fiscal and social convergence and social [. . .] sustainability" are the order of the priorities in the European Union since the Maastricht Treaty. This is probably why the project that seems to have appealed spontaneously as the most important to this assembly has been the creation of a working group on "harmonizing French and German business and bankruptcy law" in order to "improve the competitiveness of their economies in the face of competition on a global scale." At the same time, the creation of working groups on social and fiscal harmonization between France and Germany, supported in particular by Fabio De Masi (Die Linke) and Danièle Obono (France Insoumise), unfortunately did not obtain a majority.

However, this draft European Business Code, already very advanced in truth among the experts and professors of specialized law and for which parliamentary value-added seems quite questionable, appears far from up to the task, given the enormous challenges facing the Union today. At a time when social inequalities and environmental emergencies shatter the last safeguards of Western democracies, the emphasis on this project is reminiscent of the business as usual of the single market of the 1990s and its main winners.

On the contrary, the creation of this Franco-German Assembly, a "genuine" "normative laboratory," should be an opportunity to attempt an outright reversal in the European Union's customary hierarchies. It has the legitimacy of the national parliamentary assemblies in our democracies on issues of tax and social law. These are the issues that should now be placed at the top of its to-do list in order to deal with the emergencies that confront us today and to respect to the letter the first article of the Treaty of Aix-la-Chapelle (Aachen). In fact, an assembly of this type could thus compensate for the original design fault in European construction by loosening the hold of the member states' unanimity on taxation. With different political majorities, it would then constitute a "utopia," as Richard Ferrand asserted, but in a different meaning from the one he invoked of "premature truth," quoting Lamartine (who said that "utopias are often just premature truths"). Instead it would be a "genuine utopia," as invoked by Erik Olin Wright, that is, an institution or practices that can be built here and now, foreshadowing an ideal world, and thus can help us move beyond the current stage of the European Union.

This Assembly, which is historically unprecedented, has the legitimacy to propose, for example, a Franco-German alignment with respect to direct taxation on corporations, which would complement the European Business Code. This has been the dream of the European Union since the 1960s! With this Franco-German alignment of taxation on companies, the issue becomes one of breaking the vicious circle of tax and social dumping which has plagued the European Union since the mid-1980s and would "work toward *ascendant* social and economic convergence within the European Union," as advocated by the preamble to the Treaty of Aix-la-Chapelle. This is one of the keys to combating the fiscal and social inequalities that disrupt the cohesion of our European societies by colliding with their underlying moral economies and fueling populist and authoritarian protests.

Similarly, an assembly working group should be set up to consider the introduction of a tax on very large fortunes, at the very moment when this debate is raging in Germany; the Social Democratic Party (SPD) has publicly supported it (including Finance Minister Olaf Scholz), as well as the OECD, and in a recent *Die Welt* poll, 58% of Germans expressed support for it. This Franco-German assembly would reverse the ripple effect that has been created in the frantic and unambiguous pursuit of the lowest standards; and the critical mass of over 50% of the Euro area's GDP, constituted by the combined economies of the Franco-German engine, could impose these tax themes at the very heart of European policy, which would encourage other European partners to join the virtuous circle of a more advantageous and equitable tax system.

The revenues thus generated could help finance, as we demonstrate in our Manifesto for the Democratization of Europe, a number of joint European PROJECTS, financed by long-term investments, such as universities and research, conversion to new forms of energy, or all the Franco-German or European projects that the assembly would identify and which

seem to be once again on the agenda of the German government at the end of a cycle of austerity. As the European Union
prepares once again to convene a conference for the future of
Europe, the assembly could offer the path to political renewal . . . if it decided to share the social and fiscal crises in
the societies which its members represent and not reiterate the
usual old complaints about Europe. Then, in the words of
Wolfgang Schaüble during the signing of the parliamentary
agreement, it would be our turn to encourage the 100 German
and French parliamentarians who are the pioneers of this un-
usual assembly—who on this side of the Rhine are so scorned
and despised—to accept the challenge!

Sanders to the Aid of Democracy in the United States

March 10, 2020

L et it be said at once: The treatment received by Bernie Sanders in the leading media in the United States and in Europe is unjust and dangerous. Everywhere on the main networks and in the major daily papers we read that Sanders is an "extremist" and that only a "centrist" candidate like Biden could triumph over Trump. This biased and somewhat unscrupulous treatment is particularly regrettable when a closer examination of the facts actually suggests that only a full-scale reorientation of the type proposed by Sanders would eventually rid American democracy of the inegalitarian practices which undermine it and would deal with the electoral disaffection of the working classes.

Let's begin with the program. To say emphatically, as Sanders does, that a public, universal health insurance would enable the American population to be cared for more efficiently and more cheaply than the present private and extremely unequal system is not an "extremist" statement. It is on the contrary a declaration perfectly well documented by many research studies and international comparisons. In these difficult times when everyone deplores the rise of "fake news," it is right and

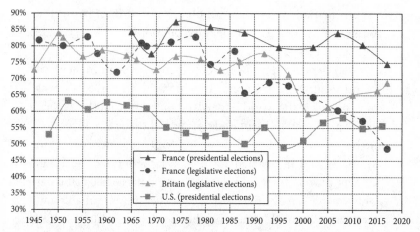

Figure 37. Evolution of voter turnout, 1945–2020. Voter turnout has been relatively stable at around 80–85% in French presidential elections since 1965 (with, however, a small fall to 75% in 2017). The fall has been much stronger in legislative elections, which was around 80% until the 1970s and less than 50% in 2017. Electoral participation dropped in Britain before rising again since 2010. In the United States, it has generally fluctuated around 50–60%. *Sources and series:* see piketty.pse.ens.fr/ideology.

proper for some candidates to rely on established facts and not resort to obscure language and complex tactics.

Similarly, Sanders is right when he proposes large-scale public investment in favor of education and public universities. Historically the prosperity of the United States has relied in the twentieth century on the educational advance of the country over Europe and on a degree of equality in this field, and definitely not on the sacralization of inequality and the unlimited accumulation of fortunes which Reagan wished to impose as an alternative model in the 1980s. The failure of this Reagan-style rupture is evident today with the growth of national income per capita being halved and an unprecedented rise in inequality. Sanders simply proposed a return to the sources of the country's model for development: a very wide diffusion of education.

Sanders also proposes a considerable rise in the level of the minimum wage (a policy in which the United States was for a long time the world leader) and to learn from the experiences in co-management and voting rights for employees on the boards of directors of firms implemented successfully in Germany and in Sweden for decades. Generally speaking, Sanders' proposals show him to be a pragmatic social-democrat endeavoring to make the most of the experiences available and in no way a "radical." And when he chooses to go further than European social democracy, for example, with his proposal for a federal wealth tax rising to 8% per year on multi-billionaires, this corresponds to the reality of the excessive concentration of wealth in the United States and the fiscal and administrative capacities of the American federal state, which has already been demonstrated historically.

Now, let's deal with the question of opinion polls. The problem of the repeated assertions that Biden would be better placed to beat Trump is that they have no objective factual basis. If we examine the existing data, such as those compiled by RealClearPolitics.com, it is clear in all the national opinion polls that Sanders would beat Trump with the same differential as Biden. These polls are of course premature, but they are just as much for Biden as for Sanders. In several key states, we find that Sanders would come out ahead of Trump, for example, in Pennsylvania and Wisconsin.

If we analyze the surveys on the primaries which have just taken place, it appears clearly that Sanders mobilizes the working-class electorate more than Biden does. It is true that the latter attracts a considerable share of the Black vote, an inheritance of the Obama-Biden ticket. But Sanders mobilizes

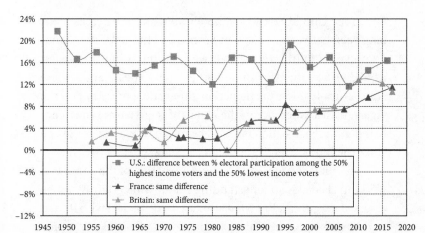

Figure 38. Voter turnout and social cleavages, 1945–2020. During the 1950–1980 period, electoral participation in France and Britain was at most 2–3% higher among the 50% highest-income voters than among the 50% lowest-income voters. This gap has grown significantly since the 1980s and reached 10%–12% in the 2010s, thereby approaching the levels historically observed in the United States. *Sources and series:* see piketty.pse.ens.fr/ideology.

the vast majority of the Latino vote and crushes Biden among the eighteen- to twenty-nine-year-old age group, as he does in the thirty- to forty-four-year-old group. Above all, all the polls indicate that Sanders has the best scores among the underprivileged (annual incomes below $50,000, no higher education qualification), whereas Biden, on the contrary, has the best scores among the most privileged (annual incomes above $100,000, higher education diploma), regardless of whether they are white voters or those from minority backgrounds, independent of age.

Now it so happens that the highest potential for mobilization is among the most underprivileged social categories. Generally speaking, voter turnout has always been relatively low in the United States: just barely above 50%, whereas it has long been between 70–80% in France and in the United Kingdom, before falling recently. If we examine things in greater detail, we also find that on the other side of the Atlantic, there is structurally lower participation among the poorer half of the voters, with a difference in the region of 15–20% from the richer half (a difference which has also begun to be visible in Europe since the 1990s, even if it remains less marked).

To put it clearly: This electoral alienation of the American working classes is so longstanding that it will certainly not be reversed in one day. But what else can we do to deal with it than to undertake a far-reaching reorientation of the election program of the Democratic Party and to discuss these ideas openly in national campaigns? The cynical, and unfortunately very commonplace, view among the Democratic elites, that nothing can be done to mobilize further the working-class vote, is extremely dangerous. In the last resort, this cynicism weakens the legitimacy of the democratic electoral system itself.

Avoiding the Worst
April 14, 2020

Will the Covid-19 crisis precipitate the end of the financial and liberal globalization of markets and the emergence of a new model of development which would be more equitable and more sustainable? It is possible, but nothing is guaranteed. At this stage, the most urgent concern is primarily to grasp the extent of the current crisis and to do everything possible to avoid the worst, which is a full-scale hecatomb.

Let me remind you of the forecasts in the epidemiological models. Without intervention, Covid-19 could have caused the death of some 40 million people in the world, of which 400,000 would be in France, or approximately 0.6% of the population (there are over 7 billion people in the world, of which almost 70 million are in France). This corresponds to almost one additional year of deaths (550,000 deaths per year in France, 55 million in the world). In practice, this means that for the most-affected regions and during the darkest months, the number of coffins needed could have been five or ten times more than usual (which we have unfortunately begun to observe in some of the Italian clusters).

However uncertain these estimates may be, these are the forecasts which have convinced governments that it was not

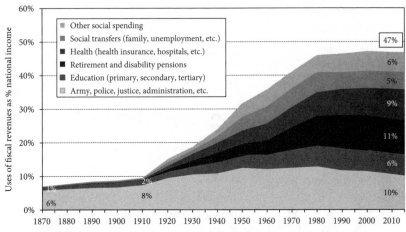

Figure 39. The rise of the social state in Europe, 1870–2015. In 2015, fiscal revenues represented 47% of national income on average in Western Europe and were used as follows: 10% of national income for regalian expenditure (army, police, justice, general administration, basic infrastructure: roads, etc.); 6% for education; 11% for pensions; 9% for health; 5% for social transfers (other than pensions); 6% for other social spending (housing, etc.). Before 1914, regalian expenditure absorbed almost all fiscal revenues. *Note:* The evolution depicted here is the average of Germany, France, Britain, and Sweden. *Sources and series:* see piketty.pse.ens.fr/ideology.

a question of a simple case of flu and that it was essential to confine populations as a matter of urgency. True, nobody really knows exactly how high the losses in human life will rise to (at the moment, almost 100,000 deaths in the world, of which almost 20,000 in Italy, 15,000 in Spain and the United States, and 13,000 in France), nor how high they might have risen without confinement. The epidemiologists hope that they will succeed in reducing the final figure by a factor of 10 or a factor of 20 in comparison with the initial forecasts, but there is still considerable uncertainty. According to the report published by Imperial College (London) on March 26, 2020,[1] only a policy of mass testing and isolation of those infected would enable a strong reduction in these losses. In other words, confinement will not suffice to avoid the worst.

The only historical precedent to which we can refer is that of the Spanish flu in 1918–1920.[2] We now know that there was nothing "Spanish" about it, and that it caused some 50 million deaths in the world (almost 2% of the world population at the time).[3] On the basis of civil registration data, researchers have shown that this average mortality concealed huge social disparities: between 0.5% and 1% in the United States and in Europe, compared with 3% in Indonesia and in South Africa and over 5% in India.

This is what we should be concerned about: The epidemic could rise to record numbers in poor countries where the health systems are not able to cope with the shock, particularly as they have been subjected to austerity policies imposed by the prevailing ideology in recent decades. Confinement implemented in fragile ecosystems may moreover prove to be

1. Summary of March 26, 2020, Imperial College Report, https://www .imperial.ac.uk/mrc-global-infectious-disease-analysis/covid-19/report-12 -global-impact-covid-19/.

2. On mortality during the Spanish flu of 1918–1920, see Christopher Murray, Alan D. Lopez, Brian Chin, Dennis Feehan, and Kenneth H. Hill, "Estimation of Potential Global Pandemic Influenza Mortality on the Basis of Vital Registry Data from the 1918–20 Pandemic: A Quantitative Analysis," *The Lancet* 368, no. 9554 (2007): 2211–2218.

3. See Robert J. Barro, José F. Ursúa, and Joanna Weng, "The Coronavirus and the Great Influenza Pandemic: Lessons from the 'Spanish Flu' for the Coronavirus's Potential Effects on Mortality and Economic Activity," National Bureau of Economic Research, March 2020, Working Paper 26866, https://www.nber.org/papers/w26866.pdf.

totally inappropriate. In the absence of a minimum income scheme, the poorest will rapidly have to go out to seek work, which will re-launch the epidemic. In India, confinement has primarily consisted of driving rural people and migrants out of towns, which has led to violence and mass displacement, at the risk of heightening the spread of the virus. To avoid the hecatomb, what is required is a social state, not a prison state. The right reaction to the crisis should be to revive the rise of the social state in the North, and most importantly to accelerate its development in the South.

In response to the emergency situation, the requisite social expenditure (health, minimum income) can only be financed by borrowing and money creation. In West Africa it is an opportunity to re-think the new common currency and use it to serve a development plan based on investment in young people and infrastructure (and not use it to serve the capital mobility of the richest). The whole structure should be supported by a more successful democratic and parliamentary structure than the opacity that is still the norm in the euro-zone (where ministers of finance continue to meet behind closed doors with the same inefficiency as they did at the time of the financial crisis).

In a short space of time, this new social state would demand a fair tax system and an international financial register to enable it to involve the richest and biggest firms as much as is necessary. The present regime of free circulation of capital, set up as from the years 1980–1990 under the influence of the richest countries (and especially of Europe) encourages evasion by the millionaires and multinationals from all over the world. It prevents the fragile fiscal administrations in the poor countries from developing a fair and legitimate tax system, which seriously undermines the construction of the state.

This crisis is also an opportunity to consider a minimal provision in public health and education for all the world's inhabitants financed by a universal right for all countries to a share of the tax revenues paid by the wealthiest economic actors in the world: major firms and households with high incomes and personal wealth (for example, ten times higher than the world average, or the 1% richest in the world). After all, this wealth is based on a world economic system (and incidentally on several centuries of ruthless exploitation of the human and natural resources of the planet). It therefore demands regulation at the world level to ensure its social and ecological sustainability, with in particular the implementation of a carbon card enabling the prohibition of the highest emissions.

It goes without saying that a transformation of this nature demands the reconsideration of a number of issues. For example, are Macron and Trump ready to cancel the fiscal gifts made to the wealthiest at the beginning of their mandates? The answer will depend on the mobilization of both the opposition and of their own supporters. We can rest assured of one thing: The major politico-ideological upheavals are only just beginning.

The Age of Green Money

May 12, 2020

C ould the Covid-19 crisis accelerate the adoption of a new, more equitable, and more sustainable development model? The answer is yes, but only under certain conditions. There must be a clear change in priorities, and a certain number of taboos in the monetary and fiscal sphere must be challenged. This sector must work to the benefit of the real economy and be used to serve social and ecological goals.

In the first instance, we must use this forced shutdown to restart on a different footing. After a recession of this type, the public authorities are going to have to play a pivotal role to restore growth and employment. But this has to be done by investing in new sectors (health, innovation, the environment) and by deciding on a gradual and lasting reduction in the most carbon-creating activities. In material terms, millions of jobs have to be created and salaries raised in hospitals, schools, and universities, thermal renovation of buildings, community services.

In the immediate future, this can only be financed by debt and with the active support of the central banks. Since 2008, central banks have created massive amounts of money

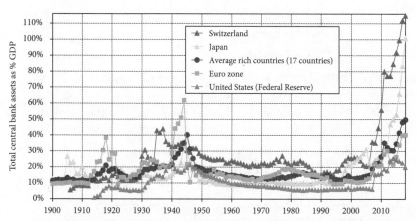

Figure 40. Central banks and financial globalization. Total assets of the central banks of rich countries rose from 13% of GDP on December 31, 2000, to 51% on December 31, 2018. The assets of the central banks of Japan and Switzerland exceeded 100% of GDP in 2017–2018. *Note:* The average of rich countries is the arithmetic average of the following seventeen countries: Australia, Belgium, Britain, Canada, Denmark, France, Finland, Germany, Holland, Italy, Japan, Norway, Portugal, Spain, Sweden, Switzerland, and the United States. *Sources and series:* see piketty.pse.ens.fr /ideology.

to save private banks from the financial crisis which they themselves had provoked. The Eurosystem balance sheet (the network of European central banks, guided by the ECB) rose from 1,150 billion euros at the beginning of 2007 to 4,675 billion euros at the end of 2018, that is, from barely 10% to almost 40% of the eurozone GDP (12,000 billion euros). This policy probably enabled the avoidance of the series of bankruptcies which led the world into the Great Depression in 1929. But this monetary creation, decided behind closed doors, and without an adequate democratic foundation, has also contributed to boosting the stock market and property prices, and to making the richest even richer, without resolving the structural problems of the real economy (lack of investment, rise in inequality, and environmental crisis).

Now there is a real risk that we will simply continue in the same direction. To address the Covid-19 crisis, the ECB launched a new asset-purchasing program. The Eurosystem's balance sheet shot up, rising from 4,692 billion euros on February 28 to 5,395 billion euros on May 1, 2020 (according to the data published by the ECB on May 5).[1] Despite the amount, this massive monetary injection (700 billion euros in two months) is not going to be sufficient: The spread in interest rates, which had fallen in mid-March following the ECB's announcements, rose again very rapidly, to the detriment of Italy.[2]

What should be done? In the first instance, we must realize that the eurozone will remain fragile as long as it chooses to continue to submit its nineteen interest rates to market speculation. Adopting the means to issue a joint debt with one and the same interest rate is a matter of urgency. Contrary to what one sometimes hears, the aim is primarily to mutualize the interest rate and not to force some countries to repay the debts of others. The countries that are considered to be the most advanced on this question (France, Italy, and Spain) must formulate a precise and operational proposal, and concomitantly, a parliamentary assembly must be created that enables

1. "Eurosystem Balance Sheet May 1st 2020: 5395 Billions," https://www .ecb.europa.eu/press/pr/wfs/2020/html/ecb.fst200505.en.html; "Eurosystem Balance Sheet February 28 2020: 4692 Billions," https://www.ecb.europa .eu/press/pr/wfs/2020/html/ecb.fst200303.en.html.

2. This is due both to the new asset purchasing program (PEPP, Pandemic Emergency Purchase Programme) and to the increased use of previous programs (especially PSPP, Public Sector Purchase Programme). https://www.ecb.europa.eu/mopo/implement/omt/html/index.en.html.

the democratic supervision of the system (along the lines of the Franco-German Assembly created last year but with real powers and open to all those countries that wish to join). Germany, which is being urged by its constitutional judges to clarify its relation with Europe, will probably choose to participate once a solid proposal is on the table and its main partners are ready to go forward. In any event, the urgency is such that we cannot sit back with folded arms waiting for a unanimous decision which will never come.

Then, and more importantly, we must make clear that the new money creation must be used to finance the relaunch of a green and social economy and not to boost the stock market. The Spanish government proposed the issue of between 1,000 and 1,500 billion euros of joint debt (approximately 10% of the eurozone GDP) and that this interest-free debt be included in the ECB balance sheet on a perpetual basis (or on a very long-term basis). In this connection, we should bear in mind that the German external debt was frozen in 1953 (and definitively waived in 1991) and that the remainder of the huge postwar public debt was extinguished by a special levy on the highest financial wealth holdings (which will also be necessary this time). The Spanish proposal must be supported, and repeated if necessary, for as long as inflation remains moderate. I would like to point out that the European treaties do not give any definition of the price stability objective (it is the ECB which fixed the target at 2%: it could equally well be 3% or 4%). These same treaties indicate that the ECB must work toward the implementation of the general aims of the European Union, which include full employment, social progress, and the protection of the environment (Article 3 of the Treaty on European Union).

What is certain is that it is impossible to raise amounts of this sort without resorting to loans. The people in Brussels who talk in terms of enormous numbers in relation to the Green Deal without proposing any financing do nothing for the reputation of politics. By definition, this means that they are recycling sums of money already earmarked for something else (for example, by taking back resources from the meager budget of the European Union, which is barely 150 billion euros per year, or 1% of the European GDP); perhaps they are counting the same expenditure several times, or else adding together public and private expenditure (with a leverage effect which would turn all the speculators on the planet green with envy), and in most instances, all at the same time. These practices must stop. Europe is in mortal danger if it does not demonstrate to these citizens that it is capable of mobilizing in the face of Covid, at least to the same extent as it did for the banks.

Confronting Racism, Repairing History

June 16, 2020

The wave of mobilization against racism and racial discrimination poses a crucial question: that of reparations for a past history involving slavery and colonization. This is an issue which has still not been fully confronted. No matter how complex the question may be, it cannot be eluded forever, either in the United States or in Europe.

In 1865, at the end of the American Civil War, the Republican, Abraham Lincoln, promised the freed slaves that after the victory, they would get "40 acres and a mule" (roughly sixteen hectares). The idea was both to compensate them for decades of ill treatment and unpaid labor and to enable them to look to the future as free workers. If this program had been adopted, it would have represented an agrarian reform of considerable dimensions at the expense, in particular, of the leading slave owners.

But as soon as the war was over, the promise was forgotten: No text for compensation was ever adopted, and the forty acres and a mule became the symbol of the deception and hypocrisy of the Northerners (so much so that the film director

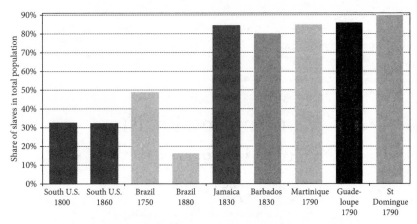

Figure 41. Atlantic slave societies, eighteenth and nineteenth centuries. Slaves made up about one-third of the population in the southern United States between 1800 and 1860. This proportion dropped from about 50% to less than 20% in Brazil from 1750 to 1850. It was higher than 80% in the slave islands of the British and French West Indies in 1780–1830 and exceeded 90% in Saint-Domingue (Haiti) in 1790. *Sources and series:* see piketty.pse.ens .fr/ideology.

Spike Lee ironically made it the name of his production company). The Democrats regained control of the South and imposed racial segregation and discrimination for over a century, until the 1960s. There again no compensation was ever applied.

Curiously, other historical episodes have nevertheless given rise to quite different treatment. In 1988, Congress adopted a law granting $20,000 to the Japanese-Americans interned during World War II. The compensation applied to those who were still alive in 1988 (approximately 80,000 persons of the 120,000 Japanese-Americans interned between 1942 and 1946); the cost amounted to $1.6 billion. Compensation along the same lines paid to the African-Americans who were victims of segregation would have a strong symbolic value.

In the United Kingdom, as in France, the abolition of slavery was accompanied on each occasion by compensation of the owners paid out of public funds. For the "liberal" intellectuals, like Tocqueville or Schoelcher, this was obvious: If these owners were deprived of their property (which after all had been acquired legally) without fair compensation, where would this dangerous situation end? As far as the former slaves were concerned, their apprenticeship of liberty involved extremely hard work. Their only compensation was the obligation to obtain a long-term work contract with a landowner, without which they were arrested for vagrancy. Other forms of forced labor were applied in the French colonies until 1950.

During the British abolition of slavery in 1833, the equivalent of 5% of the British national income (in present-day currency, 120 billion euros) was thus paid to some 4,000 slave owners, the average indemnity being 30 million euros, which was the origin of numerous fortunes still visible today. Compensation to the owners was also paid in 1848 in Réunion, Gaudeloupe, Martinique, and French Guyana. In 2001, during the debates on the question of the recognition of slavery as a crime against humanity, Christiane Taubira made an unsuccessful attempt to convince her fellow members of parliament to set up a commission to study the issue of compensation for descendants of slaves, in particular in terms of access to land and to property, which was still highly concentrated in the hands of the descendants of planters.

The most extreme injustice is undoubtedly the case of Saint Domingue, the jewel of the French slave islands in the eighteenth century, before their insurrection in 1791 and their proclamation of independence in 1804 under the name of Haiti. In 1825, the French state imposed a considerable debt on the country (300% of the Haitian GDP at the time) to compensate the French owners for their loss of slave property.

Threatened with invasion, the island had no other choice but to comply and to repay this debt, which the country dragged like a millstone until 1950, after multiple refinances and interest paid to French and American bankers. Haiti is now requesting that France refund this iniquitous tribute (30 billion euros today, which does not include the interest), and it is difficult not to agree with them. France refuses all discussion on the subject of a debt which France had imposed on Haitians (as a fine) for having wanted to put an end to their slavery. The payments made from 1825 to 1950 are well documented and are not challenged by anybody. Today compensation payment is still being made for spoliation, which occurred during the two world wars. There is inevitably a risk of creating a huge feeling of injustice.

The same applies to the question of street names and statues, like that of the slave trader which has just been torn down in Bristol. Of course, it will not be easy to fix a frontier between the good and bad statues. But just as for the redistribution of property, we have no other choice than to trust to democratic discussion to endeavor to fix rules and criteria which are just. All refusal of discussion amounts to perpetuating injustice.

Over and above this difficult but necessary discussion concerning compensation, we must also, and primarily, turn to the future. To repair the damage done to society by racism and colonialism, we must change the economic system and establish a foundation of reduction of inequalities and equal access for all women and men to education, employment, and property ownership (including a minimal heritage), independent of origins, for both Black people and whites alike. The present mobilization, which brings together citizens of all backgrounds, can contribute thereto.

Reconstructing Internationalism
July 14, 2020

C an we restore positive meaning to the idea of internationalism? Yes, but on condition that we turn our backs on the ideology of unfettered free trade which has until now guided globalization and adopt a new model for development based on explicit principles of economic and climatic justice. This model must be internationalist in its final aims but sovereigntist in its practical modalities, in the sense that each country, each political community, must be able to determine the conditions for the pursuit of trade with the rest of the world without waiting for the unanimous agreement of its partners. The task will not be simple, and it will not always be easy to distinguish this sovereigntism with a universalist vocation from nationalist-type sovereigntism. It is therefore particularly urgent to indicate the differences.

Let's suppose that one country, or a political majority within it, considers it would be desirable to set up a highly progressive tax on top incomes and wealth holders to bring about a major redistribution in favor of the poorest socioeconomic groups while at the same time financing a program for social, educational, and ecological investment. To move in

Table 8. A novel organization of globalization: Transnational democracy

Transnational Assembly In charge of global public goods (climate, research, etc.) and of global fiscal justice (common taxes on high wealth and income holders and large corporations, carbon taxes)				
National Assembly Country A	National Assembly Country B	National Assembly Country C	National Assembly Country D	. . .

Source: see piketty.pse.ens.fr/ideology.

Interpretation: According to the proposed organization, the treaties regulating globalization (flows of goods, capital, and individuals) will henceforth include the creation between the signatory states and regional unions of a Transnational Assembly in charge of global public goods (climate, research, etc.) and global fiscal justice (common taxes on high wealth and income holders and large corporations, carbon taxes).

Note: Countries A, B, C, D can be states like France, Germany, Italy, Spain, etc., in which case the Transational Assembly will be the European Assembly; or countries A, B, etc., could be regional unions like the European Union, the African Union, etc., in which case the Transnational Assembly would be that of the Euro-African Union. The Transnational Assembly could be formed of deputies from the national assemblies and/or of transnational deputies especially elected for this purpose, depending on the situation.

this direction, this country is considering a taxation at source on corporate profits and most importantly, a system of financial registry that would enable the identification of the ultimate owners of the shares and dividends and thus the application of the desired progressive tax rates at the individual level. The whole package could be completed by an individual carbon card, thus encouraging responsible behavior, while taxing the highest emissions heavily; those who benefit from the profits of the most-polluting firms would also be taxed. Once again this would demand a knowledge of the owners.

Unfortunately, a financial registry of this type has not been provided for by the treaties for the free circulation of capital established in the 1980s–1990s, in particular in Europe in the framework of the Single European Act (1986) and the Maastricht Treaty (1992), texts which have strongly influenced those adopted thereafter throughout the world. This ultra-sophisticated legal architecture, still in force today, has de facto created a quasi-sacred right to get rich by using the infrastructures of one country, then by one click on a laptop, transferring one's assets to another jurisdiction, with no possibility provided for the community to find any trace of them. Following the crisis in 2008, as the excesses of financial deregulation came to light, agreements on the automatic exchange of banking information have been developed within the OECD, true. But these measures, established on a purely voluntary basis, do not contain the slightest sanction for recalcitrant countries.

Let us suppose, therefore, that a country wishes to accelerate the movement and sets up a redistributive form of taxation and a financial registry. Now, let's imagine that one of its neighbors does not share this point of view and applies a ridiculously small profit tax and carbon tax on firms based on its territory (whether in actual fact or fictitiously), while refusing to transmit the information as to their owners. In these circumstances, the first country should in my view impose commercial sanctions on the second; the amount would vary, depending on the firm and the extent of the fiscal and climatic damage caused. Recent research has shown that sanctions of this type would bring in substantial revenues and would encourage other countries to cooperate.[1] Of course, we would

1. For a first estimate of the possible amount of anti-dumping sanctions, see Ana Seco Justo, "Profit Allocation and Corporate Taxing Rights: Global and Unilateral Perspectives," Paris School of Economics, June 2020.

have to plead that these sanctions are merely correcting un-fair competition and the non-respect of the climate agree-ments. But the latter are so vague and, in contrast, the treaties on the free circulation of goods and capital are so sophisticated and absolute, particularly at European level, that a country which adopts this approach stands a considerable risk of be-ing condemned by European or international bodies (the Court of Justice of the European Union, the World Trade Organization). If such were the case, the country should leave the treaties in question unilaterally, while at the same time sug-gesting new ones.

What is the difference between the social and ecological sovereigntism which I have just outlined and nationalist sov-ereigntism (for example, of the Trump; Chinese; Indian; or to-morrow, the French or European variety) based on the defense of identity of a specific civilization and of interests deemed to be homogenous within it?

There are two. First, before taking possible unilateral measures, it is crucial to propose to other countries a model for cooperative development based on universal values: social justice, reduction of inequality, conservation of the planet. It is also important to describe in detail the transnational assem-blies (such as the French-German agreement created last year, but with real powers) which ideally would be in charge of global public property and common policies for fiscal and climatic justice.

Second, if these social-federalist proposals are not taken up at the moment, the unilateral approach should neverthe-less remain incentive-based and reversible. The aim of sanc-tions is to encourage other countries to exit from fiscal and climatic dumping; the aim is not to establish permanent pro-tectionism. From this point of view, the sectoral measures with no universal basis, such as the GAFA tax, should be avoided, because they easily lend themselves to ratcheting up sanctions (wine taxes versus digital taxes, etc.).

To claim that this type of path is easy to follow and well signposted would be absurd: It all still has to be invented. But historical experience demonstrates that nationalism can only lead to exacerbating inegalitarian and climatic tensions and that there is no future for unfettered free trade. One more reason for thinking, as from today, about the conditions for a new internationalism.

The Fall of the U.S. Idol,
2020–2021

Can the Left Unite on Europe?

September 15, 2020

In France, as in Germany and most other countries, the left is heavily divided on the European question, and more generally on the strategy to adopt in the face of globalization and the transnational regulation of capitalism. While national deadlines are fast approaching (2021 in Germany, 2022 in France), many voices are calling for these political forces to unite. In Germany, however, the three main parties (Die Linke, the SPD, and the Greens) are likely to find it difficult to reach agreement, particularly on Europe, and some already predict that the Greens will end up governing with the CDU. In France, the different forces have started talking to each other again, but there is no guarantee for the moment that they will manage to unite, especially on European policy.

The problem is that each side is convinced that they alone have got it right. In France, La France Insoumise (LFI) likes to remind everyone that the PS (Parti Socialiste) and its ecological allies had already promised before the 2012 elections to renegotiate the European rules. However, as soon as they were elected, the majority at the time hastened to ratify the new budgetary treaty, without modifying anything, for lack of a precise plan on what they really wanted to obtain. *Les Insoumis* also insist that the Socialists have still not indicated how their strategy and objectives have changed and could lead to a different result next time. It has to be admitted that their criticism is justified.

But on the side of PS, EELV (Europe-Ecologie-Les Verts), and other left forces not attached to LFI (like Generations, the PCF [French Communist Party], etc.), it is pointed out that the plan of the *Les Insoumis* to change Europe is far from being as precise and convincing as they claim, and that Jean-Luc Mélenchon sometimes seems more interested in criticizing (or even purely and simply leaving) the current European Union than in its reconstruction along social-federalist, democratic, and internationalist lines. Unfortunately, this criticism is not completely false either.

In theory, the LFI strategy has been based on the articulation of "plan A/plan B" since 2017. In other words, either we convince all the other countries to renegotiate the European treaties (plan A), or we leave the existing treaties and build new ones with a smaller group of countries (plan B). The idea is not necessarily a bad one, except that the *Les Insoumis* spend more time brandishing the threat of exit than describing the new treaties they would like to propose to the other countries, whether in plan A or plan B. In concrete terms, the LFI, like the whole of the left, has for a very long time defended the idea of social, fiscal, and environmental harmonization from above in Europe, which includes ending the unanimity rule in fiscal and budgetary matters. The problem is that the LFI does not say which democratic body should, in its view, be empowered to take such decisions by majority rule.

One could simply propose that tax decisions within the Council of Ministers should henceforth be taken by majority vote, with the risk, however, of perpetuating an opaque body, operating behind closed doors and favoring country-to-country confrontations. Another solution would be to give the last word to the European Parliament, with the risk this time of cutting themselves off entirely from national democratic bodies. A more innovative formula would be to set up a genuine European Assembly based on national MPs in proportion to the respective national populations and political groups.[1]

Let's be clear: these are complex issues to which no one has a perfect solution. All the more reason for the different political forces to talk to each other and come up with a strategy together. In particular, it is essential that specific proposals be made to other countries. For even if it is unlikely that the twenty-seven member states will accept the end of the unanimity rule from the outset (especially states such as the Netherlands, which have relied heavily on tax dumping), it would still be a bit of a problem if on coming to power, the French left were to fail to convince at least a few countries (for example, Spain or Italy) of the possibility of moving forward together in this direction. In any case, it is crucial to give a chance to genuine social-federalist proposals based on transnational assemblies before arriving at possible unilateral sanctions against countries practicing dumping (not to mention that such sanctions will be more effective if they are applied jointly by several countries).

Finally, both the French and the German left must take into account that the Europe of 2022 will not be the Europe of 2012. In particular, they will have to situate themselves in relation to the recovery plan adopted this summer, which, despite its limitations, constitutes a major innovation, especially

1. Manifesto for the Democratizaton of Europe, https://tdem.eu/en/manifesto/.

with the joint loan of 390 billion euros intended to supplement national budgets. Its main flaw remains its small size (less than 3% of the European GDP) and its subordination to the unanimity rule, which prevents any reactivity and change of direction. It should be noted in passing that the plan has yet to be ratified by the national parliaments, which de facto each have a right of veto. Here again, in order to go further, it will be necessary to move to majority rule, ideally in the framework of a genuine European Assembly, even if this means moving forward with a subset of countries.

What is certain is that there is an urgent need to overcome old disputes and false certainties and to get out of this situation where every fraction of the left thinks it can be right about Europe on its own.

What to Do with Covid Debt

October 13, 2020

How are countries going to deal with the accumulation of public debt generated by the Covid crisis? For many, the answer is clear: Central banks will take on their balance sheets a growing share of the debts, and everything will be settled. In reality, things are more complex. Money is part of the solution but will not be enough. Sooner or later, the wealthiest will have to be called upon.

Let's recap. In 2020, money creation has taken on unprecedented proportions. The Federal Reserve's balance sheet jumped from $4,159 billion as of February 24 to $7,056 billion as of September 28, or nearly $3 trillion in monetary injection in seven months, which has never been seen before. The balance sheet of the Eurosystem (the network of central banks piloted by the ECB) rose from 4,692 billion euros on February 28 to 6,705 billion euros on October 2, an increase of 2,000 billion euros. In relation to the GDP of the eurozone, the Eurosystem's balance sheet, which had already risen from 10% to 40% of GDP between 2008 and 2018, has just jumped to almost 60% between February and October 2020.[1]

---

1. On central bank balance sheets, see "The Age of Green Money," May 12, 2020.

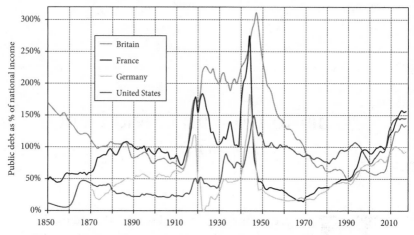

Figure 42. The vicissitudes of public debt, 1850–2020. Public debt rose sharply after each world war and reached between 150% and 300% of national income in 1945–1950, before falling sharply in Germany and France (debt cancellations, high inflation) and more gradually in Britain and the United States (moderate inflation, growth). Public assets (especially real estate and financial assets) have fluctuated less strongly over time and generally represent around 100% of national income. *Sources and series:* see piketty .pse.ens.fr/ideology.

What is all this money used for? In calm weather, central banks are content to make short-term loans to ensure the liquidity of the system. As the inflow and outflow of money in and out of the various private banks never balance exactly to the day, the central banks lend for a few days, amounts which the institutions then repay.

Following the 2008 crisis, central banks started lending money at increasingly longer maturities (a few weeks, then a few months, or even several years) in order to reassure financial players, who were petrified at the idea that their gambling partners would go bankrupt. And there was a lot to be done, because, for lack of adequate regulation, financial gambling has become a gigantic planetary casino over the past few decades. Everyone has started lending and borrowing in unprecedented proportions, with the result that the total private financial assets and liabilities held by banks, companies, and households now exceed 1,000% of GDP in rich countries (without even including derivative securities), compared to 200% in the 1970s. Real wealth (i.e., the net worth of real estate and businesses) has also increased from 300% to 500% of GDP, but much less strongly, illustrating the financialization of the economy. In a way, the balance sheets of central banks have only followed (slightly later) the explosion of private balance sheets, in order to preserve their capacity to act in the face of the markets.

The new activism of the central banks has also allowed them to buy back a growing share of public debt securities, while bringing interest rates down to zero. The ECB already held 20% of the public debt of the eurozone at the beginning of 2020, and could hold nearly 30% by the end of the year. A similar development is taking place in the United States.

As it is unlikely that the ECB or the Fed will ever decide to put these securities back on the markets or to demand their repayment, the decision to no longer count them in the total public debt could be taken now. If registration of this guarantee in legal form is desired, which would be preferable, then this might take a little more time and debate.

The most important question is the following: Should we continue along this path, and can we envisage that central banks will in future hold 50% and then 100% of public debts, thereby lightening the financial burden on states? From a technical point of view, this would not pose any problem. The difficulty is that by resolving the question of public debt on one hand, this policy creates other difficulties elsewhere, particularly in terms of increasing inequalities of wealth. The orgy of money creation and the purchase of financial securities in fact leads to an increase in stock and property prices, which contributes to the enrichment of the richest. For small savers, zero or negative interest rates are not necessarily good news. But for those who can afford to borrow at low rates and who have the financial, legal, and tax expertise to find the right investments, excellent returns are possible. According to *Challenges*, France's 500 largest fortunes have thus risen from 210 to 730 billion euros between 2010 and 2020 (from 10% to 30% of GDP). Such a development is socially and politically unsustainable.

It would be different if monetary creation, instead of fueling the financial bubble, were mobilized to finance a real social and ecological recovery (i.e., by assuming strong job creation and wage increases in hospitals and schools, thermal efficiency, and local services). This would alleviate debt while reducing inequalities, investing in sectors useful for the future and shifting inflation from asset prices to wages and goods and services.

However, this would not be a miracle solution either. As soon as inflation becomes substantial again (say, 3–4% per year), we would have to put a stop to money creation and use fiscal means. The whole history of public debt shows this: Money alone cannot offer a peaceful solution to a problem of this magnitude, because it leads in one way or another to uncontrolled distributive consequences. It was by resorting to exceptional levies on the better-off that the large public debts of the postwar period were extinguished and that the social and productive pact of the following decades was rebuilt. Let's bet that the same will be true in the future.

Global Inequalities:
Where Do We Stand?

November 17, 2020

Thanks to the combined efforts of 150 researchers from all continents, the World Inequality Database has just put new data online on the distribution of income in the different countries of the world. What does it tell us about the state of global inequality?[1]

The main innovation is that the data collected make it possible to cover almost all countries. Thanks to research carried out in Latin America, Africa, and Asia, 173 countries representing 97% of the world's population are now covered. The new data also make it possible to analyze for each country the detailed evolution of the overall distribution, from the poorest to the richest.

In concrete terms, we already knew that the widening in inequalities has been made at the top over the past few decades, with the well-known rise in the numbers of the richest 1%. The innovation is to propose a systematic comparison of the situation of the poorest classes in different parts of the world. It

---

1. World Inequality Database, https://www.wid.world.

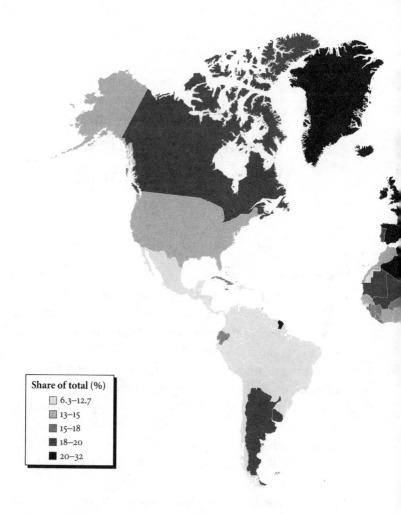

Figure 43. Bottom 50% of national income share. *Source:* World Inequality Database; www.wid.world.

can be seen, for instance, that the share of the poorest 50% varies considerably from country to country: It varies between 5% and 25% of total income.[2] In other words, for the same national income, the standard of living of the poorest 50% can vary by a factor ranging from 1 to 5. This underlines the urgent need to go beyond GDP and macroeconomic aggregates to focus on concrete social distributions and groups.

It should also be noted that inequalities are high in all countries. The share of the richest 10% represents between 30% and 70% of total income. It is always significantly higher than that of the poorest 50%. The gap would be even greater if we looked at the distribution of wealth (what you own) and not income (what you earn in a year). The poorest 50% own almost nothing (usually less than 5% of the total), even in the most egalitarian countries (such as Sweden). However, the data available on wealth is still insufficient and will be updated in 2021.

With regard to income distribution, there are very wide variations between countries, including within a given region and at the same level of development. This shows that different policies can make a difference. In Latin America, for example, Brazil, Mexico, and Chile have historically been more unequal than Argentina, Ecuador, and Uruguay (where more ambitious social policies have been implemented for several decades), and the gap between these two groups of countries has widened over the past twenty years. In Africa, the most extreme inequalities are in the south of the continent, where no real redistribution of land and wealth has taken place since the end of Apartheid.

2. Bottom 50% national income share, World Inequality Database, https://wid.world/world/#sptinc_pop50_z/US;FR;DE;CN;ZA;GB;WO /last/eu/k/p/yearly/s/false/5.2355/30/curve/false/country.

In general, the map of global inequality reflects both the effects of longstanding racial and colonial discrimination and the impact of contemporary hypercapitalism and more recent sociopolitical processes. In several of the world's most unequal countries, such as Chile or Lebanon, social movements in recent years hold out hope for profound transformations.

The Middle East appears to be the most inegalitarian region on the planet, both because of a system of borders concentrating resources on petro-monarchical territories and because of an international banking system which allows the transformation of the oil rent into an eternal financial rent. In the absence of a new, more balanced, social-federal and democratic model of regional development, it is to be feared that the totalitarian and reactionary ideologies currently at work will continue to occupy the field, as in Europe a century ago.

In India, where the gap between the top and the mass of the population has reached levels not seen since the colonial period, Hindu nationalists believe they can alleviate socioeconomic frustrations by stirring up identity and religious tensions, resulting in increased discrimination faced by the Muslim minority, which is threatened with long-term impoverishment and marginalization.

There has also been a steady rise in inequality in Eastern Europe since the 1990s. At the fall of communism, the inequality shock had been much more brutal in Russia, which in a few years has become the world capital of oligarchs, tax havens, and financial opacity, after having been the country of the total abolition of private property. But almost thirty years later, Eastern Europe seems to be gradually approaching the level of inequality observed in Russia. The stagnation of wages and the scale of the flow of profits out of these countries are fueling a frustration that the western part of the continent finds hard to understand.

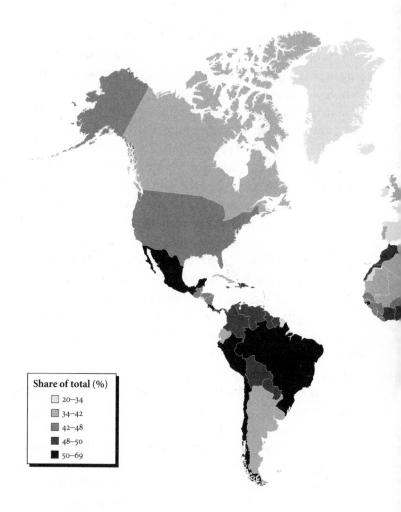

Figure 44. Top 10% of national income share. *Source:* World Inequality Database; www.wid.world.

At the global level, the share of the world's poorest 50% of the world's population has clearly increased from 7% of total world income in 1980 to around 9% in 2020, thanks to the growth of emerging countries. However, this progress must be put into perspective, as the share of the world's richest 10% has remained stable at around 53%, and that of the richest 1% has risen from 17% to 20% of total world income. The losers are the middle and working classes of the North, which is fueling the rejection of globalization.

To sum up: The planet is criss-crossed by multiple unequal divides, which the pandemic will further aggravate. Only an increased effort of democratic and financial transparency, which is currently very insufficient, would make it possible to develop solutions acceptable to the greatest number of people.

The Fall of the U.S. Idol

January 12, 2021

After the invasion of Capitol Hill, the bewildered world wonders how the country that has long presented itself as the self-proclaimed leader of the "free" world could have fallen so low. To understand what has happened, it is urgent to leave the myths and idolatry aside and to go back to history. In reality, the republic of the United States has, since its beginnings, been run through by weaknesses, violence, and considerable inequalities.

The Confederate flag, the emblem of the pro-slavery South during the American Civil War of 1861–1865, which was waved a few days ago by the rioters on the floor of the U.S. Congress, was not there by chance. It refers to very serious conflicts that need to be confronted.

The system of slavery played a central role in the development of the United States, and indeed of Western industrial capitalism as a whole. Of the fifteen presidents who succeeded one another until Lincoln's election in 1860, no fewer than eleven were slave owners, including Washington and Jefferson, both of whom were born in Virginia, which in 1790 had a population of 750,000 (of which 40% were slaves), equivalent to

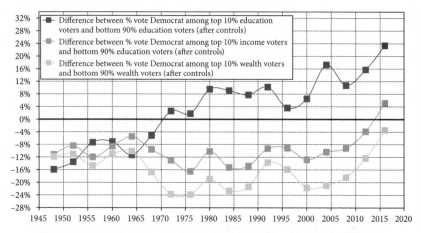

Figure 45. Social cleavages and political conflict: The United States, 1948–2020. During 1950–1970, the Democratic vote was associated with voters with the lowest levels of education and the lowest levels of income and wealth. During 1980–2010, it became associated with the voters with the highest levels. During 2010–2020, it is perhaps close to becoming associated with voters with the highest income and wealth. *Sources and series:* see piketty.pse.ens.fr/ideology.

the combined population of the two most populous northern states (Pennsylvania and Massachusetts).

After the 1791 revolt in Santo Domingo (the jewel in the French colonial system and the biggest concentration of slaves in the Atlantic world at the time), the South of the United States became the world center of the plantation economy and underwent rapid growth. The number of slaves quadrupled between 1800 and 1860; cotton production increased tenfold and fed the European textile industry. But the Northeast of the United States and especially the Midwest (the birthplace of Lincoln) developed even more rapidly. These two groups relied on a different economic model, based on the colonization of the West and free labor, and they wanted to block the expansion of slavery in the new territories in the West.

After his 1860 victory, Lincoln, a Republican, was ready to negotiate a peaceful and gradual end to slaveholding, with compensation for the owners, as had happened during the British and French abolitions in 1833 and 1848. But the Southerners preferred to play the secession card, like some of the white settlers from South Africa and Algeria in the twentieth century, in an attempt to preserve their world. The Northerners refused their departure, and the war began in 1861.

Four years later, and after the death of 600,000 persons (as many as the cumulative total of all the other conflicts in which the country took part, including the World Wars, Korea, Vietnam, and Iraq), the conflict ended with the surrender of the Confederate armies in May 1865. But the Northerners did not consider the Black population to be ready to become citizens, let alone property owners, and they let the whites regain control of the South and impose a strict system of racial segregation, which was to allow them to retain power for another century, until 1965.

In the meantime, the United States became the world's leading military power and was able to put an end to the cycle of nationalist and genocidal self-destruction which posed the European colonial powers against one another between 1914 and 1945. The Democrats, who were the party of the erstwhile pro-slavery South, managed to become the party of the New Deal. Driven by the communist challenge and African-American mobilization, they conceded civil rights without reparations.

But from 1968, the Republican Nixon recovered the white Southerners' vote by denouncing the social largesse that the Democrats would grant to Blacks through clientelism (a little like the way in which the right-wing in France suspects the left of Islamo-leftism when it evokes anti-Muslim discrimination).

A major reversal of the alliance then took place, amplified by Reagan in 1980 and Trump in 2016. Since 1968, Republicans have won a clear majority of the white vote in all presidential elections, while Democrats have always obtained 90% of the Black vote and 60–70% of the Latino vote. Meanwhile, the share of whites in the electorate has steadily declined from 89% in 1972 to 70% in 2016 and 67% in 2020 (against 12% for Blacks and 21% for Latinos and other minorities), fueling the hardening of the Capitol's Trumpists and threatening to plunge the republic of the United States into an ethno-racial conflict with no way out.

What can we conclude from all this? According to a pessimistic reading, supported by many of the most educated groups, who henceforth have voted for the Democrats (which allows the Republicans to present themselves now as anti-elite, even though they continue to include a good part of the business elite, if not as yet appealing to the intellectual elite), Republican voters are described as "deplorable" and "beyond redemption." Democratic administrations are said to have done everything they could to improve the lot of the most disadvantaged, but the racism and acrimony of the white working classes apparently prevents them from seeing this.

The problem is that this vision leaves little room for a democratic solution. A more optimistic approach to human nature might be as follows. For centuries, people from different ethno-racial backgrounds have lived with no contact with each other except through military and colonial domination. The fact that they have recently been living together in the same political communities is a major civilizational advance. But it continues to give rise to prejudice and political exploitation that can only be overcome by more democracy and equality.

If the Democrats want to regain the socially disadvantaged vote, whatever its origin, then more needs to be done in terms of social justice and redistribution. The road ahead will be long and arduous. All the more reason to get started now.

Index

Locators in *italics* indicate figures and tables.

Alvaredo, Facundo, 37
Apple Inc., paying tax on Irish profits, 31–32
Arendt, Hannah, 280
Atkinson, Anthony B. (Tony), 37; retrospective on work of, 58–61

basic income, 54–57, 197; in India, 235–239
Beveridge, William, 242
Bezos, Jeff, 229
Bharti, Nitin, 237
Biden, Joseph, 19, 288–289
Black Americans: Democratic Party and, 262–263, *264*, 331–332; reparations and, 24, 25, 301–302
Bolsonaro, Jair, 202
Bouju, Manon, 109
Bozio, Antoine, 267
Brazil, under threat, 200–203
Brexit, 83, 109, 211, 231, 240, 241, 276–277, *277*, 278, 279–280
Britain, compensation paid to slaveholders after abolition of slavery, 303. *See also* United Kingdom
British Labour Party, nationalization agenda, 11–12
budgetary policy, democratic eurozone assembly and, 104
budgetary surplus, in eurozone, 193–194
Budget Project, for Europe, 211, *212*, 213–214
business leaders, deduction of income tax at its source and, *127*, 130–131

Cadiot, Juliette, 179
Cage, Julia, 139–140, 206
capital: public *vs.* private, 95–98; in Russia, 178–181; tax system and restricting power of, 56
capital code, reform of French, 138–141
Capital in the Twenty-First Century (Piketty), 33, 38, 60
capitalism: need for social regulation of, 221; new socialism as alternative to, 2

carbon emissions, 51, *245*
carbon tax, 14, 213, 221, 231–232, 247
Catalonia, crisis in, 154–158
central banks: buying back public
    debt securities, 319; financial
    globalization and, *297*; holding
    public debt, 319–320; policies to
    address Covid-19 crisis, 296–298
centrist ecology, illusion of,
    244–248
CFDT (Conféderation française
    de travail), 139
Chancel, Lucas, 161, 237
China: control on outflows and
    private accumulation, 180;
    inequality in, 88–91; lack of
    inheritance tax, 258–259;
    mobilizing resources to raise
    level of training and health of
    population, 237
Churchill, Winston, 242
CICE (Tax Credit for
    Competitiveness and
    Employment), deferral of
    replacement of, 74, 134–137
circular economy, 257–261
class cleavage, in Europe, 240–243
climate change: inequality and,
    161, 274–275. *See also* global
    warming
Clinton, Bill, 50
Clinton, Hillary, 29, 31, 32, 50
colonial discrimination, map of
    global inequality reflecting, 325
co-management systems, 10–12,
    56, 139–140, 204–205
Comprehensive Economic Trade
    Agreement treaty, 161–162
Confederate flag, 329
Constitutional Treaty (2005),
    French referendum on, 240,
    241, *279*

corporate income tax scandals,
    92–93
corporate profits, taxes on, 122,
    159, 160, 213, 284; minimum
    rates, 31–32, 51, 52–53
Council of Finance Ministers,
    92, 93
Covid-19 crisis, 8; Covid debt,
    317–320; deaths from, 291–294;
    new model of social state and,
    291, 293–295, 296
CSG (Generalized Social
    Contribution) (France), 57, 119,
    127–131, 137

deficit, secondary, 223–224. *See
    also* trade deficit
Delevoye, Jean-Paul, 254
Delevoye Report, 254–255, 267,
    270, 271
De Masi, Fabio, 282–283
democracy: Bernie Sanders and,
    286–290; transnational, *306*
democratic eurozone assembly,
    composition of, 99–109, *101,
    103, 105*
Democratic Party: Black
    Americans and, 262–263, *264,*
    331, 332; composition of
    electorate, 123–124; regaining
    socially disadvantaged vote, 333
democratic socialism, 242
democratization, Manifesto for
    the Democratization of Europe,
    211–216
Democratization Treaty for
    Europe, 211, 212, 214, 215
disempowerment, rise in sense
    of, 98
*The Distribution of Personal
    Wealth in Britain* (Atkinson &
    Harrison), 59–60

Eastern Europe, 325; inflows *vs.* outflows in, *165*, 165–166; Western investment in, 166–167

East-West divide, 164–165

ecological sovereigntism, 307–309

economic activity (GDP), 2007–2015, *155*

economic crisis of 2008, 43, 66, 108, 163, 184, 198, 221, 234, 273, 307

economic indicators, redefinition of, 14, 16

economic research, IMF, inequality debate, and, 33–42

education: Covid-19 crisis and, 295; French system of, 114, 118–119, 152–153, 170, 171–172; inequality in, 55–56; labor productivity and, 68–69; public investment in, 9, 76, 237, 287–288

educational justice, 266

EELV (Europe-Ecologie-Les Verts), 314

Elysée Treaty (1963), 231, 282

The Emergence of Globalism (Rosenboim), 243

employment: gender and ethno-racial discrimination in, 24; hours worked and, *72*, 72–76, *73*, *75*

endowments, American university, 40, *41*, 205–206

entrepreneurs, Reagan policies and, 259

environmental policy based on reduction of inequality, circulation of power and property, and redefinition of economic indicators, 14, 16

equality, march toward participatory socialism and, 4–7

equal rights, social state as vehicle for, 7–10

ethnicity, divisions in Europe based on, 263–266, *265*

ethno-racial discrimination in employment, 24

Eurogroup, 214

Europe: challenges in 2018, 163–167; class cleavage in, 240–243; division on basis of ethnic origin in, 263–266, *265*; left in, *196*, 313–316; Manifesto for the Democratization of Europe, 211–216; minimum tax rate on multinationals' profits, 31–32; need for reform of, 120, 186–189; populism in, 173; reduction of inequalities in, 7–10; rise of social state in, 1870–2015, *292*

European Assembly, creation of new, 176–177, 214–215

European budgetary rules, French right and, 43–46

European Budgetary Treaty (2012), 85, 87

European Business Code, 283, 284

European Central Bank (ECB), 106, 225, 298; balance sheets, 249, *250*, 251–252; money creation and, 249–252, 297–298

European PROJECTS, 284–285

European Stability Mechanism, 106, 187

European Union: competition between countries, 241; individual states and taxation, 232; joint budget and free circulation of persons in, 278–279; strengthening political and fiscal union in, 176–177

European Union-Canada
    Comprehensive Economic and
    Trade Agreement (CETA),
    51–52
eurosystem balance sheet, 297,
    298, 317
eurozone: allocation of
    population *vs.* allocation of
    GDP, 106, *107*; budget, 45–46,
    189; democratization of, 187;
    need for a democratic eurozone
    government, 92–94
eurozone parliamentary assembly,
    45, 82–83, 186; based on
    national parliaments, 93–94,
    176–177; composition of,
    99–109, *101, 103, 105*
exit tax, 227

Federal Franco-British Union,
    proposed, 242
Federal Reserve balance sheet,
    Covid debt and, 317
Federal Union movement,
    241–243
feminist socialism, 22–26
Ferrand, Richard, 283
Ferreras, Isabelle, 139
Fillon, François, 85, 104
Finance Act 2017 (France), 126, 129
Finance Laws (France), 148–149
financialization of the economy,
    319
fiscal decentralization, Catalonia
    and, 154–155
fiscal dumping, 51, 52, 159, 184, 277
fiscal justice, US 2020 presidential
    campaign and, 227–228
fiscal revolutions, political
    revolutions and, 128
Five Star Movement (M₅S),
    coalition with Lega, 195–198

flat tax, 197, 221, 256, 270
France, 106; abolition of slavery
    and compensation of slave
    owners, 24–25, 303–304;
    attitudes toward Muslims in,
    265–266, 278; basic income *vs.*
    living wage, 54–57; budget 2018,
    147–153; commonalities with
    Germany, 83; concentration of
    property in, 5, *6, 7*; denial of
    inequality in, 272; disinterest in
    making fundamental changes
    to Europe, 231–234; domestic
    consumption and investment,
    79–80, *80*; employment in, *72*,
    72–76, *73, 75*; European cleavage
    in, *279*; GDP per capita and
    number of hours worked, 69,
    70, 70–71, *71*; gender pay
    inequality in, 47–49, *48*;
    inequality in, 113–116; in-
    equality of property, *268*;
    investment in education, 9–10,
    147–151, *148, 150*, 170; left divided
    on European question, 313–316;
    populism in, 84–87;
    productivity in, 62–83, *64, 67*;
    public capital in, 95–98, *96*;
    reforming retirement pension
    system, 253–256; reform of
    student university admission
    system, 168–170; reforms for,
    117–120; trade deficit, 76–77, *78*;
    trade surplus, 77–78, *78*;
    unemployment in, 43–44; voter
    turnout in, 290
Franco-German Cooperation
    Treaty (2019), 282
Franco-German Parliamentary
    Assembly (APFA), 21, 231, 232,
    233, 298; tax justice and,
    281–285

Franco-German Treaty (Elysée
  Treaty), 231, 282
French Revolution, failure of, 5, 6
French right, European budgetary
  rules and, 43–46
French Socialists, nationalization
  agenda, 11–12

Gandhi, Rahul, 238
Garbinti, Bertrand, 114
GDP per capita, number of hours
  worked and, 69–72, 70, 71
gender discrimination in
  employment, 24
gender pay inequality, 23, 47–49, 48
Germany, 106; blaming South for
  problems in Europe, 188;
  co-management systems in,
  10–12, 56, 139; commonalities
  with France, 83; disinterest in
  making fundamental changes
  to Europe, 231–234; domestic
  consumption and investment,
  80, 80; employment in, 72, 72;
  external debt, 299; federal
  income tax, 157; Franco-
  German Parliamentary
  Assembly, 21, 231, 232, 233,
  281–285, 298; GDP per capita
  and number of hours worked,
  69, 70, 70–71, 71; income tax
  calculation, 132; left divided on
  European question, 313, 315–316;
  nationalism in, 278;
  productivity in, 62–83, 64, 67;
  trade deficit, 79; trade surplus,
  76–77, 78, 79, 80–82, 193
global inequalities, 273, 321–328;
  bottom 50% of national income
  share, 322–323, 324
globalization: Brexit, election of
  Trump, and, 276; changing

current path of, 50–53, 174–175,
  280; changing organization of,
  19–22; corporate, 77; Europe's
  position in, 190; inegalitarian
  challenges posed by, 160–161;
  transnational democracy, 306
global poverty, correcting
  inegalitarian tendencies of
  globalization and, 161
global warming, 221, 244, 260. See
  also climate change
Goupille-Lebret, Jonathan, 114
grand écoles, 114; needed reform
  in admission to, 152–153, 170,
  171
green money, age of, 296–300
Green New Deal, 261
Greens, 244, 247, 313
gross domestic product (GDP):
  concept of, 66; national income
  and, 274–275

Haiti, forced to compensate slave
  owners and current demand for
  reparations, 24, 25, 303–304
Hamon, Benoît, 87
Harvard University endowment,
  205–206
Hayek, Friedrich, 242, 243
health care: Covid-19 crisis and
  public, 295; Indian spending
  on, 237
Hennette, Stéphanie, 99–100, 176
higher education: endowments,
  40, 41, 205–206; French public
  investment in, 147–151, 148, 150,
  170; inequality in access to in
  United States, 68–69; needed
  reform in French, 152–153
Hollande, François, 129, 148;
  reform of CICE and, 134,
  135–136

hypercapitalism, postcommunism
and, 258
hyper-financialization, 252

IMF (International Monetary
Fund), 187; inequality debate,
economic research, and, 33–42
immigrants to European Union,
173–174, 190, *191*, 191–192
income: educational investment
and growth of average, 9; global
distribution of, 324; inequality
in French, 114–116, *115*; rise in
inequality of labor and, 35, 36;
taxation of highest European
wealth owners, 213. *See also*
national income
income tax: base in Catalonia and
Spain, 155–156; deduction of at
its source, 119, 125–133; French,
218; Russian, 180, 258; top rates
in rich countries, *227*, 228. *See
also* progressive income tax
India: basic income (NYAY) in,
235–239; BJP vote by caste and
religion, 1962–2014, *236*; Hindu
nationalists *vs.* Muslim minority,
264–265; inequality in, 325
individualism, May '68 Movement
and rise in, 182
inequalities: allocating revenue to
reducing, 229–230; Atkinson's
work on, 58–61; in China,
88–91; denial of, 272–275;
educational investment and, 9;
European drift toward, 164, 166;
in France, 113–116; high level of
productivity in United States
and, 68–69; May '68 Movement
and, 182–185; measure of, 34–36;
as "natural," 167; reduction of
over long term, 4–10; in Russia,

179, 325. *See also* global
inequalities; social inequality
Inequality: What Can Be Done?
(Atkinson), 61
inequality debate, IMF, economic
research, and, 33–42
inheritance system, reform of,
13–18
inheritance tax, 56; China's lack
of, 258–259; rates in rich
countries, 1900–2017, *229*;
reduction of in United States,
159; Russia's lack of, 180
internationalism, 20–21;
incomplete, 184–185;
reconstructing, 305–309
international trade, intensification
of, 77
international transfers, universal
system of, 25–26
Italy: employment in, *72*, *73*; labor
productivity in, *64*, *71*, *72*,
75–76, *76*; percent of population
of eurozone, 106; public debt,
222–223, *224*; social-nativism
in, 195–199; trade surplus, 193

Japan: domestic consumption and
investment, *80*; public capital in,
96, *97*; trade surplus, 77, *78*, *78*
Japanese-American internees,
compensation of, 24–25, 302
Jospin government, deduction of
income tax at its source and, 129
justice: basic income and, 54–55;
educational, 266; fiscal,
227–228; social, 19–20, 256. *See
also* tax justice

Keynes, John Maynard, 178
kleptocracy, Russia as, 180
Kuznets, Simon, 59–60

labor productivity, *64, 65, 66–69, 67, 71, 72, 75–76, 76*
Labour Code (French), 118; reform of, 138–141
La France Insoumise (LFI), 313–314
Lamartine, Alphonse de, 283
Latinos, Democratic Party and, 332
Lee, Spike, 302
left: in Europe and the United States, 1945–2020, *196;* possibility of uniting on Europe and, 313–316
Lega, coalition with Five Star Movement, 195, 196–197
Le Pen, Marine, 30, 84
life expectancy, social inequality of, 8, 179, 254, 268–269
Lincoln, Abraham, 301, 329, 330, 331
loans to finance public debt in Europe in response to Covid-19 crisis, 299–300
London Debt Agreement (1953), 224
low-income students, in French university system, 171–172
LREM *(La république en marche),* 125–126, 131, 133
Lula, 201–202

Maastricht Treaty (1992), 184, 223, 240, 241, 251, *279,* 307
Macron, Emmanuel, 85, 104, 117, 118–119, 282; Covid-19 crisis and tax policies, 295; deduction of income tax at its source and, 130–132, 134; financing social protection and taxation, 119–120; policies compared to Trump's, 159–162; reform of
CICE and, 134, 136; tax justice and, 217–221; timidity in reforming eurozone, 188; wealth tax policies, 246–247. *See also* LREM
Malthus, Thomas, 59
Manifest for a Free and United Europe (Spinelli), 243
Manifesto for the Democratization of Europe, 21, 211–216, 284
market, sacralization of, 29–30, 50
Marx, Karl, 59, 178, 181
mass incarceration, 179
May '68 Movement, inequality and, 182–185
McGaughey, Ewan, 139
McGovern, George, 123
Mélenchon, Jean-Luc, 84, 85, 104, 197, 314
meritocratic narrative, 168
Merkel, Angela, 187–188, 282
middle class, property-owning, 5, 6
Middle East, as most inegalitarian region, 325
migration, patterns of European, 190, *191,* 191–192
minimum inheritance, 13–18
minimum wage, 57, 183, 270, 288
Modi, Narendra, 238
Le Monde (newspaper), 3–4; share ownership of, 204–205, 206
monetarist illusion, 252
money creation, 320; European Central Bank and, 249–252, 297–298
Montebourg, Arnaud, 87
multicultural exchanges, migratory flows and, 192
multiracial socialism, 22–26

Muslims, French attitudes toward, 265–266, 278
Mussolini, Benito, 243

National Front, 44–45, 87, 265
national income, 274–275; to replace gross domestic product, 16; share of bottom 50%, 322–323, 324, 328; share of top 10%, 324, 326–327, 328
nationalism: global temptation of, 278; Republicans and Trump and, 123; United States and United Kingdom and, 276–277
nationalist-type sovereigntism, 305
national-liberalism vs. social-federalism, 276–280
national parliaments, European Assembly and, 93–94, 176–177
nativism, social, 195–199
Nixon, Richard, 123, 263, 331–332
nonprofit media organizations (NMO), 206
North-South divide, 164
Novokmet, Filip, 166, 179

Obama, Barack, 30, 50
Obamacare, Trump and, 122, 123
Obono, Danièle, 283
Ocasio-Cortez, Alexandria, 227
offshore assets, of wealthy Russian, 180–181
Orbán-Salvini meeting, anti-immigrant solidarity and, 198
Organisation for Economic Co-operation and Development (OECD), 260, 284, 307; database, 64–65
ownership: decrease in concentration of, 5–6, 6, 7; participatory socialism and circulation of, 10–18

Parcoursup, reform of system, 168–172
Paris Accords, 52, 246, 247
Paris Climate Change Conference, 162
participatory socialism, 3–7; circulation of power and ownership and, 10–18; feminist, multiracial, and universalist socialism, 22–26; march toward equality and, 4–7; social federalism, 19–22
patriarchy, failure to take into account in previous socialist experiences, 22–23
Peillon, Vincent, 87
Pétain, Philippe, 242
Philippe, Edouard, 134
pluto-communism, China and, 90
Polanyi, Karl, 280
political change, changes in structure of property owner-ship and, 98
political revolutions, fiscal revolutions and, 128
poorest: income of in China, 89–90; share of total income, 5–6
populism: European, 173; in France, 84–85
postcolonialism, failure to take into account in previous socialist experiences, 22–23
Postel-Vinay, Gilles, 37
poverty: fall in Brazilian, 202–203; global, 161
power, participatory socialism and circulation of, 10–18
private capital, 95–98, 175
private wealth, rise in, 97
productivity: in France, 62–83, 119; in Germany, 62–83; use of, 79–80

progressive income tax, 56–57; adoption in France, 113–114; circulation of property and, 14, *15*; in United States, 121–122, 156–157

progressive inheritance tax, greater circulation of property and, 13–14

progressive property tax, 56; greater circulation of property and, 13–14, *15*

property: composition of French, 2015, *145*; concentration of private property in China, 90; decline in public, 95, *96*; inequality of in France, *268*; reduction in property inequalities and concentration of, 5–6, *6, 7*; reform of tax and inheritance system and circulation of, 13–18, *15*

property tax: American, 229–230; French, 116, 145–146, 220

public capital, 95–98; in capitalist countries, 90–91; fall of, *175*

public debt: European Union regulations on, 222–223; for investment in climate and training, 252; Italy and, 222–223; referendum on cancellation of, 222; response to Covid-19 crisis and, 296–297, 298–300, 317–320; Revolution of 1789 and, 224–225; of richest countries, *318*; rise in, 95

racial cleavage in United States, 262–263, *264*

racial discrimination, map of global inequality reflecting, 325

racial segregation, in American South, 331

racism, confronting, 301–304

Reagan, Ronald, 17, 50; tax policies, 228, 258, 259, 276, 287; Trump policies as continuation of Reagan's, 121–122, 123; white vote and, 263, 332

redistribution, pension schemes and, 269–270

redistributive form of taxation, 307

reparations, 304; to Black Americans, 24, 25, 301–302; to Japanese-American internees, 24–25, 302

Republican Party: composition of electorate, 123; white vote and, 263, 331–332

retirement pension systems: French, 74, 117–118, 131; setting up fair, 253–256; universal retirement schemes, 267–271

r-g (return on capital-rate of growth) gap, 34, 35–37; measurement of, 38–41

Ricardo, David, 59

richest 10%, share of wealth of, 5, *6, 7*

richest countries: private and public capital, *175*; public debt, *318*

Robbins, Lionel, 242

Roosevelt, Franklin D., 122

Rosenboim, Or, 243

Rosenthal, Jean-Laurent, 37

Roussef, Petrobras, 202

Russia: capital in, 178–181; income tax, 180, 258; inequality in, 179, 325; offshore assets of wealthy, 180–181; trade surplus, 180

Sacriste, Guillaume, 99–100, 176

Saez, Emmanuel, 37, 226, 260

Salvini, Matteo, 197, 198
sanctions, commercial, 307–308
Sanders, Bernie, 19, 30, 50, 85, 227,
    260; democracy in the United
    States and, 286–290
Sarkozy, Nicolas, 148, 217, 247
Sautter, M., 129
Schaüble, Wolfgang, 281, 285
Schoelcher, Victor, 303
Scholz, Olaf, 284
secondary deficit, 223–224
shareholder power, 10–12,
    12–13n14, 12n13
*Shares of Upper Income Groups in
Income and Savings* (Kuznets),
    59
Single European Act (1986), 307
slavery: abolition in Brazil,
    200–201; Atlantic slave
    societies, *302*; in United States,
    329–330
social cleavage in United States,
    262–263, *265*, 329–330, *330*
social democracy in crisis,
    184–185
social dumping, 241, 277, 284
social economy, money creation
    for, 298
social federalism, 19–22; national-
    liberalism *vs.*, 276–280
social inequality: global warming
    and, 245; historical reduction
    of, 257–258; of life expectancy,
    8, 179, 254, 268–269
socialism, 1, 2. *See also*
    participatory socialism
socialists and social-democrats,
    responsibility for breakdown of
    political system, 247–248
social justice, Macron government
    and, 256
social-nativism in Italy, 195–199

social protection, modernization
    and unification of French,
    117–118, 119
social regulation of capitalism, 221
social sovereightism, 305–309
social state: Covid-19 crisis and
    emergence of, 291, 293–295, 296;
    rise of in Europe, 1870–2015,
    292; as vehicle for equal rights,
    7–10
sovereigntism, 305–309
Spain, 106, 299
Spinelli, Altiero, 242–243
Stalin, Josef, 179
statues and street names,
    confronting slavery and, 304
sustainable development, 51,
    52–53, 83, 159, 175, 248, 296
Sweden, co-management systems
    in, 10–12, 139

Taubira, Christiane, 303
taxation: on corporate profits, 122,
    159, 160, 213, 284; European, 213,
    215, 225, 232–233; Macron and
    French, 217–218; redistributive
    form of, 307; reform to
    encourage greater circulation of
    property, 13–18, *15*; restricting
    power of capital and, 56; of very
    large fortunes, 284
tax justice: in France, 217–221;
    Franco-German Parliamentary
    Assembly and, 281–285
tax reforms: Trump's, 121, 174, 228,
    295; Trump *vs.* Macron, 159–160
3% rule, 222–223
Tocqueville, 178, 303
*Top Incomes in France in the
Twentieth Century* (Piketty), 60
trade deficit, 76–79, *78*; defined,
    79; French, 76–77, *78*, *78*

trade surplus, 76–82, *78*; defined, 79; eurozone, 192–193; German, 76–77, *78*; Russian, 180
transferunion, Europe and, 186–189
transnational democracy, *306*
Treaty for Stability, Coordination, and Governance (TSCG), 223
treaty for the democratization of the governance of the eurozone (T-Dem), 99–100, 109
Treaty of Aix-la-Chapelle, 283, 284
The Triumph of Justice (Saez & Zucman), 260
Trump, Donald: Biden *vs.*, 288; continuation of long-term trends under, 121–124; election of, 29–30, 50–51, 163; nationalism of, 259, 276–277; policies compared to Macron's, 159–162; tax policies, 121, 174, 228, 295; trade sanctions by, 174; white vote and, 263, 332

underemployment, 43, *75*, 76
unemployment in France, 43–44, 118, 138
United Kingdom: Brexit, 276–277, *277*, 278, 279–280; compensation paid to slaveholders, 24–25, 303; domestic consumption and investment, *80*; employment in, 69, *70*, 71, *71*, *72*, *73*; labor productivity in, *64*, *67*, 68; public capital in, *96*, 97; reduction of debt, 86; voter turnout in, 290
United States: access to higher education, 9, 68–69, 168, *169*; Bernie Sanders and democracy in, 286–290; Civil War, 331;

compensation of former slaves in, 24–25, 301–302; domestic consumption and investment, *80*; employment in, 69, *70*, 71, *71*, *72*, *73*; federal income and inheritance tax, 203; growth and progressive taxation, 1870–2020, *258*, *259*–260; income per capita after fiscal progressivity halved in 1980s, 17; inequality in, 6, 68–69; labor productivity in, *64*, 65, 66–68, *67*; left in, *196*; migration flow to, 191, *191*, 192; net public wealth, *175*; progressive federal income tax, 56–57, 132, 156–157; public capital in, *96*, 97; slavery in, 329–330; social and racial cleavages in, 262–263, *264*, *265*; social cleavages and political conflict, 1948–2020, 329–333, *330*; toward social justice and redistribution in, 19–20; trade deficit, *78*, 78–79; universal health insurance coverage, 30, 122, 123, 286; voter turnout in, *287*, *289*, 289–290; wealth tax, 19–20, 226–230
universal capital endowment (minimum inheritance), 13–18
universalist socialism, 22–26
universal retirement schemes, 267–271
universal system of international transfers, 25–26
university endowments, American, 40, *41*, 205–206

Valls, Manuel, 87
Vauchez, Antoine, 100, 176
vocational training, French government investment in, 118–119

voter turnout, *287, 289*, 289–290
voting, in Brazil, 200, 201–202

wages: basic income or fair,
    54–57, 197; minimum, 57, 183,
    270, 288
Warren, Elizabeth, 19, 226–227,
    229, 260
wealth: growth rate of top global,
    1987–2013, *39*, 39–40; measure
    of inequality of, 36, 37; of
    richest 1% in France, 144
wealth tax, 13–14; in America,
    226–230, 288; on billionaires,
    19–20; for Europe, 213; French,
    18, 56, 85, 116, 142–146, 147, 152,
    160, 218–221, *219*
welfare state, 8, 10, 20, 178
West African Economic and
    Monetary Union (WEAMU),
    21–22

West African response to
    Covid-19 crisis, 294
Wooton, Barbara, 242
working class, alienation of, 174,
    289, 290
world fortunes, rise in, 144–145
World History of France
    (Boucheron), 86
World Inequality Database, 3, 321
World Inequality Report, 161
World Wealth and Income
    Database (WID.world),
    37–38, 60
Wright, Erik Olin, 283

Yang, Li, 89
"yellow vests," 217, 222

Zuckerberg, Mark, 229
Zucman, Gabriel, 37, 89, 179, 226,
    260